Education in Indigenous, Nomadic and Travelling Communities

Also available in the Education as a Humanitarian Response Series

Also available from Bloomsbury

Education in Indigenous, Nomadic and Travelling Communities

Education as a Humanitarian Response

Edited by

Rosarii Griffin

B L O O M S B U R Y

LONDON · NEW DELHI · NEW YORK · SYDNEY

Bloomsbury Academic
An imprint of Bloomsbury Publishing Plc

50 Bedford Square	1385 Broadway
London	New York
WC1B 3DP	NY 10018
UK	USA

www.bloomsbury.com

First published 2014

British Library Cataloguing-in-Publication Data
A catalogue record for this book is available from the British Library.

ISBN: HB: 978-1-4725-1314-4
     PB: 978-1-4725-1360-1
  ePDF: 978-1-4725-1119-5
  ePub: 978-1-4725-1246-8

Library of Congress Cataloging-in-Publication Data
Education in indigenous, nomadic and travelling communities / edited by Rosarii Griffin.
pages cm. – (Education as a humanitarian response)
ISBN 978-1-4725-1314-4 (hardback) – ISBN 978-1-4725-1360-1 (paperback)
1. Indigenous peoples–Education–Case studies. 2. Nomads–Education–Case studies. 3. Multicultural education–Case studies.

LC3715.E378 2014
371.829–dc23

2013048782

Typeset by Integra Software Services Pvt. Ltd.
Printed and bound in Great Britain

Contents

Notes on Contributors

Sheila Aikman is Senior Lecturer in Education and International Development at the University of East Anglia, UK. Prior to this, she was Education Policy Advisor for Oxfam GB and Lecturer at the Institute of Education, University of London. She researches on education and indigenous peoples, social movements and rights in education and has published on indigenous knowledges and languages, particularly in relation to debates and developments in intercultural bilingual and plurilingual education in the Amazon. Her other areas of research and writing include gender equality, social justice and education and the policy/practice interface in a wide range of countries across Latin America, Africa and Asia.

Lorenzo Cherubini is a professor in the Faculty of Education, Brock University, St. Catherines, Ontario, Canada. His research is concentrated primarily in the areas of teacher development and policy analysis and is funded by the Social Science and Humanities Research Council of Canada (SSHRC). He has published more than 95 refereed articles and proceedings, has authored eight book chapters, written six books and edited three others. He has also presented more than 60 refereed conference papers across Canada, the United States and abroad. He is the former Director of the Tecumseh Centre for Aboriginal Research and Education at Brock University.

Rosarii Griffin is a lecturer, researcher and administrator at University College Cork (UCC), Ireland. Rosarii Co-Chairs an Irish-African initiative (CREATE) promoting capacity building between Mzuzu University and UCC. A former UCC Governor and Director of a Centre for Global Development, Limerick, Rosarii initially won the British ESRC Scholarship and read for a doctorate at St Hugh's College, Oxford University, subsequently winning the Oxford Vice Chancellor's Award for her doctoral research. Rosarii's research interests are in teaching, learning and e-learning; educational research methods; inclusion and social justice in education, particularly in relation to developing countries. This is Rosarii's fifth book on education in the global context.

Máirín Kenny, an independent scholar, is a former principal of a primary school for Traveller children and has lectured in pre-service and ongoing teacher education. She is involved in Pavee Point Travellers' Centre and the Wicklow Travellers Group. Her research includes studies of Travellers' engagement with the school system; sectarianism in Early Years education; ethnicity and racism in Irish schools; the experience of people with disabilities in the education system; and education for showground children in Australia. In 2009, she was co-editor of and contributor to a Routledge (Research in Education) publication: *Traveller, Nomadic, and Migrant Education* (edited by P. A. Danaher, M. Kenny and J. Remy Leder).

Pigga Keskitalo, PhD, works as the associate professor at the teacher training section of the Sámi University College (Sámi allaskuvla) in Kautokeino, Norway. Along with participating in the developmental projects of teaching, Keskitalo became interested in culturally sensitive teaching arrangements, and did her doctoral research about Sámi primary school issues, 'Cultural sensitivity in the Sámi School through educational anthropology' at the Faculty of Education, University of Lapland, Finland. She has published numerous articles and books about Sámi education in many languages. Her latest publication is *Sámi Education* (authored by P. Keskitalo, K. Määttä and S. Uusiautti, Peter Lang, Frankfurt am Main).

Hema Letchamanan obtained her master's degree from the University of Oxford, UK. She is currently a doctoral student at the Faculty of Education, University of Cambridge, UK. Her research interests include education for marginalized communities, education in developing countries and curriculum development. She is also a project consultant with UNHCR Malaysia, where she develops the curriculum for refugee learning centres and provides teacher training to the refugee teachers in Malaysia. Previously she has taught in both a rural primary school and a higher education institution in Malaysia.

Kaarina Määttä, PhD, is the professor of educational psychology at the Faculty of Education, University of Lapland, and deputy vice-chancellor at the University of Lapland, Finland. During her career, she has supervised over 50 doctoral theses, written hundreds of articles and dozens of textbooks, especially about love, human strengths, early childhood education and student guidance, and teacher training and teacherhood. Her latest publications include *Obsessed with the Doctoral Theses. The Supervision and Support in the Phases of Dissertation Process* (edited by K. Määttä, 2012) and *Many Faces of Love* (authored by K. Määttä and S. Uusiautti, 2013).

Piaras MacÉinrí is lecturer in migration studies in the Department of Geography, University College Cork (UCC). He was Director of the Irish Centre for Migration Studies from 1997 – 2003 and Principal Investigator for the Irish Research Council-funded Emigre project, the first major representative survey of current emigration from Ireland, in 2012/13. With Dr Caitríona Ní Laoire and Dr Allen White he was responsible for UCC's taught *MA in Contemporary Migration and Diaspora Studies*, now in its seventh year, and chairs the Board of Studies for the programme. He has lectured, published and broadcast widely on emigration, immigration, integration and related issues.

Juliet McCaffery, PhD, has, specialized in literacy, gender and equalities for 30 years working in the US, Brighton and London. She was the first gender and development officer at the British Council. She is now an education consultant and has worked in Sub-Saharan Africa, in Egypt and Yemen and also the Indian sub-continent. She first became involved in the situation of English Gypsies and Irish Travellers as an elected Councillor and is cofounder of Sussex Traveller Action Group. She has a number of publications on literacy including Developing Adult Literacy coauthored with Merrifield and Millican (2007) and Access, Agency and Assimilation: exploring literacy among Gypsies and Travellers (2012).

Christine O'Hanlon has taught in a range of schools at all levels before becoming a researcher and educator in higher education. She is interested in 'marginalized' communities and educational segregation for pupils with special needs, Travellers and others. She has an international reputation through her publications, lectures and presentations in Europe, Asia and South America. She supports change in community projects through action research and pursues these aims both informally and formally through her role as Honorary Reader in Education at the University of East Anglia, UK. She has published an action research guide for teachers entitled *What Is Your School Doing for Traveller Children?* (1996) – a staff development pack, published by EFECOT with the co-operation of the Commission of the European Union DG XXII.

Firdaus Ramli lectures at Taylor's University, Malaysia. He has a vast experience with the Orang Asli community, which includes teaching and engaging in community services for many years. His research interests are policy planning, development studies and history and he is currently pursuing his doctoral degree in public policy. He is also a life member of the Malaysian History Association.

Judith Smith is Outreach Support Officer at Minority Ethnic and Traveller Attainment Service, (METAS), UK. While having little qualifications beyond average grade O levels, Judith is currently undertaking a Foundation Degree in Learning Support to enhance her work for the METAS. Judith has 25 years of experience working with a variety of Gypsies and Travellers throughout the East Riding of Yorkshire. This work has been provided through a holistic approach, working within all types of educational establishments as well as a variety of projects with families, the wider community and other services.

Satu Uusiautti, PhD, Adjunct Professor at the University of Helsinki, works as a specialist at the University of Lapland, Finland, and as a post-doctoral researcher in the research project Love-based Leadership – An Interdisciplinary Approach (http://www.ulapland.fi/lovebasedleadership). Her personal research interests are in positive psychology and human strengths, happiness, success and well-being in life in general but especially in education and teacherhood, and in diverse educational contexts. Her latest publications include *Early Child Care and Education in Finland* (edited by K. Määttä and S. Uusiautti, 2013).

Helen Worrell is a Family and Early Years Learning Officer. Helen has a BA (Hons) Sociology and Social Anthropology from the University of Hull and utilizes training in Counselling and Systemic Practice to inform her approach to working practice with Minority Ethnic and Traveller Attainment Service (METAS). Helen has a particular interest in the concept of identity and its impact on the sense of belonging, specifically in relation to Gypsy/ Roma/Travellers, and additionally how marginalization has a lifelong impact on the positive outcomes for formal and informal educational chances and recognition. Helen also is Vice Chair of Governors for Middleton, Beswick and Watton Federation of Schools in the East Riding of Yorkshire.

Series Editor's Preface
Colin Brock

Underlying this entire series on *Education as a Humanitarian Response* is the well-known adage in education that 'if we get it right for those most in need we will likely get it right for all if we take the same approach'. That sentiment was born in relation to those with special educational needs within a full mainstream system of schooling.

In relation to this series, it is taken further to embrace not only the special educational needs of those experiencing disasters and their aftermath, whether natural or human-made, but also to other groups who may be significantly disadvantaged. Indeed, much can be learned of value to the provision of mainstream systems from the holistic approach that necessarily follows in response to situations of disaster. Sadly very little of this potential value is actually perceived, and even less is embraced. Consequently, one of the aims of the series, both in the core volume *Education as a Global Concern* and in the contributing volumes, is to bring the notion of education as a humanitarian response to the mainstream, and those seeking to serve it as teachers, other educators and politicians.

Among human groups that are very significant in educational terms are those addressed in this book, the indigenous, nomadic and traveller communities. They are something of a paradox in that their disadvantage is often dual, partly in relation to accessing the formal systems of countries, and partly resisting efforts by those formal systems to participate and conform. Rosarii Griffin has done a splendid job in gathering together a range of cases that illustrate this paradox individually and collectively. Not only are such communities often overlooked, merely tolerated or in many cases oppressed, all of which is of global concern in terms of human rights, majority global societies and nations fail to understand the wisdom often exhibited by these communities in terms of positive relationships between human beings and the natural environment. They often also exhibit the power of continual informal education, another form of learning that also exists throughout humanity but is disregarded and denigrated by national formal systems of education.

This aspect is of special significance as the majority of humanity stumbles into potential environmental catastrophe through the twenty-first century.

Colin Brock
Honorary Professor of Education
University of Durham, UK

Acknowledgements

I would like to thank most sincerely all the contributors to this volume who gave of their time and expertise so generously in delivering very interesting and informative chapters in a timely fashion. It is your unique contributions that make this timely volume so special. Míle buíochas.

I would like to thank the Series Editor, Dr Colin Brock, for his unfailing support and generosity of spirit, which, as always, goes well beyond the call of duty. Colin, my heartfelt thanks and appreciation for your patience, kindness and advice. Without you, this book would not have been possible. I'd also like to thank Rosie Pattinson from Bloomsbury Publishing House for her support during the beginning of this project and I'd like to wish her well in her future career at Cambridge. I'd also like to thank Anna Fleming from Bloomsbury, and to congratulate her heartily on the recent arrival of her bundle of joy. I would particularly like to thank Balaji Kasirajan, Claire Cooper and Avinash Singh at Bloomsbury for their collective advice, support and assistance during the compilation and completion of this volume, sincere thanks indeed.

I'd like to thank my UCC colleague and friend, Dr Piaras MacÉinrí, for his ongoing friendship and support during the editing process, and his stalwart contribution to the introductory chapter. Again, míle buíochas. On a similar vein, I'd like to thank Dr James Urwick, a colleague and friend, for his unfailing support and sterling assistance during the editing process. Nothing was left to chance with James reviewing the final manuscript. If any mistakes occur within, these are my responsibility and mine alone.

Finally, I'd like to thank my family and friends for sustaining me through this process, particularly Fintan, and my two beautiful daughters, Catherine and Miriam. I wish to reserve a special thanks to my mother, Carmel Griffin, for instilling in me a belief in the age-old adage that 'the pen is mightier than the sword' when wishing to exact change, especially change for a better world. Grá agus céad míle buíochas!

To conclude, this book is dedicated to all those who fight for the rights of marginalized groups, particularly indigenous, nomadic and travelling communities around the world.

Rosarii Griffin
University College Cork
Ireland

Educational Issues for Indigenous, Nomadic and Travelling Communities: A Global Overview

Rosarii Griffin and Piaras MacÉinrí

University College Cork, Ireland

Modern nation states – the dominant global form of territorial political organization today – are less than adequate containers for the full expression of the multiple varieties of competing individual and communal identities found in all parts of the inhabited world, nor do they necessarily facilitate the negotiation and vindication of equal rights and liberties for all. This inadequacy is complex and multifaceted. It is illustrated by the scarring experiences, notably by indigenous peoples worldwide (Fanon, 1963), of imperialism, colonialism and systematic doctrines of pseudo-scientific racism; earlier moral panics about 'miscegenation' and the more recent emergence of the 'racial state'(Goldberg, 2001); the inferior status of minorities, including nomadic peoples, migrants and trans-nationals in unitary ethno-national polities; the after-effects of the forced movement of peoples following war, famine or other crises; and the effects of explicitly genocidal policies perpetrated against specific peoples such as the Jews of Europe and the Armenians of Ottoman Turkey (Akçam, 2006). Finally, the specific ways in which the various actors have positioned themselves, in terms of gender and social class as well as 'race' and ethnicity, generate their own patterns of discrimination and exclusion (Krenshaw, 1991).

Many of these factors arise from surprisingly modern ideologies and movements, but the reification of difference is not a modern phenomenon at all. Inequalities of treatment between nomadic and settled cultures constitute one of the oldest examples of this process. Greek historian/geographer Herodotus' unflattering descriptions of the equestrian, nomadic Scythians contrasted them unfavourably with his own sedentary and therefore allegedly superior Greek culture. 'Scythian' became a byword for barbarity; Edmund Spenser, poet and colonist in English-occupied early modern Ireland, linked the allegedly uncivil Irish directly back to their supposed ancestors, the aforementioned Scythians (Coughlan, 1989, p. 52), a trope taken up by other cultural commentators in other parts of Europe when discussing other supposedly inferior peoples.

Nomadism, then, became associated with the notion that nomadic people had an inherently inferior culture and civilization. Many found themselves on the margins of society, following trades or occupations which set them apart, and routinely denied civil or social rights or equality with members of mainstream society. Although nomadic people came from a variety of ethnic backgrounds and did not necessarily share the same linguistic, cultural or religious roots, the processes of exclusion and marginalization which they suffered were sometimes remarkably similar. The advent of modernity brought about even higher levels of discrimination on occasions, together with the effects of urbanization in shrinking or even erasing the spaces and places where traditional occupations and ways of life could be pursued.

The development of mass education systems from the early nineteenth century onwards proved a particular challenge. Mass education was not the same thing as universal education and many children from nomadic backgrounds found themselves unable to access education on equal terms and thus to compete with their peers in order to meet the requirements, in terms of literacy and other kinds of formal knowledge, of life in the modern technocratic state. Indigenous children faced similar challenges in dealing with a 'one size fits all' educational model which ignored or was actively hostile to indigenous knowledge and culture.

The process of European expansion and conquest which began with the Spanish and Portuguese colonizations of the 'New World', which reached its peak in the late nineteenth-century 'Scramble for Africa' (Pakenham, 1992) and which did not finally begin to be dismantled, for the most part, until the 1950s, constitutes the second major source of conflict. The occupation, conquest and exploitation of so many parts of the world by European powers proceeded in part via the racialization of relations between conquering and subject peoples, a process which also occurred, as has been seen above, within Europe itself. A new power paradigm emerged, whereby the original peoples were pushed to one side and became the 'indigenous' oppressed within their own land. While the institution of slavery was not an exclusively European invention, it too, literally coloured the forced migrations of the Middle Passage. The rise of pseudo-scientific racism, underpinned by social Darwinism in the late nineteenth century, served as the perfect pretext for self-justifying doctrines of colonial conquest. Since Europeans saw themselves as more 'evolved', it was argued that it was in the interests of conquered peoples to be ruled by the representatives of a superior civilization. The allegedly benign view expressed in Kipling's famous poem 'White Man's Burden' (1899) notwithstanding, European expansion also led to genocide on an industrial scale against native peoples in countries and regions as far apart as the United States, Tasmania and the Herero lands of German-occupied South West Africa. Within Europe itself, the identification of a racialized 'enemy within' reached its culmination with the mass scapegoating of the Jews of Europe and their collective murder in the *Shoah*. Today, Roma and other nomadic peoples continue to be the subject of discrimination and exclusion in many parts of Europe.

Much of the long legacy of European expansionism is still unfinished business. Native Americans did not receive full citizenship rights until 1924 (Indian Citizenship Act, 1924), but many continue to be marginalized members of US society to the present day. It was not until the 1970s that Maori inhabitants of Aotearoa/New Zealand began effective legal action, using the 1840 Treaty of Waitangi to vindicate many rights which had been guaranteed to them and subsequently withdrawn by land-grabbing Pakeha (settlers of European origin) in the late nineteenth century (Larner and Spoonley, 1995). The many debates across the Americas concerning the manner in which Columbus' 'discovery' of the region in 1492 should be commemorated, including the re-naming of the event as Indigenous People's Day in some parts of the USA, is evidence of the ongoing contestation of these underlying histories of conquest and colonization. Even the casual visitor to certain Central and South American countries cannot but be struck by the clear, if informal, hierarchy of colour in public life, whereby persons 'of colour' are more likely than others to be doing the most menial work. But the same region, from Chiapas to Venezuela to Bolivia, has also seen the growth of strong movements emphasizing rights and equality for indigenous peoples (Boel, 2001).

A third source of conflict lay in the very political ideology which thinkers and writers as far apart as Italian Giuseppe Mazzini and Irish activist Patrick Pearse saw as the way of the future: nationalism itself, a powerful ideology for embattled peoples such as the Czechs, Basques and Irish. It drew strongly on Gottfried Herder's vision of the nation as a unique and homogenous community possessing its own *volkgeist*, sharing common ethnic and cultural traits. This view was a driving factor in what might be termed the antiquarian revolution of the nineteenth century, an interest in language and cultures which explains, for instance, the major contribution made by German scholars to Irish philology. In the Herderian tradition all nations are distinct and tribal and, in the strict sense, incommensurable. The only way in which the nation can realize itself and find its highest expression of identity is through political independence and the control of that territory which it regards as its natural home. The state, therefore, is an 'organic state', rather than one based on political citizenship. To a greater or lesser extent this political philosophy underpins most nineteenth-century European nationalist thinking and also represents an explicit rejection of the universalist thinking of the Enlightenment and of the French and American Revolutions.

There was a difficulty, of course, with this view of the 'organic state'. What would happen to migrants and minorities or those other trans-national individuals and communities which owed allegiance to no one nation or whose claims were not accepted by their co-citizens?

One possible answer, following the French tradition, lay in part in defining the nation in political rather than ethno-national terms. Renan's famous question *Qu'est ce qu'une nation?* (what is a nation?) in his 1882 Sorbonne conference (Renan, 1882), sought explicitly to refute the notion that race or religion could be the basis of the modern nation, which, rather, was based on a 'daily plebiscite' of those who gave it their allegiance, although also accompanied by a degree of unavoidable violence and 'necessary forgetting'. Herein lies a core problem, because the 'necessary forgetting' necessarily meant the elimination of difference and the homogenization of what it meant to be French.

The twentieth century was the great age of modernity, increasing state interventionism, mass migration and globalization. The *laissez faire* policies of Victorian Britain, for instance, gave way to a far more powerful state, intervening increasingly in all walks of public life – and nowhere more so than in education. In France, the iconic school text *Le Tour de France par deux enfants* (the Tour of France by Two Children) (Bruno, 1887) first published in

1877 and still in use in the 1950s, was not a travelogue for French school children as much as top-down, ideologically driven project to make the many regions and cultures of France into one. Education and universal male conscription were seen as key tools of integration and assimilation in a country where many people still spoke languages other than French as their daily vernacular. The very concept of treasuring 'minority' or 'indigenous' rights or cultures could have formed no part of such an approach.

While space does not allow a more extensive treatment of the themes evoked above, they may be seen as forming part of a continuum of views which saw the issue of 'race' in society in hierarchical and central terms. Such views profoundly affected the construction of difference, entitlements and rights, whether the groups in question were indigenous peoples, nomadic peoples, minorities or migrants. The responses to such differences in white settler societies were matters of on-going debate in all such societies throughout most of the twentieth century, although in many cases the issues were constructed, not so much in terms of whether certain groups were seen as inferior – that was read as a given – but rather whether, in certain contexts, they could be 'civilized'.

The role of education came to be seen as a central part of the 'civilizing process' and the extirpation of any vestigial remnants of 'indigenous' culture became, for instance, a key element in the education of Australian Aboriginal children. The most egregious element of all, in the Australian case, was the forcible separation and removal of Aboriginal children from their parents and their schooling in circumstances far removed from their home environment. Similar policies were implemented in Canada. Not all colonial education policy was assimilationist. There were 'adapted' variants, especially in parts of the British Empire that had few European settlers. These variants, however, like their modern counterparts, tended to have low status.

Returning to the more general issue, the prevailing tenor of debates concerning what would nowadays be called 'integration' in the early part of the twentieth century was strongly assimilationist in most countries. By implication, it was up to the 'outsider' – whether indigenous or incomer – to 'fit into' (or be excluded from) a dominant culture, in which 'natural insiders' would always possess the upper hand in terms of cultural capital.

Early definitions of assimilation theory are associated with the influential Chicago School of Sociology of the 1920s. Full assimilation was the end point of several stages – contact, conflict, accommodation and acculturation – and was seen as not only inevitable but desirable, whether those to be assimilated were migrants or Native Americans. In numerous countries, policies of a more or less forced assimilation, reflecting the hegemonic ideology of those who dominated the state, were the rule rather than the exception, even if sometimes inspired by a benign belief that integration and social harmony were best achieved by stressing shared core cultural values rather than diversity.

Such ideas began to be challenged more actively by the 1960s. For one thing, it became evident in societies such as the USA and the UK that 'ethnicity' and 'difference' did not disappear over time, that racism was an on-going reality and that the rights and opportunities of migrants, minorities and indigenous peoples were not equal to those of the mainstream. Moreover, the 1960s were a decade which emphasized difference, with the rise of the Civil Rights Movement, the women's movement and the 'events' of 1968 in France and elsewhere. Some African Americans even made common cause with the Viet Cong, the supposed enemy of the United States. As boxer Muhammed Ali famously put it in 1966, 'I Ain't Got No Quarrel with The VietCong…No VietCong Ever Called Me Nigger' (Haas, 2011, p. 27).

Meanwhile, in a number of industrialized countries, assimilationist doctrines were being tested and questioned. UK Home Secretary Roy Jenkins famously rejected assimilation as a policy in 1965, noting that the UK approach was 'not a flattening process of assimilation but equal opportunity accompanied by cultural diversity in an atmosphere of mutual tolerance' (Lester, 2004, p. 142). Even with this phrase, there were those who argued that something stronger than 'tolerance' was called for, but it was a start. Real change, however, began in Canada.

Identity politics in Canada were already highly complex. Apart from the traditional divide between French- and English-speaking Canada, which had persisted since the eighteenth century, notably in Québec, Aboriginal Canadians, including First Nations peoples, Inuit and Métis, were beginning, notably in the twentieth century, to seek greater autonomy as well as a range of social, economic and cultural rights. Ironically, it was a third element in Canadian society which spurred the introduction of what became a new multicultural template for co-existence. This was the arrival in Canada in recent decades of increasing numbers of non-British, non-French immigrants, beginning with people from other parts of Europe but also including other groups from Lebanon to various parts of Asia. Ukrainian-Canadian academic and politician Paul Yuzyk is generally credited as the originator of modern multiculturalism, a policy championed in the early 1970s by then Canadian prime minister Pierre Trudeau. To quote the Canadian government's official website for the Paul Yuzyk Award:

According to Mr Yuzyk, Canada could succeed in building a strong nation through adherence to the principles of Confederation, compromise and 'unity in diversity'. He challenged the prevailing view that Canada was a bilingual and bicultural nation (in addition to Canada's native peoples). He argued that Canadian society also included Canadians who were of neither British nor French descent. He also predicted that Canada would become a role model for other nations faced with the challenge of integrating peoples of diverse faiths and cultures. (Citizenship and Immigration Canada)

Both Canada and Australia legislated for the new multiculturalism, and variations of multiculturalism were introduced in a number of other countries, including Britain, the Netherlands and Sweden. These have been contested in the past decade, notably in the aftermath of social unrest in the Netherlands (relating to the murders of Pym Fortuyn and Theo Van Gogh in 2002 and 2004 respectively), Britain (riots in UK Midlands cities of mixed communities at the beginning of the 2000s) and France (the 2005 riots in the *banlieux*). Certain European politicians, including the UK's David Cameron and Germany's Angela Merkel, have declared, without advancing any credible proof, that multiculturalism is a 'failure'.

The rise of violent, xenophobic new movements (such as *Jobbik* in Hungary and *Golden Dawn* in Greece), targeting nomadic people, immigrants and minorities, cannot be denied. Moreover, multiculturalism has been criticized by some who argue that it reduces real differences in rights and equality to soft-core debates about the politics of identity or who argue, as Ghassan Hage powerfully does, that an enduring fantasy of a 'white nation' persists even among liberal multiculturalists (Hage, 1998). In France and other countries, there are still lively debates about how to find the right balance between *intégration, tolérance* and an alleged excessive multicultural *relativisme* of a kind which might destroy the role of the school in promoting social harmony and mutual understanding (Haut Conseil à l'Intégration, 2011). Indeed, these debates have proved so divisive that the *Haut Conseil* itself has now been disbanded (Le Bars, 2013).

Perhaps the last word on multiculturalism, and one of particular relevance to this book, is suggested by a comment of Shohat and Stam on the link between multiculturalism and a necessary critique of Eurocentrism:

The celebration of multiculturalism and the critique of Eurocentrism are for us inseparable concepts. Multiculturalism without the critique of Eurocentrism runs the risk of being merely accretive – a shopping mall summa of the world's cultures, while the critique of Eurocentrism without multiculturalism runs the risk of simply inverting rather than profoundly unsettling and rearticulating existing hierarchies. The goal of what we call 'polycentric' multiculturalism is to eliminate, as far as possible and in our own specific sphere of action, the long-term cultural legacies of Eurocentrism and white supremacy. (Shohat and Stam, 2001)

Summing up, it should be difficult for any multicultural, multiethnic state nowadays, whatever its composition, to advance educational, social, economic and political policies which do not seek to recognize the specificity and historical basis of the identity claims being staked out by disparate indigenous, minority, nomadic and migrant groups. Of necessity, this must be the starting point for a volume such as this one, which focuses on such issues through a single prism: the provision of education. This book, therefore, is a global exploration of the provision of formal and non-formal education for indigenous, nomadic and travelling communities in their home countries. Through case study exploration, *Education in Indigenous, Nomadic and Travelling Communities* highlights various factors that significantly affect the provision of indigenous peoples and travelling communities' education. Within this volume, special attention is given to the socio-cultural notion and processes of 'integrating' travelling, nomadic and indigenous communities. 'Integration' is not understood as *assimilation* or absorption – perhaps 'respectful incorporation in diversity' might be closer (Mac Éinrí, 2007). Similarly, the purpose of providing formal and non-formal education at the school and university level to indigenous, nomadic and travelling communities within the culture of the dominant 'settled' people and the received wisdom behind this idea are also explored. Some attention is paid to other issues, such as the structure of the type of education provided. Less attention is paid specifically to curriculum content or pedagogical approaches, unless deemed essential to the wider context.

This book posits the importance of providing a contextually suitable educational system while respecting the identity of the indigenous, travelling or nomadic community and sustaining livelihoods. How this can be achieved within the modern context, and in the face of increasing bureaucratic government models of engaging, remains to be determined. However, it is important to expand the debate on these matters, and to broaden understandings around the cultural complexities raised within the variety of situations highlighted in this volume. In doing so, this book also wishes to highlight the aspirations of some case-specific travelling, nomadic and indigenous community groups – children, youth and adults – and examine ways of promoting increased access to sustainable livelihoods through the medium of education, in a way that is culturally sensitive and self-directed.

Within the broader international frame of reference, Article 4 of the UNESCO *Convention Against Discrimination in Education* (1960) obliges governments to develop and apply policy in such a way as to 'promote equality of opportunity and of treatment in the matter of education'. The convention also states that 'children of minority communities and indigenous peoples have the right to enjoy their own culture, to practice their own religion and to use their own language'. In line with the *UN Convention on the Rights of the Child* (1989), Articles 2, 28, 29 and 30, indigenous, nomadic and traveller children have the right to adequate accommodation; respect for their cultural identity and values; appropriate education; and freedom and protection from discrimination. However, there is a lot of tension between these two cited goals, which presents many dilemmas for the providers of education, some of which are examined herein. In this volume, the authors show different degrees of emphasis on each of these goals. For instance, Cherubini and Keskitalo et al. emphasize cultural goals over equal educational opportunity issues, while Lechamanan and Ramli prioritize equal educational opportunity issues and do not appear to expressly favour a special curriculum for Orang Asli pupils. Meanwhile, Kenny appears to give equal weighting to both goals, notwithstanding the tensions therein. Against the background of past injustices as outlined at the beginning of this chapter, there is always the danger that curricula that are culturally adapted for minority or indigenous groups will not give opportunities for improved livelihoods and fuller participation in public life. (The same dilemma, incidentally, sometimes occurs in a special needs educational context.) The book, however, makes these dilemmas more evident and also suggests that there is, of necessity, no 'one best way' of responding to them (Urwick, 2013).

Education in Indigenous, Nomadic and Travelling Communities: A Global Overview examines current case studies of educational provision to Travelling communities and indigenous peoples in their homeland or in host countries. Education is usually under-utilized during phases of transition. In many instances, indigenous groups and travelling people, including nomads, do not have educational opportunities equal to that of their settled counterpart-citizens of their country and this results in early school leaving, high school drop-out rates, low school attendance and low success rates resulting in such groups beginning their working life at an early age and finding difficulty penetrating the formal employment arena. This volume looks at the factors affecting educational provision to travelling, nomadic and indigenous groups. Other global case studies will result in a comparative examination of similar cases.

Measures are needed to tackle discrimination which affects the development of the full potential of traveller, nomadic and indigenous children. Such measures need to be put in place urgently. Within this frame of reference, the voice of the traveller, nomadic and indigenous child needs to be heard in policy development. These understandings need to be derived through culturally attuned deeply qualitative and ethnographic approaches. This book attempts to highlight these issues, examining in some depth a range of factors that affect decisions concerning the provision of education.

This volume uses case studies to discuss the provision of, and the policies around, the education of travelling, indigenous and nomadic communities in Ireland, the UK, the EU and Russia, Asia, and South and North America. This book provides a current account and source of information for students and academics in the field of education as a humanitarian response. It also provides a thorough understanding of the importance of the role of education in assisting travelling, nomadic and indigenous peoples to overcome experiences of social and economic exclusion, to gain access to social capital, to alleviate issues arising from the adjustment required when catering to the demands of a modern economy and to find educational pathways into higher education levels and associated professions. Thus the following collection of chapters arose from an interest in, and a dearth of knowledge about, education in indigenous, nomadic and traveller communities around the globe. What makes this volume particularly important is the inclusion of many groups which are often excluded from common discourses on and about education. The chapters herein force us to reimagine education, and to create a vision of education which goes beyond schooling, especially beyond schooling for inclusion in the workforce, an education driven by neoliberal concerns within a Eurocentric educational paradigm. What this volume does is to open our eyes to the diversity of people within our midst, and to show that the drive to homogenize and make others like ourselves is, at best, mistaken and, at worst, a form of genocide. There are, as highlighted in all the chapters – but particularly those by Cherubini and Aikman – many different epistemes and ways of knowing. There are other dimensions to knowledge, and other reasons to be educated, that stretch far beyond the economic. For far too long, perhaps, education has been dominated by industrial and post-industrial concerns. The chapters in this book highlight a growing disconnect between people and the land and their culture. And then there are indigenous peoples, fighting for their culture, language and heritage, at risk of losing precious intergenerational knowledge which has sustained them for millennia. The loss of identity has already been a major concern following decades, if not centuries, of assimilationist policies within education – the dominant paradigm demonizing and estranging the 'other'. In some places, this has translated into overt racial policies and discrimination practices, or into inadequate provision, or indeed, into indifference within national educational systems with unspoken and hidden messages transmitted through mainstream curricula which can prove difficult to prevent.

What follows exemplifies academic debates around theories of inclusion, exclusion, intercultural, intra-cultural or assimilationist policies through an exploration of various case situations facing different indigenous groups around the world, and of approaches that have been taken to educate in a way that is inclusive, holistic and meaningful, as well as providing adequate preparation for full participation in modern democracies. The case material presented herein may also be useful for such debates as well as the development of policy and practice which is a real challenge and one that is being met with varying degrees of success by different governments who have different levels of awareness and cognizance of the issues at stake. This book is an eclectic collection about the fate of Gypsies, Travellers, nomadic groups and indigenous peoples within the educational sphere. While different countries address their respective ethnic groups differently, it appears that there is much to be learnt from 'thinking outside the box' and looking to our counterparts in the global South. There, we see many novel approaches to education in the broadest sense, and perhaps, for us in the West, there is much to be learnt therein.

A volume as this could not possibly expect to cover all countries or areas of the globe. Surprisingly, perhaps, the Aboriginal people of Australia or Maori of New Zealand (Aotearoa) are not discussed in this book, but neither are the many indigenous, travelling and nomadic groups in India, Pakistan, the Middle East or Africa. Rather, what follows is a selection and variety of diverse cases which may provoke further thought and reading on the different approaches to education. What is important is that countries look beyond themselves, and learn from other cultures and contexts, and allow those impacted by educational policies to dictate the terms of reference of the education they wish for themselves, for it is only through self-determination that people do become in control of their own destinies.

The following is a brief synthesis of the chapters herein, which is intended to guide readers and researchers towards cases most relevant to their research interests.

In her incisive chapter, 'Cross-Cultural Communication and Change: Travellers and Roma, and the Irish Education System', author Máirín Kenny has as its central focus Irish Travellers within the Republic of Ireland. Kenny highlights that while the current education system's intercultural policy is ostensibly inclusive, it is 'ultimately assimilationist'. In an interesting twist, Ireland does not recognize the Travellers as a separate ethnic group, but rather views this group as being 'culturally distinct', though sharing the same rights and entitlements as an 'ethnic minority group'. Kenny believes that, as in other places, Irish Travellers, though long established, are not necessarily a 'wanted' group being treated as a 'subtle and silenced' sub-culture. Perhaps, Kenny posits, this group appears to present a latent threat to the sedentary dominant settled majority. Whatever the reasons, the growth of capitalism and the rise of property ownership have contributed to Irish Travellers' experiencing discrimination and assimilation policies similar to that of their EU counterparts. Kenny then explores the many narratives, both positive and negative, around Travellers and their heritage. Some popular narratives play on common stereotypes of the Travelling community. Kenny comments that data on Traveller education is patchy. Unfortunately, it appears they tend to cluster into more disadvantaged schools and areas. Though enrolment figures have increased – particularly at second level – overall Traveller participation, attainment and progression in the formal schooling sector remains low. Kenny explores the reasons for this, which vary from cultural alienation, to racism, to bullying. Education does not appear to offer the same cultural capital to Traveller children as to settled children. Kenny points out that Travellers do value and want further education. However, the provision on offer does not appear to accommodate their needs or value their culture. Kenny suggests that the increasing influence of neoliberalism, pushing an economically driven notion of inclusive education, has forced the concept of identity 'to take a backseat'. She concludes that the tensions between sedentary and nomadic relations remain unresolved, with opportunities on both sides to negotiate. Kenny concludes that for the Travelling community within Ireland, more work needs to be done, especially by education providers.

In her chapter 'Education as Cultural Conflict: Gypsies and Travellers in the South of England', Juliet McCaffery takes us on an ethnographic journey through her research of the Gypsy and Traveller communities in Southern England, including some interactions with Irish Travellers. The documentary evidence that forms the basis of her chapter derives from a myriad of sources, including minutes of meetings, the media and face-to-face interviews-involving what McCaffery describes as the varied 'discourses' of different participants. McCaffery highlights the mismatch between the Gypsy and Traveller tradition of educating their children through the practical process of induction which is very different from the formalized abstract learning required in school. She highlights the cultural tensions this mismatch creates for children from these communities. McCaffery highlights that the educational attainment of the Gypsy and Travelling communities, as measured in standardized tests, is very much lower than their settled counterparts. Literacy, the ability to read and write, was not perceived by previous generations of Gypsies or Travellers to be socially or economically important, although this is slowly changing and a greater value is placed on literacy as essential for modern day living, though secondary education is still frequently regarded as irrelevant. McCaffery makes a clear case that these ethnic minority groups are under-represented in education and under-valued by society. Indeed, as a result of a combination of ignorance and misunderstanding of their ethnic culture, discrimination occurs directly and indirectly against such groups. Interestingly, McCaffery also suggests that non-literacy is sometimes used by Gypsies and Travellers as a defensive mechanism to reinforce social cohesion within their culture, and as a way of avoiding assimilation. Whilst some do perceive literacy and education as a means for participating more fully in a democratic society, there are still problems with formal schooling. Cultural training for teachers and the inclusion of Gypsy and Traveller culture within the curriculum might assist in enabling Gypsy and Traveller children retain their culture and achieve their educational potential.

The chapter 'A Case Study of Gypsy travellers in the East Riding of Yorkshire, UK' by Judith Smith and Helen Worrell gives a colourful account of the recent history of Gypsies and Travellers in the East Riding area of Yorkshire, UK. Smith and Worrell give an in-depth description of the Gypsy and Traveller way of life, and their acceptance (or not) by the settled community. Mostly, due to well-established patterns, these groups were by and large well received by local settled communities. Smith and Worrell highlight the importance of intergenerational informal learning which typically occurs within such groups. An act 'to restrict the eviction from caravan sites of occupiers of caravans and make other provision for the benefit of such occupiers; to secure the establishment of such sites by local authorities for the use of Gypsies and other persons of nomadic habit...' changed the patterns of travel for both Gypsies and Travellers alike. Smith and Worrell describe further acts of legislation which served to further restrict their movement from place to place, directly or indirectly enforcing settlement policies on these nomadic groups. The authors further describe the educational system and local attempts to include the Travelling community within their formalized structured. Such local attempts were mildly successful. Smith and Worrell are at pains to point out that, while the Gypsy and Travelling communities do recognize the increasing importance of education, they are naturally suspicious of the curriculum, of the formalized processes which define schooling life and of the effect that this may have, directly and indirectly, on their culture and heritage as a Travelling community. Smith and Worrell also point out how traditional gender roles, norms and patterns long established within Travelling communities, which play a strong part in their culture and identity formation, have also been challenged through education. Resistance to change often takes the form of self-exclusion. However, as Smith and Worrell report, the evidence shows too that this is often as a result of overt racism and exclusion directed towards them by the settled community.

Smith and Worrell highlight some case examples to illustrate the complexities of the dilemmas and issues facing the Gypsy and Traveller communities within the current climate. They are sympathetic to the cross-roads that these groups face in trying to sustain their collective and individual identities within the current climate. Their chosen examples – not elaborated on here – lend themselves to very interesting insights. Suffice to say that what the chosen vignettes illustrate beautifully is that when the local education community (i.e. educational projects and organizations) are working in harmony and partnership with the Gypsy-Traveller community, and when the subject matter is genuinely inclusive and when real attempts are made to enhance the Gypsy-Traveller culture, this model appears to work extremely well and to be enormously successful for all concerned. More importantly, as pointed out by Smith and Worrell, barriers to building trust are broken down, and bonds of friendship are strengthened between both communities accordingly. However, the researchers still point out that while the primary education sector goes a long way to supporting the Gypsy and Travelling communities, at the secondary level, such children can experience exclusion and bullying and become disaffected. As Smith and Worrell highlight, there are good examples of success stories, but there are still enormous challenges to be met within the education sector in overcoming prejudice and cultural differences between the settled and Travelling communities.

Moving northwards, the chapter on the Sámi nomadic group spans across four countries: Norway, Sweden, Finland and Russia, in descending order of numeric presence. 'Multi-Dimensional Sámi Education – Towards Culture-Sensitive Policies', by Pigga Keskitalo, Satu Uusiautti and Kaarina Määttä, based on the fate of the Sámi, proves to be another very interesting chapter in this volume. Originating from hunter-gatherer tribes, the Sámi have traditionally been involved with fishing, hunting and reindeer herding (in small numbers). Today, the Sámi have, to some degree, embraced urbanization. However, according to the authors, this has been highly influenced by centuries of assimilationist policies in operation in all four countries. In effect, Keskitalo, Uusiautti and Määttä warn us that all Sámi indigenous languages are endangered. The authors highlight how positive discrimination is warranted in order to protect the Sámi community, its languages and culture. Historically, assimilation policies have had a detrimental effect on the traditional Sámi way of life. Keskitalo, Uusiautti and Määttä believe that 'the position of the indigenous language and a culture-based approach should be adopted at the core of teaching and language planning' and call for 'transformative solutions' and a 'pedagogical revolution' that is appropriate. So too do the authors warn against the dangers of idealizing the Sámi past, and ignoring their skilful adaptations to modern life whilst preserving their Sámi culture and heritage. The authors remind us to be mindful of the Sámi's right to progress and integrate within society and that this should be valued in an inclusive and intercultural way. Ironically, the Sámi way of life, and education, is holistic in nature and is reminiscent of Rousseau's child-centred and naturalistic approach to education along with Montessori's notion of independent thinking and reflection. However, given the endangered position of Sámi languages and culture, the authors call upon the four aforementioned countries to sensitize their curricula and pedagogical approaches in order to secure, revitalize and preserve Sámi culture into the future.

Within the broader EU context, Christine O'Hanlon's chapter, 'Roma and Traveller Inclusion in Europe: Why Informal Education is Winning', explores the situation of the Roma and similar groups within Europe and how they have been affected by past and present policies. O'Hanlon explores this from a macro perspective, examining policies and processes which have had direct implications for disparate groups living in the EU region. In fact, in some ways, O'Hanlon's chapter complements McCaffery's chapter, where the latter illustrates how macro policies can play out at the grassroots level, in this case in Southern England. O'Hanlon also describes the recent, and not-so-recent, rise of right wing politics in Europe, coinciding with the inclusion of the Eastern European accession states as part of the greater EU, often giving rise to racism. Institutional racism has historically been supported by government decrees. This was particularly evident against the Roma community of Travellers in the earlier part of the twentieth century. O'Hanlon highlights that the Roma community, in particular, has suffered various forms of persecution from different EU states since then, in spite of the laws that are there to protect them. O'Hanlon points out, for instance, that the tendency to assign Roma children to special schools (i.e. schools for children with disabilities) has been a problem in Eastern Europe until relatively recently. Nevertheless, the situation for Roma has improved considerably in the twenty-first century. Concrete strategies, such as early childhood education and intervention, have been viewed as an effective means of overcoming social exclusion and marginalization in relation to such groups. However, *access* to early education still remains problematic for Roma.

O'Hanlon also highlights how the provision and structure of education is often in direct conflict with Roma culture, tradition and values. Very little accommodation is made to facilitate ethnic minority groups who do not fit the majority mould. In fact, O'Hanlon shows that, while provision is made, the kind of provision is neither suitable nor accommodating. Hence, the Roma community and others are suspicious of the drive to 'integrate' and 'assimilate' at the perceived cost of their cultural heritage. Such groups are not willing to forfeit generations of received wisdom and apprentice-type educational experience. As a result, the Roma community do not fare well in traditional educational settings nor is their performance reflected well in formal examinations. Not surprisingly, Roma underperform compared to their settled counterparts – drop-out rates remain high and literacy levels low. By and large, O'Hanlon points out, Roma are, with good reason, 'suspicious of authority'. Nevertheless, the relatively disadvantaged position of Roma and other similar groups is well documented. They are also disadvantaged linguistically, with little or no credence paid to their mother tongue, creating further barriers along linguistic lines. Aside from institutional discrimination practices, poverty is a further issue that causes Roma to self-segregate, not having the necessary funds for books, uniforms, transport to school or schooling expenses.

Despite EU rules and regulations, local governments still often rule in favour of discrimination practices. O'Hanlon highlights too that the media sometimes sensationalize a negative portrayal of Roma and Traveller life, further inciting hostile attitudes to such ethnic minorities. This 'othering' of such groups can create a false dichotomy of 'them' versus 'us', generating perceived threats to stability. Moreover, the Roma way of life, typically divided along traditional gender roles and expectations, often appears to fly in the face of more 'progressive' societies and ways of life. O'Hanlon believes that the Roma community is generally under-researched when it comes to its educational welfare, especially in light of recent EU reports that highlight the comparative educational disadvantage of Roma and Traveller groups. Action on EU recommendations to states to improve the social inclusion of such groups remains an ongoing battle. O'Hanlon wonders if the EU's dedicated decade of Roma inclusion, due to end by 2015, will make any real difference to the educational lives of this ethnic group.

The next chapter moves swiftly beyond Europe towards South-east Asia and is based on the Orang Asli (OA), and is authored by Hema Letchamanan and Firdaus Ramli. 'Orang Asli' is the name given to the eighteen indigenous minority ethnic groups (clustered in three main groups) from Peninsular Malaysia. Like other indigenous, traveller and nomadic groups, these groups are affected both by poverty and by a low level of educational attainment. Access to education that is culturally appropriate and relevant is a cross-cutting theme amongst all the ethnic minority groups represented in this book, and the OA are no different. The OA as a group appear to have been excluded from any privileges which might assist them to progress in modern-day life. Drawing on Maslow's 'hierarchy of needs' theoretical framework, Letchamanan and Ramli explore the reasons for the high attrition rates of OA children within the schooling system and they apply Maslow's work to examine what factors might affect the motivational levels of the OA children in relation to school attendance. While Maslow's theoretical lens provides one way of viewing the difficulties that arise for OA children in respect of school attendance, Letchamanan and Ramli also call on the 4A framework, which in some ways offers a way forward for educational planners to think about education from the perspective of OA indigenous groups. This framework includes notions of 'Availability, Accessibility, Acceptability and Adaptability' (SUHAKAM, 2009) and is a framework often used to understand truancy and low educational attainment levels. It may also go some way to address the overarching factor for non-educational attendance: acute poverty. Letchamanan and Ramli highlight how in spite of the Malaysian government's attempts, in conjunction with certain NGOs, to address the lower educational attainment of OA, evidence shows that far more needs to be done with this community to reap relevant benefits from their educational experience. The authors of this chapter urge that the OA should be included more effectively in discussions, decision-making and policies about their effective inclusion within the educational domain.

Returning westward, in a fascinating chapter, Lorenzo Cherubini gives a very passionate account of the fate of the Aboriginal and American Indian and Alaska Native (AI/AN) people within Canada and the USA. His chapter, entitled 'Indigenous Groups' Education: The Case of North America', highlights how the Aboriginal and AI/AN culture and heritage and self-taught educational system have been systematically and brutally oppressed – overtly and perhaps inadvertently – through ongoing Western and Eurocentric policies of assimilation. Mainstream models of education have been based on individualism, in direct conflict with Aboriginal and AI/AN communitarian educational and cultural practices. Cherubini highlights, for example, that within the North American system of education, there are internal contradictions between the official recognition of Aboriginal and AI/AN differences and the inadequate measures put in place to accommodate them, either through pedagogical practices or though the provision of appropriate curricula and assessment procedures. Cherubini gives a comprehensive whistle-stop historical tour of the various pieces of legislation and policy making, both in Canada and in the USA, which attempted to assimilate in an attempt to accommodate the Aboriginal and AI/AN people into the melting pot that is North America. These essentially assimilationist policies did more to homogenize rather than to officially recognize legitimate cultural differences and opposing educational traditions. However, Cherubini points out that, following certain watershed reports, the endangered position of Aboriginal culture has finally been recognized and such groups are encouraged to rediscover their long-oppressed identities and heritage. Yet, Cherubini reports that the problems facing such groups are profound, including huge problems around the decline of their native languages. Citing Bourdieu, Cherubini highlights how 'dominant languages can embody the exercise of power in socio-political arenas', distorting and affecting the Aboriginal and AI/AN relationship with its own culture and worldview. Nevertheless, strides are being made to tackle educational disadvantage within Aboriginal and AI/AN groups through a transformative and participatory model of education which extends beyond the classroom, endorsing their traditional episteme and way of life. Cherubini concludes his chapter by making a number of recommendations to ensure that the Aboriginal and AI/AN worldview and culture are valued and cherished within society.

Heading South, in her very insightful chapter, 'Intercultural Bilingual Education, Self-Determination and Indigenous Peoples of the Amazon Basin', Sheila Aikman describes the struggles faced by such marginalized groups. Aikman's chapter 'considers the growth of intercultural bilingual education (IBE) in the Peruvian Amazon' and she asks about 'the nature of the expectations of IBE for those debating and shaping the concept' as well as for 'those drafting the policies... not least indigenous leaders, parents and learners engaging with IBE as a practice'. Aikman reports how many Latin American countries have embraced many different forms of intercultural education, along with indigenous languages, to support their educational aspirations.

However, Aikman, argues that these aspirations are diverse and contradictory. She examines intercultural bilingual education in the Peruvian Amazon context through three theoretical lenses - education for economic and social development, education and decolonisation, and education for indigenous self-determination. It distinguishes between educational modalities and aims of education for indigenous peoples and contrasts this with indigenous peoples' own diverse responses and demands in fast changing local, national and global contexts, including indigenous peoples' active engagement with international rights through UN Declaration on the Rights of Indigenous Peoples. Aikman discusses variants of intercultural bilingual education in different contexts and notes that though there not just one model, intercultural bilingual education can offer good practice and quality education for inclusive schooling for young indigenous learners, but this is dependent on many factors. These factors include the policy aims for education, learners' aims and the nature of the intercultural relationship. Her chapter considers two examples of intercultural bilingual education programmes in the region and considers some of the challenges to the practice of intercultural bilingual education and of the need for ongoing reflection and critique of the process of doing intercultural bilingual education in contexts characterized by weak democratic structures, economic exploitation and structural inequalities.

These examples are discussed in relation to analyses of post-coloniality and historically informed critiques of education and education systems in the region which challenge neoliberal hegemonies and dominant education agendas. Aikman notes, moreover, that concepts and practices of intercultural bilingual education have been critiqued for the ways that they can serve the majority or dominant systems. The chapter provides insights into the complex and diverse contexts in which indigenous people lives today and discusses the situation of the Arakmbut of SE Peruvian Amazon where attempts to introduce intercultural bilingual education have been seen by community members as being assimilationist and marginalizing. She shows how different indigenous communities, within the same country and region, can have very different priorities for formal education and for the Arakmbut intercultural education symbolizes the resurgence of a colonial form of exclusion, which labels them as different and `inferior'.

Whilst this volume criss-crosses the globe, representing the unique situations of various indigenous, nomadic and traveller groups, some cross-cutting themes emerge. As aforementioned, at the macro level, there is a case for reimagining education beyond the traditional educational system: reimagining educational structures and settings, pedagogical methods, curricular content and assessment procedures and modes of examination that are more culturally attuned and appropriate to indigenous, nomadic and traveller group settings. At the more micro level, there is a case for decentralizing education so as to encourage groups to generate systems of indigenous education that are inclusive of their traditions, mores and beliefs whilst also preparing them, if they so desire, for the challenges of modern-day life and full participation in democratic processes. This is particularly important where indigenous groups make up a considerable percentage of the local population. Nonetheless, the concept of equal educational opportunity is inescapably important, and for minorities it is affected by the wider economy and society.

In such societies, there is also a case for tackling the underlying causes of poverty, and not blaming minority groups for being 'other' and not mirroring the dominant society. Particularly in the Western context, there is a case for looking beyond 'educational disadvantage', 'truancy', 'high attrition rates' and 'low educational performance' and for reflecting back on society's modes, methods and mechanisms for determining success and failure within the educational sphere.

The question remains about 'who is failing whom' within education. And this question goes back to the very foundation of education. Education for what purpose? Education for whom? Has it become education for education's sake? There are many factors that need to be considered when thinking about education, including the sociological, historical, economic, geographical, cultural, linguistic, spiritual, ritualistic, community and spatial context of education, for instance (Brock, 2011). Historically, since the industrial era, education has been packaged and delivered in linear fashion. Today, in most Western democracies, educational systems are highly centralized with a high degree of control over curricula and assessment procedures, the results of which are the accepted currency for social success, for promotion and for progression within set systems and institutions. Perhaps, as this volume suggests, it is time to put a mirror to the soul of education and ask, 'Mirror, mirror on the wall, which is the fairest of them all?' And maybe, the mirror will reflect back that it is the travelling, indigenous nomad who instinctively understands how education might be reconceived in a holistic way. Maybe, just maybe, this volume will teach us to reimagine education, not just for the sake of those marginalized (either by or through education – by default or by design) but also to assist educators to imagine a different way of being, so that education might truly become a 'drawing out' as opposed to a 'filling up'. To paraphrase Mahatma Gandhi, education is and should be about drawing out the best in a person – mind, body and spirit.

It is our hope that this volume will contribute some understanding to the broader macro debate, as well as create a greater appreciation of the precarious predicaments that confronts all travelling, nomadic and indigenous peoples around the world. Ideally, it is highly desirable that education be harnessed to assist their progression in the life that they chose to live. Education must not be used as a weapon to destroy or belittle such unique cultures, belief systems and heritage that have served these communities well over time. If this happens, then we shall all be collectively responsible, and we shall all be the poorer for it. Rather, education must be conceived as a vehicle to appreciate different forms of knowledge, understanding and being. What form schooling and its provision takes is a related matter. And the marriage of the two? Well, therein lies the challenge.

References

Akçam, T. (2006), *A Shameful Act: The Armenian Genocide and the Question of Turkish Responsibility.* London: Constable.

Boel, N. (2001), 'Talking to Eduardo Galleano: The open veins of mcworld', The UNESCO Courrier, pp. 47–51.

Brock, C. (2011), *Education as a Global Concern.* Education as a Humanitarian Response Series. London: Continuum Books.

Bruno, G. (1887), *Le Tour de France par Deux Enfants.* Retrieved from http://www.gutenberg.org/files/27782/27782-h/27782-h.htm on 22 October 2013.

Citizenship and Immigration Canada. 'About Paul Yuzyk', Retrieved from http://www.cic.gc.ca/english/multiculturalism/paulyuzyk/paul.asp on 23 October 2013.

Coughlan, P. (1989), "'Some secret scourge which shall by her come unto England": Ireland and incivility in Spenser', in P. Coughlan (ed.), *Spenser and Ireland: An Interdisciplinary Perspective*. Cork: Cork University Press.

Fanon, F. (1963), *The Wretched of the Earth*. New York: Grove Press.

Goldberg, D. T. (2001), *The Racial State*. New York: Wiley-Blackwell.

Haas, G. (2011), *The Assassination of Fred Hampton*. Chicago: Chicago Review Press.

Hage, G. (1998), *White Nation*. Annandale, NSW: Pluto Press Australia.

Haut Conseil à l'Intégration. (2011), "'Le relativisme dans lequel nous vivons": Conversation avec Alain Finkelkraut', *Hommes et Migrations*, 1294, 100–110.

Indian Citizenship Act. (1924), Retrieved from http://www.nebraskastudies.org/0700/frameset_reset.html?http://www.nebraskastudies.org/0700/stories/0701_0146.html.

Kipling, R. (1899), *The White Man's Burden*. Retrieved from http://www.fordham.edu/halsall/mod/kipling.asp on 23 October 2013.

Krenshaw, K. (1991), 'Mapping the margins: Intersectionality, identity politics and violence against women of color', *Stanford Law Review*, 43, (6), 1241–1300.

Larner, W. and Spoonley, P. (1995), 'Post-colonial politics in Aotearoa/New Zealand', in D. Stasiulis and N. Yuval-Davis (eds), *Unsettling Settler Societies: Articulations of Gender, Race, Ethnicity and Class*. London: Sage.

Le Bars, S. (2013), 'Laïcité: Matignon signe l'avis de décès du Haut Conseil à l'intégration', Le Monde, 25 September.

Lester, A. (2004), 'The home office again', in A. Adonis and K. Thomas (eds), *Roy Jenkins: A Retrospective*. Oxford: Oxford University Press.

Mac Éinrí, P. (2007), 'Integration models and choices', in B. Fanning (ed.), *Immigration and Social Change in the Republic of Ireland*. Manchester: Manchester University Press, pp. 214–236.

Pakenham, T. (1992), *The Scramble for Africa: White Man's Conquest of the Dark Continent from 1876 to 1912*. New York: Avon.

Renan, E. (1882), *Qu'est ce qu'une Nation?* Retrieved from http://classiques.uqac.ca/classiques/renan_ernest/qu_est_ce_une_nation/qu_est_ce_une_nation.html on 22 October 2013.

Shohat, E. and Stam, R. (2001), 'French intellectuals and the U.S. culture wars', *Black Renaissance/Renaissance Noire*, 3, (2), 90.

UN. (1989), *Convention on the Rights of the Child*. Articles 2, 28, 29 and 30.

UNESCO. (1960), *Convention Against Discrimination in Education*. Article 4.

Urwick, J. (2013), Email conversations with R. Griffin and P. MacÉinrí debating issues and associated editorial concerns around education for indigenous, nomadic and travelling communities and associated chapters in this volume. October 2013.

Cross-Cultural Communication and Change: Travellers and Roma and the Irish Education System

1

Máirín Kenny

Chapter Outline

Introduction

> For more than a thousand years, Roma people (including Travellers, Gypsies, Manouches, Ashkali, Sinti, etc.) have been an integral part of European civilisation. Today, with an estimated population of 10 to 12 million in Europe (approximately six million of whom live in the EU), Roma people are the biggest ethnic minority in Europe. (Opening statement, European Commission's Roma website, 2012)

In the EU, the term 'Roma' is officially used to denote the range of peoples mentioned in the quote above; however, in Ireland, the dual term 'Travellers and Roma' is used because the two groups are distinct. The Commissioner for

Human Rights (CHR) of the Council of Europe also uses the dual term (CHR, 2012).

Traveller communities in the two jurisdictions on this island – Republic of Ireland (ROI) and Northern Ireland – are closely interlinked, and this has implications for education provision. However, within the scope of this chapter the complexities of this cannot be discussed adequately. This chapter will focus on the situation of Irish Travellers in the ROI education system, contextualizing that in the general European setting.

Irish Travellers comprise a small population in a small nation: there are about thirty-six thousand Travellers, according to the All Ireland Traveller Health Study Team (AITHST, 2010), in a state population of about 4.5 million (Central Statistics Office (CSO), 2012). There are no official data on the recently arrived Roma: their estimated number is about three thousand (Pavee Point, 2013), an estimate cited by the Government of Ireland (2011). In national censuses and other official data records, Roma identity vanishes under nationality, birthplace and broad ethnic category – probably 'White Other' ('other' = not Irish). As regards Roma children in the ROI school system, there are no data other than fragments of anecdotal evidence from Roma and teachers. These fragments indicate that their experience is fraught with difficulty, resonating with the historic experience of Travellers.

The experience of Travellers and Roma and the debates that rage around them at popular, policy and academic levels are very similar across Europe (CHR, 2012; Liégeois, 2007). Diversity and change in current Irish society and in the educational system frame the experience of Travellers and Roma and it is useful to visualize this overall context. Review of policy documents suggests that attempts to include Travellers and Roma in ROI education policy, curricula and practice are defeated by a conceptual fracture at their core.

The broader societal and institutional context shapes Travellers' experience in education, so the core issue regarding their prospects in the system is not about them, but about the dominant society and its institutions. Analysis of recent documents will show that current intercultural policy is ostensibly inclusive, but ultimately assimilationist – perhaps particularly for Travellers and Roma. Historic racism has left its mark, and supports are required to ensure true equality of access, participation and attainment for Travellers and Roma. How such supports are conceptualized and delivered is crucial. There remains an outstanding need to challenge racism, particularly institutional racism; a key element in this is to ensure systemic understanding, recognition and respect for Traveller and Roma identities.

MACMILLAN TERMS

The following terms and conditions apply to all orders for goods that we receive from you, unless otherwise agreed in writing signed by an authorised representative of MDL, and supersede any previous correspondence or discussions between MDL or any authorised agent of MDL and the customer. Customers' terms of purchaser will not apply.

1. Orders

1.1. No order submitted to MDL shall be deemed to be accepted by MDL unless and until confirmed in writing (by invoice submitted with goods delivered, or otherwise) by MDL or by an authorised agent or representative of MDL.

1.2. By accepting delivery of any goods the customer acknowledges receipt of and agrees to be bound by these terms and conditions. All goods are supplied by MDL, unless the relevant invoice expressly states otherwise.

2. Risk and Title

2.1. Risk of damage to or loss of any particular goods supplied by MDL to the customer will pass to the customer on delivery of those goods or, if the customer wrongfully fails to take delivery of those goods, the time when those goods are tendered for delivery. Title and property in any goods, including full legal and beneficial ownership, shall not pass to the customer until MDL has received full payment (in cash or cleared funds) for all goods delivered to the customer under this and all other contracts between the customer and MDL. Full payment of the goods shall include the amount of any interest or other sum payable under the terms of this and all other contracts between the customer and MDL.

3. Charging and Selling

3.1. All books are sold subject to the condition that they shall not, by way of trade or otherwise, be lent, re-sold, hired out or otherwise circulated without our prior consent in any form of binding or cover other than that in which it is published and without a condition to the same effect as this condition being imposed on the subsequent purchase.

4. Payment

4.1. The price of goods is the published price as shown on the invoice less such discount (if any) shown on the invoice. The price is exclusive of any applicable value added or other tax which the customer shall be additionally liable to pay to MDL as shown on the invoice

4.2. No settlement discounts or other deductions may be made against amounts due on MDL's invoice(s) or statement(s).

4.3. If the customer fails to make any payment on the due date then, without prejudice to any other right or remedy available to MDL, MDL shall be entitled to charge the customer interest (both before and after any judgement) on the amount unpaid at the rate of 3% per annum above National Westminster Bank Plc base rate from time to time, until payment in full is made.

4.4. MDL reserves the right to withhold further supplies in the event of amounts payable being overdue, breach of any of the conditions of this agreement, or any other reason which at MDL's discretion warrants such action.

5. Liability

5.1. The agreement for the supply of goods shall be governed by the laws of England and these terms and conditions will be interpreted in accordance with those laws.

5.2. MDL shall not be liable for any failure in performing any of its obligations under the agreement if the failure was due to any cause beyond MDL's reasonable control.

5.3. Save as expressly provided in these terms and conditions all warranties, conditions or other terms implied by statute or common law are excluded to the fullest extent permitted by law.

5.4. Where the goods are sold to a co[...] are not affected by these terms and conditi[...]

5.5. Except in respect of death or perso[...] or the negligence of any employee or auth[...] any fraudulent misrepresentation by MD[...] of MDL or any implied term as to title[...] liable to the customer by reason of any[...] condition or other term or any duty at c[...] the agreement or otherwise for any los[...] loss of business or any indirect or cons[...] which arises out of or in connection [...] resale by the customer except as expres[...]

6. Insolvency

6.1. If:- (a) the customer make[...] creditors, becomes subject to an adm[...] firm) becomes bankrupt or (being a[...] than for the purposes of amalgamatio[...] (b) an encumbrancer takes possessio[...] property or assets of the customer; or [...] (c) if the customer, being a trade custo[...] business; or (d) MDL reasonably believes that a[...] without prejudice to any other right or[...] entitled to cancel the agreement or s[...] agreement without incurring any liabil[...] been delivered but not paid for the [...] payable.

7. General

7.1. If any provision of these terms [...] ineffective or unenforceable in whole o[...] enforceability of the other provisions o[...]

7.2. No waiver by MDL of any breach [...] treated as a waiver of any subsequent bre[...]

7.3. Variations to these terms and co[...] and signed by an authorised representativ[...]

7.4. MDL's employees or agents are no[...] concerning goods unless confirmed by M[...]

8. Information to be provided by M[...]

8.1. Where an order is placed by tele[...] obligation to give certain information to [...] medium in relation to such order at th[...] information is provided either on the [...] conditions. In particular a description o[...] being supplied, the price (including all [...] will be set out on the relevant invoice.

9. Cancellations

9.1. Subject to the exceptions set out[...] statutory right under the Consumer Protec[...] ("the Regulations") to cancel any order [...] giving notice in writing to the address sh[...] attention of the Customer Service Manage[...]

Always quote invoice number on

For a downloadable version of these terms and conditions,

A D V I C E   N O T E
Inside

Swansea

NUMBER	77266871
DATE & TAX POINT	02-06-14
PICK LIST	75105/009 - ISG
PAGE NO.	1

CUSTOMER INFORMATION:-

ACCOUNT NO.	002140004
CONTACT NAME	
DIRECT TEL NO. (DDI)	
PREFERRED DAY	Not Applicable
CARRIER / ROUTE	07 09
DESCRIPTION	2nd Cl. Post
VAT NO.	GB 199 4406 21

'E

AND RAISE QUERIES IMMEDIATELY

PRINTED BOOKS UNLESS OTHERWISE STATED

	AUTHOR	TYP	PRICE	TRADE DISC %	VALUE	VAT	SOU
ment required.							
digenous, Nomadi	Griffin,Rosarii	P	24.99		No Charge		

Items Zero Rated Unless Otherwise Stated	TOTAL		No Charge
	SUNDRIES		No Charge
	VAT		No Charge
	INVOICE TOTAL	£	No Charge

e4books
BIC commended

Order & Payments To:-
MACMILLAN DISTRIBUTION (MDL)
HOUNDMILLS, BASINGSTOKE,
HANTS, RG21 6XS, ENGLAND
Giro No. - 206 4057
Registered Number 785998 England

Telephone +44 (0) 1256
Fax (Home) +44 (0) 1256
+44 (0) 1256 &
Fax (Export) +44 (0) 1256 &

Bank - NATIONAL WESTMIN
Code - 60-02-49
Account No. - 47301759
Email - mdl@macmillan.co.uk
Swift Code - NWBKGB2L
IBAN - GB10NWBK60024947

Macmillan Publishers Ltd trading as Macmillan Distribution (MDL)

PLEASE REMIT TO THE ABOVE ADDRESS

600

CHARGE TO

Kate Hoskins
DEPT OF EDUCATION
FREOBEL Col Univ
ROEHAMPTON ROEHAMPTON LANE
LONDON SW15 5PJ

DESPATCHED TO
PP0002

Kate Hoskins
DEPT OF EDUCATION
FREOBEL Col Univ
ROEHAMPTON ROEHAMPTON
LONDON SW15 5PJ

SEE REVERSE FOR TERMS & CONDITIONS OF SUPPLY AND FOR NET BOOK AGREEMENT.   ALWAYS QUOTE INV

INTERNAL USE ONLY	ORDER REF.	QTY	ISBN	ED	C O M	C of O	PUB	TITLE
								Review copy,
7B6391	REVIEW	1	9781472513601	01	BK	GB	BLM	EHR:Educatic

INTERNAL ONLY

BOOKS	1	KEYED BY	JMO	
LINES	1	BATCH	89209/011	
WEIGHT	0.344	BRICK	0103	
CARTONS		TYPE	A ADPR	
INV. DISTR.	101000	SPOOL FILE NAME	XWPRHA5105SI	

www.macmillandistribution.co.uk

AND CONDITIONS:

sumer the consumer's statutory rights
ns.

Injury caused by MDL's negligence
ed agent or representative of MDL,
authorised agent or representative
iet enjoyment, MDL shall not be
sentation or any implied warranty,
m law or under the express terms of
out, loss of sales, loss of goodwill,
nd loss or damage howsoever caused
th apply of the goods or their use or
ly ded in these terms and conditions.

mposition or arrangement with its
n order, or (being an individual or
ny) goes into liquidation (otherwise
r onstruction) or;
receiver is appointed of any of the

ceases or threatens to cease to carry on

these events is about to occur then
edy available to MDL. MDL shall be
nd any further deliveries under such
to the customer, and if the goods have
e shall become immediately due and

conditions is held for any reason to be
part this shall not affect the validity or
se terms and conditions.

the agreement by the customer will be
h of the same or any other provision.

ions will only be effective if in writing
of each of MDL and the customer.

authorised to make any representations
L in writing by one of its Directors.

hone or by fax, MDL has a statutory
e customer in writing or other durable
latest at the time of delivery. This
evant invoice or in these terms and
the main characteristics of the goods
es) and delivery costs (if applicable)

n clause 3 below, the customer has a
on (Distance Selling) regulations 2000
hich has been accepted by MDL by
wn on the invoice and marked for the

Unless any other time limit applies under the Regulations, the notice must be received with 7 working days following the day on which the goods which are the subject of order being cancelled are delivered, unless the reason for such cancellation is shortage, damage, defect in quality or condition, failure to correspond with order or non-delivery in which case should be given and must be received within 30 days following the day on which the goods are delivered.

9.2.   The customer may not cancel any order which has been accepted by MDL where such order is for the supply of newspapers, periodicals or magazines. The customer may not cancel any order which has been accepted by MDL, where such order is for an audio or visual recording (including audio books) or computer software if such recording or software has been unsealed by the customer.

9.3.   If an order is cancelled the customer must return the goods concerned to the address shown on the invoice marked for the attention of the Customer Service Manager within 14 days of giving notice of cancellation of the order. Where such return is for reasons other than shortage, damage, defect in quality or condition, failure to correspond with order or non-delivery this will be at the customer's expense and liability.

9.4.   MDL will reimburse any sum paid by the customer for or in relation to the goods as soon as possible following receipt of notice of cancellation given in accordance with the appropriate time limit and in any case within 30 days of receipt of such notice. Other than in the case of cancellation for shortage, damage, defect in quality or condition, failure to correspond with order or non delivery (where the reasonable costs of returning the goods by the mechanism agreed with MDL will be reimbursed) this will not include reimbursement of the costs of returning the goods.

9.5.   Any complaints should be sent in writing to the address shown on the invoice marked for the attention of the Customer Services Manager.

10.   Payment
10.1.   Unless payment has been made at the time of order in a form acceptable to MDL, orders received from consumers will be invoiced by MDL and payment will be due immediately upon receipt of the invoice or goods (whichever is the later). Where goods are ordered by a consumer for delivery to a third party the invoice will be sent separately to the consumer and not with the goods to the third party.

11.   Delivery
11.1.   Delivery of goods is at the customer's expense and liability, unless otherwise agreed in writing by MDL or an authorised agent or representative of MDL, delivery charges being invoiced at the same time as the invoice of the goods.

11.2.   MDL will use its reasonable endeavours to deliver all goods within 30 days of receipt of the order for such goods and will in any case deliver all goods within 90 days of receipt of such order. If for any reason MDL is unable to deliver any goods within such 90 day period, it will notify the customer of this. Unless otherwise requested by the customer the relevant order will be treated as cancelled from the point of notification and MDL will reimburse any sum paid by or on behalf of the customer for or in relation to such goods. MDL will reimburse any such sum as soon as possible following notification to the customer and in any case within 30 days following the day after the expiry of the 90 day period.

11.3.   If any goods ordered by the customer are to be delivered to a third party, then delivery to such third party shall be treated as delivery to the customer and all relevant provisions of these terms and conditions shall apply accordingly.

orrespondence or with returns.

Travellers and Roma in ROI law

The mid-1990s ushered in an unprecedented economic boom in this country. The immigration levels this boom attracted were also unprecedented (at least since the last major waves of colonization); asylum seekers and refugees were also seeking residence here. All this brought to the surface identity debates, racism and an appalling move towards tightening borders: the ROI was a good member of 'Fortress Europe' (Mac Éinrí, 2002). Until the mid-1990s, the prevailing identity discourse in the ROI was narrowly nationalist: inclusion meant absorption in a monochrome White Catholic Irish society and in its schools (Bryan, 2009). Lentin and McVeigh (2006, p. 12) call this 'the ordering zeal of modernity'.

With the widespread social change, a new official self-definition began to emerge; diversity within the nation was officially recognized and protected. The ROI is signatory to a range of international agreements on equality, human rights and minority rights. Key instruments to which the ROI is signatory include the European Union (EU) *Charter of Fundamental Rights* (2000) and the Council of Europe *Framework Convention for the Protection of National Minorities* (1994). The state's equality and anti-discrimination legislation has been brought into conformity with these international agreements. The Equal Status Acts of 2000–2004 (Government of Ireland, 2004) forbid discrimination, harassment or victimization across nine 'grounds' (social categorizations). The 'ground of race' covers biological, national and ethnic identities; however, the 'Traveller community ground' is listed separately. Right to equal treatment in the provision of goods and services (including education provision) is equally protected under any of the grounds. The Equality Authority and Equality Tribunal were established to support and monitor compliance with this legislation. A significant number of cases regarding education access heard by these bodies have been brought by Travellers. The government established a High Level Group (HLG) of senior public servants and officials to monitor and advise on policy and practice on Traveller issues. However, the following comment in its report illustrates how legal protection frameworks can be reshaped, to domesticate the inclusion process:

> The Government is aware that many Travellers feel that the Traveller community has suffered a number of high profile reversals such as the amendment of the public order legislation..., the removal of discrimination cases involving licensed premises from the Equality Tribunal to the District Court... (Government of Ireland, 2006, p. 16)

Irish Travellers have ethnic status in the UK and in Northern Ireland, but not in the ROI: here they are recognized as culturally distinct, but not as ethnic (Government of Ireland, 2006, p. 6). This does not compromise their legal right to equal treatment (insofar as the state systems ensure this, as noted above). The 'social group' framing enables the HLG to identify outcomes of discrimination (within an ethnicity framework, racism):

> ... accommodation provision is not some golden key ... to social integration ... Travellers in permanent accommodation, like those in unauthorised sites, can also have very limited education achievements, suffer poor health, and be in long term unemployment. (Government of Ireland, 2006, p. 6)

The Irish government reported in 2011 to the EU on Traveller and Roma integration strategies; it states that it 'supports the participation of Travellers in mainstream social and economic life, while continuing to acknowledge and respect the legitimate expression of Traveller culture and identity' (Government of Ireland, 2011, Sec. 2). It states that legally resident Roma are protected under EU and Irish law; however, there is no reference to the situation of many Roma from Hungary and Bulgaria who live in a limbo, prevented by the complex Habitual Residence Condition (Free Legal Aid Centres, 2004) from seeking employment or accessing more than minimal and erratic social supports (Pavee Point, 2011). Living in such precarious conditions, their children attend school irregularly; in school they face the double barrier of a problematized Roma identity, hostility and a language difference (they are entitled to English Language Support, but provision levels for this are overstretched). As regards the overall report, Pavee Point (2011) argues that it is a review of existing policy; no new initiatives are outlined.

In these often heated debates about Travellers, there is a marked focus on origins/identity and numbers. These two foci can also structure further critical review of the situation and of the thinking informing it.

Ethnicity and racism, Travellers and Roma

Constructions of Travellers and Roma are deeply embedded in the current discourses, both of diversity and of racism; Lentin and McVeigh (2006, p. 189) argue that the Traveller support movement moulded Irish anti-racism for years (see also Bryan, 2009; Fanning, 2002; Lentin, 2007). Recognition of Travellers' ethnicity, while it would not garner Travellers additional legal protection, would have symbolic value, strengthening the recognized status of their cultural identity. That would arguably have an impact on education policies, programmes and practice regarding nurturing children's cultural identities. As will be argued below, cultural identity issues need protection in the current neo-liberal climate.

The diverse range of Traveller and Roma people share a nomadic heritage (Liégeois, 2007). Some still travel; others have settled, some for centuries. However, whether or not they have remained nomadic, the nomadic/sedentary divide fuels virulent racism against them in all countries in Europe (CHR, 2012); they have historically been targets of institutional and communal violence (including killings, pogroms, forcible sterilization of women, culminating in the Nazi camps where an estimated half million Roma were killed). Anti-Roma racism is intensifying across Europe, and persists in institutional provision, including education (CHR, 2012; Liégeois, 2007; McVeigh, 1997). The Irish historical record is not so severe, perhaps because the majority population were so deeply dispossessed of power by colonization (Kenny, 1997), but the same virulent hostility informs it, and recent events suggest that the potential for extreme violence is present (Lentin and McVeigh, 2006).

Travellers have long been present, needed but not wanted, in Irish society. 'Tynkeres' were first mentioned in official records in the twelfth century. Recent analysis of Travellers' DNA indicates that they are not Roma; their genetic profile is broadly Irish, but they have been a separate, endogamous population in Ireland for at least a thousand and perhaps two thousand years (Blood of the Travellers, 2011). Roma began migrating to Ireland, at least in any significant numbers, only in the late 1990s. However, similar issues arise in debate about them elsewhere in Europe (Liégeois, 2007; McVeigh, 1997), and here since their arrival was first noticed (Lentin and McVeigh, 2006).

Historically, Traveller and Roma groups have lived on boundaries, distinct from the sedentary populations through which they moved or among which they lived. Travellers and Roma are predominantly entrepreneurs, providing goods, services, entertainment and, in some cases, temporary labour to the local populations. They identify and respond to local needs; flexibility rather than any specific trade, such as tinsmithing, is the hallmark of their economic activities. Judith Okely (1983) calls them 'bricoleurs': they adopt local customs and practices into their lifestyle. Their languages (the Irish Travellers' Gammon or Shelta, and the Romani family of languages) are deeply intermixed with words adopted from local languages, but as Alice Binchy (1994) found in her analysis of the status and functions of Shelta/Gammon, that language is a powerful group identity marker, particularly in boundary situations. Given their historic experience of sedentary hostility, many Roma and Travellers have learned to hide their identity in boundary situations. Perhaps particularly in the case of indigenous ethnic groups such as the Irish Travellers, theirs is a subtle and silenced culture, offering no easy indicators for the non-Traveller/Roma to grasp.

O'Connell (1994) identified five often intersecting 'models' or concepts of Travellers, in discourse about them: they were 'like ourselves'; criminals/deviant; tragic and impoverished; romantic; an ethnic group. This framework has been powerful in enabling critique of state policy: most show a mix of models, but the driving force is rarely so diffuse. Travellers also draw on it in their 'analysis from within':

> For too long Travellers have been unaware of the theories that have been constructed about them … we see ourselves as an ethnic group. This enables us to put into words and to have concepts which explain our experiences and what has been happening to us. (Collins, 1994, pp. 130–132)

Liégeois identifies nomadism, even for Roma/Traveller groups who are long settled, as a 'fundamental part of their culture, colouring the whole' (2007, p. 66). Michael McDonagh, Traveller activist, says:

> Country people organise every aspect of their lives … on the fact of sedentarism, the fact that they live permanently side by side with a fixed group of people. Travellers … organise every aspect of their lives around family ties; how far away other family members may be is of no importance, any more than how physically close non-family may be. The Traveller's very identity requires 'keeping in touch' and this in turn requires travel … (1994, p. 98)

'Race' and nomadism/sedentarism

The biological concept of race has been proven spurious, but the passionately held social construct of it is a real and powerful basis for racism. Likewise, nomadism is constructed as inferior, anarchic, utterly 'Other' from sedentarism; this construct fuels prejudice and discrimination against Roma, Travellers and others of nomadic heritage. Whether they still travel or not, they are viewed with hostility, as if they had only arrived (in suspicious circumstances) yesterday, and cannot be trusted to stay until tomorrow. They should settle, but not here. From being a people on the move, they are driven to being a people on the run. However, colour-based racism posits the Others' inferiority on their bodies, whereas anti-nomadic racism posits it on a practice. So, hostile pressure on Irish Travellers to assimilate can be validated by claims that they are 'just Irish', 'racially'/ethnically the same as 'us', ought to conform and settle down. And it fuels the level of anger that often attends ethnicity claims by Travellers and Traveller organizations. The comments following recent articles on Traveller identity (Irish Times Online, 2013) highlight how historical research and recent DNA findings do not suffice to challenge the view of those who believe that Travellers are neither different enough nor separate enough for long enough to qualify as ethnic.

Bryan (2009) analyses the connections between discourses of nationalism, colonialism and racism; colonialism, international or internal, drove the marginalization and even extermination of Travellers and Roma. McVeigh (1997) takes this argument back to the far more ancient nomadic/sedentary divide. In all societies at some point, transition occurred from hunter-gathering to pastoralism and agriculture; in the ensuing dominant sedentary narrative this transition was constructed as inevitable, unproblematic progress, and nomadism was reconstructed as a curse (for instance: Cain killed Abel, and so his descendants were cursed to wander). However, McVeigh points to ample evidence that the transition was far from tidy or irreversible. Nomadic societies were not all powerless and primitive; in many times and places they held the dominance, and were the more culturally sophisticated. Settlement came at a price, evidenced in the reverence for lost values inherent in nomadism, for instance, in the sacred status of pilgrimage and of wandering holy men. But the sedentary won out eventually – or maybe just thus far in history. McVeigh argues that the virulence of opposition to New Travellers in the UK is because they threaten the presumed innate superiority of settlement with its roots in place and property.

To summarize McVeigh's depiction, the sedentary stole the ground from under the nomads' feet. Assuming ownership of land itself, the sedentary, with their enclosures and boundaries, stole the nomads' travel paths and thus their means of livelihood – the nomads needed those paths with their stopping points, to move along their flocks, goods and services. And subsequently, the victors rationalized this history by focusing on the nomads' depredations. Thievery is a central motif of the negative narratives, along with disquiet at the nomads' exotic but dangerous fecklessness. In the 'Vagrancy Acte' of 1597, the English Parliament criminalized numerous categories of people for 'wandring abroade': included were 'Tynkers' and 'Egipcians' (Gypsies) (Mayall, 1988, cited in Helleiner, 2000, p. 35). With the rise of capitalism, the sedentary–nomadic divide widened. 'The civilized man lives not in wheeled houses' (Carlyle, 1843, cited in Hansen, 2004). The communist system equally sought to fix the nomad into a controllable place (Liégeois, 2007; McVeigh, 1997).

In Irish society, popular arguments focus on the notion of 'real' Travellers, and narratives of old-time harmonious Traveller–settled relations. Two accounts of Travellers have coexisted in literature and in traditional rural Irish society (Bhreatnach, 2006; Helleiner, 2000). They were romanticized (as remnants of the ancient Irish, as carefree rovers), but to a far greater extent they were 'tabooed and dreaded', viewed 'as frost in spring or blight in harvest' (Samson, 1894 and Lady Gregory 1976, cited in Helleiner, 2000, p. 43). Thus categorizations of people develop into clusters of potentially contradictory expectations and perceptions (Potter and Wetherell, 1989). This interweaving of positive and negative is why people can be so surprised at attributions of racism. Similar accretions at a systemic level require serious attention. MacPherson, citing the British Commission for Racial Equality, identifies as institutionally racist 'organizational structures, policies, processes and practices which result in ethnic minorities being treated unfairly and less equally, often without intention or knowledge' (Macpherson, 1999, paragraph 6.30).

'History is always written from a sedentary point of view and in the name of a unitary State apparatus, at least a possible one, even when the topic is nomads' (Deleuze and Guattari, 1987, cited in Trumpener, 1992, p. 863). Challenging the dominant sedentary narrative, there is a growing body of research in disciplines including history, literature and of course the social studies. McDonagh's words quoted earlier highlight how Travellers prioritize network over place. Travellers also weave romantic and harsh pictures of their experience and of their relations with settled people, into their accounts of life in the old days (Kenny and Mac Neela, 2005). For a people without written history or accumulated cultural artefacts, their memories furnish the materials for analytic and archival work which is going on currently in a number of local Traveller heritage projects. Travellers are also actively involved in exploring their contribution to Irish culture generally and in disseminating and preserving folklore and music (Ní Laodhóg and Collins, 1995; Munnelly, 1975; Mac Gréine, 1932). All this will document their positive self-identity and their perspective on relations, hostile and otherwise, with the sedentary population. It should also inform sedentary perspectives on Travellers.

Racism is a problem of the majority; to challenge the dominant narrative calls for a profound mindset shift on the part of educators. Before we take this issue further, quantification issues and education provision for Travellers will be outlined.

Quantifying the people or the problem

Concerns about counting Travellers arise with every official census and relate predominantly to official intent to control/police and provide services for them. However, many Travellers are suspicious and hide their identity when faced with officials seeking information. Traveller organizations assert that the number registering as Travellers in the National Census is well below the reality. Substantially higher numbers registered in the two specialized censuses conducted to inform studies of Travellers' health status (AITHST, 2010; Barry et al., 1989): enumerators were people known to and trusted by the Travellers. In the AITHST census, Travellers were recruited and trained as enumerators for their own people. In the 2011 Census a total of 29,573 persons registered as Travellers; three years earlier, the AITHST Census total was 18 per cent higher, at 36,224 Travellers.

The level of diversity in contemporary Irish society and schools, particularly as regards Travellers and Roma, needs to be viewed in perspective. Figure 1.1 illustrates the nationalities profile of the population aged 0–14 years, and Irish Travellers are represented separately from the rest of the Irish national population. This is an indicator of current and potential school populations (in the ROI, children aged 6–16 years are legally obliged to attend school, but

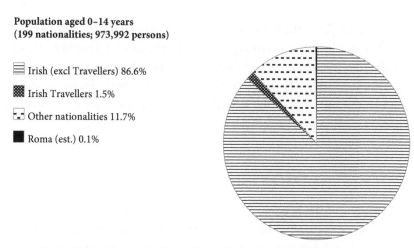

**Population aged 0–14 years
(199 nationalities; 973,992 persons)**

▤ Irish (excl Travellers) 86.6%

▨ Irish Travellers 1.5%

⬚ Other nationalities 11.7%

■ Roma (est.) 0.1%

Other Nationalities: Polish 2.3%; UK 1.1%; Rest of EU 2.0%; Asian nationalities 1.1%; African nationalities 0.8%; Irish-Other 2.0%; Other and multiple nationalities 0.7%; None/not stated 1.8%.

Figure 1.1 Child population profile by nationality, and including Irish Travellers and Roma

Data sources: Nationalities: CSO (2011). Travellers: AITHST (2010). Roma: 40 per cent of Roma Support Group estimate (Pavee Point, 2013).

most are enrolled from the age of four). The census required people to state their ethnic and national identities; the latter is used here because the 'ethnic/racial' category bands, besides being too problematic in their definitions, are too broad to be useful for this profiling.

In the state population aged 0–14 years, the nationalities profile is slightly less diverse than that of the general population, because the age profiles of most immigrant groups are skewed heavily towards working-age bands (mainly ages 25–45). However, the opposite is the case with Travellers (and probably Roma). Table 1.1 shows the differentials for the largest three of the 199 nationality groups in the ROI population, and for Travellers.

Table 1.1 Adult–child population balance: The three largest nationality groups and Travellers

Groups	Group, as % of state population (*n* = 4,525,281)	Group cohort aged 0–14 years, as	
		% of state 0–14-yr population (*n* = 9,73,992)	% of own group population
Irish excl. Travellers	84.7	86.6	22.0
Polish	2.7	2.3	18.1
UK	2.5	1.1	9.9
Travellers	0.8	1.5	42.0

Data sources: Nationalities: Census of 2011. Travellers: AITHST (2010).

The percentages of the Polish and UK nationalities in the 0–14 age band are relatively low (the UK one remarkably so). In the case of Travellers, it is the opposite: they comprise 0.8 per cent of the national population, but almost twice that (1.5 per cent) in the 0–14 age band. In short, Travellers are the second-largest minority in the school-going population; they rank fourth in the general population. Nonetheless, their numbers are small.

Education provision and Travellers

A brief review of the history of Travellers in formal education will introduce this section.[1] Travellers' education first attracted official concern in the 1960s (Department of Education, 1970; Commission on Itinerancy, 1963). School attendance and literacy levels were negligible; to address this, special classes and schools were set up, with provision for transport, hygiene and meals. The aim was to remediate extreme distress prior to integration with 'the normal children'. However, separate provision became a fixture rather than a transition tool.

Since then, services grew and so did the debate about identity and inclusion. By the 1990s, special classes were on the wane; Traveller children were in mainstream classes supported by Resource Teachers for Travellers (RTTs). By 2006, there were about 500 RTTs in the primary school system; second-level schools could claim 1.5 ex-quota teaching hours per Traveller student enrolled. Capitation grants at both levels (paid annually per pupil on roll) are the major block of state financing for operating schools; an enhanced rate is paid for Traveller pupils registered as receiving RTT support. In parallel with developments in the schools, Traveller-specific provision at other levels was established. This grew over the years, to comprise: a National Education Officer for Travellers (a senior Department of Education and Science (DES1) position) to coordinate services, identify needs and advise, monitor and report on progress; a home-school support service of forty Visiting Teachers for Travellers; fifty preschools attended by about 500 children; eleven alternative units for Travellers of second-level school age; and forty Training Centres for Travellers of post-school age. Outside the formal education sector, local Traveller organizations developed a range of adult education and community development initiatives.

Pressure from Traveller organizations and involved professionals drove a campaign for integration; this was promoted in primary and second-level schools, but specialized separate centres were a different matter. In 2006, the DES1 Traveller Education Strategy was published. It recommended full integration at all levels. Implementation has been speeded by the economic downturn (DES1, 2008), and by 2011 virtually all Traveller-specific provisions had been terminated. In 2010, almost 80 per cent of the eight thousand Travellers in primary schools were registered as receiving RTT support. This is criticized as indicating an assumption that Travellers have innate learning difficulties; but it is also significant that this registration was required in order to draw down the enhanced capitation grants. Travellers now access supports via the same assessment procedures on offer for all children; those in identified disadvantaged schools have access to augmented learning support services (Dáil, 2011).

Current school profiles: Enrolment and progression

Traveller enrolments are clustered in the school system. Darmody et al. (2012, p. 41) found that 74 per cent of all primary schools had no Traveller pupils; few were enrolled in multi-denominational or minority faith schools, or *Gaelscoileanna* (schools where Irish is the language of daily life and work).

Traveller enrolments were significantly higher in schools classified as disadvantaged. This reflects the concentration of this population in urban, disadvantaged areas (CSO, 2012), but also shows how parental choice often intensifies social stratification across schools.

Second-level education in the ROI comprises two cycles: a three-year Junior Cycle terminating with the Junior Certificate Examination (or the Junior Certificate Schools Programme for those not suited to the JCE), and a three-year Senior Cycle, comprising a Transition Year (offering a broad programme of personal and social studies and work experience) and a two-year programme leading to the Leaving Certificate or (less highly prized) Leaving Certificate Applied. Data on Travellers' participation are patchy (particularly since Traveller-targeted services were terminated). Table 1.2 gives a range of available data.

Table 1.2 Selected data on Traveller participation in second-level schooling

School year	1999/2000	2004/2005	% increase, 1999–2005	2009/2010	% increase, 2004–2010
Total enrolment	961	1845	92.0	3014	63.4
First Year enrolment	478	671	40.4	No data	
Sitting Junior Certificate	No data	292		442	51.4
Sixth Year enrolment	19	72	278.9	No data	
Sitting Leaving Certificate	No data	63		103	63.5

Data sources: DES (2006), Dáil Debates (2008, 2011).

On the positive side, it is generally agreed that currently, virtually all Traveller children of primary school age are enrolled; attendance levels range from excellent to poor, but are improving overall. Second-level enrolments grew from almost zero in the early 1980s, to 3014 in 2009–2010 – about 75 per cent of the approximately four thousand Travellers in the 13–18-year-old cohort (estimate based on Census and AITHS data). The profile of this improvement would warrant study, as differentials in increase rates in Table 1.2 indicate. This remarkable trajectory is usually forgotten in the rush to concern about the real, grave and seemingly intractable problems.

However, attainment and progression rates, though improved, are definitely unacceptably poor. The DES1 (2006) estimates a drop-out of about one hundred (about 10 per cent of the 12-year-old age band) at the point of transfer from primary school. The steep differentials from First Year through to Sixth Year (Table 1.2) indicate that drop-out rates in ensuing years (particularly severe at transition to the Senior Cycle) depress the average enrolment. The 103 sitting Leaving Certificate in 2010 comprised at most 14 per cent of the Travellers aged 17/18 years old. Consistently identified reasons for this are given by providers (DES1, 2006) and by Travellers (Kenny and Mac Neela, 2005; Pavee Point, 2005): environmental factors, absence of role models, poor attendance, cultural alienation and experience of discrimination/racism from teachers and non-Traveller peers. Roma face the same difficulties in education systems across Europe (CHR, 2012; EU Agency for Fundamental Rights, 2012).

The seriousness of the quantifiable failures to date can focus strategies to address them too closely on the surface level of delivery and performance. At the environmental level, Travellers are far more aware than the providers, of the toll that racism takes on their children and of the limited value of formal education for them: qualifications will not get them jobs unless they can hide their identity (Hourigan and Campbell, 2010). One 'successful' Traveller summarized the price thus:

> The Company I work in – I couldn't stand up and say I'm a Traveller and proud of it. If I did, people still have their ideas and prejudice and though the law protects your job, you'd be dealing with that every day ... I've chosen my life, to move away, settle, get education, get a job ... I don't consider myself to be a Traveller ... I know my family, it's a good family. But once you go out of that circle it's completely different. (Traveller interviewee in Kenny and Mac Neela, 2005, p. 32)

I suggest we need to focus on the dominant mindset that generates this alienation, predisposes students and schools to failure and frustrates welcoming school agendas.

Travellers in higher and further education

The Higher Education Authority (HEA) survey of third-level students in 2010/2011 (HEA, 2012) found that 0.2 per cent of mature respondents (aged 23 year or over) and 0.1 per cent of younger respondents self-identified as Irish Travellers (2012, p. 86). Travellers comprise about ten times that level (one per cent) of the national 18–29-year-old cohort (which would encompass most school-transfer and mature-age students).

Travellers' self-reported levels of higher and further education participation in the 2011 National Census are far higher than the available institutional data indicate. There must be reasons for this; I tentatively suggest one: many adult education programmes that Travellers attend are located in second-level school buildings; this could be constructed (at least for the benefit of the strange official with the census form) as attending college. However, the census data do strongly support what Traveller community organizations argue: adult Travellers need and want opportunities to further their education, in settings that value them, their culture and historic experience (Hourigan and Campbell, 2010). The DES1 (2008) assessment of Traveller Training Centres recognized the value of adult education to the Traveller community but advocated that provision for Travellers be integrated into local community further education initiatives. This is now the only option for Travellers; the challenge is to transfer the respect and space for cultural expression and development, into integrated adult education settings.

Conceptualization in policy and bureaucracy

Is there conceptual space and support for addressing issues of Traveller identity and racism in current education policy? Concepts, policy and practice are cyclically interrelated:

> Social texts do not merely reflect or mirror … categories pre-existing in the social and natural world. Rather, they actively construct a version of those things. They do not just describe things; they do things. (Potter and Wetherell, 1989, p. 10)

Introducing its Strategic Framework for a dynamic, well-educated Europe, the European Commission states:

> Efficient investment in *human capital* through education and training systems is an essential component of Europe's strategy to deliver the high levels of sustainable, knowledge-based growth and jobs that lie at the heart of the Lisbon strategy, *at the same time as* promoting personal fulfilment, social cohesion and active citizenship … (2009, paragraph 2, emphasis added)

The phrases emphasized suggest that economic dynamism is the core value; personal/social values are instrumental. Likewise, in the education system we have the competitiveness of the examination system uneasily co-existing with overt policies of inclusion and holistic personal growth. In DES1 education policy documents, interculturalism is increasingly being translated into cohesion-for-progress.

The first intercultural education policy texts issued at the national level were the Guidelines on Travellers in primary and secondary schools (DES1, 2002a, 2002b). The National Council for Curriculum and Assessment (NCCA), now the state body responsible for schools curriculum development, has also published general Intercultural Guidelines for primary and second-level schools (NCCA, 2005, 2006). Both open by recognizing the pioneering insights generated by the experience of Travellers and their educators in the system. The primary schools Intercultural Guidelines open with a quotation from the 2002 Guidelines on Travellers:

> Young people should be enabled to appreciate the richness of a diversity of cultures and be supported in practical ways to recognise and to challenge prejudice and discrimination where they exist. (NCCA, 2005, p. 6)

Diversity is normal, and normality is diverse: this is to be explored and celebrated; equality is a core value, and students are to become knowledgeable, just and inclusive citizens of a diverse world. Bryan (2009) questions the capacity of the current framework to deliver a critical perspective on social structures of exclusion; my focus here is on how the capacity it does have is in danger of being eroded.

The guidelines assert that 'Ireland has long been culturally diverse', and exemplify this at four levels: social (Travellers), linguistic (Irish and English), religious (Jews and Protestants mainly) and modern Irish lifestyles generally. In school curricula hitherto, apart from the privileging of the Irish language, even this very pale and limited level of diversity had been ignored in the thrust to assimilate everyone into a unified national citizenry. It is disquieting that whereas all primary teachers in the state have studied religious education throughout their four-year training, the education system's way of supporting their response to growing social diversity is the equivalent of a book in the mail. Teachers are supposed to read the main curriculum through the lens of these guidelines; but the guidelines are a physically separate book, when what is needed is that all curricula be rewritten so that all facets are saturated with an intercultural, anti-racist mindset. The same applies to teacher pre-service courses and continuing professional development: interculturalism is close to being a separate subject, rather than informing teaching of all subjects. The approach remains add-on. This shows in the discourse even of many concerned teachers, and of pupils; Travellers remain the most 'othered' group (Devine, 2005; Devine et al., 2008).

By delivering as an add-on what should be a root-and-branch transformation, the system does not achieve the required mindset shift at any level. It is not surprising, then, that system commitment to diversity principles did not percolate through all levels of policy and provision. Conceptual fractures occur erratically, but in powerful locations. References to Travellers in the annual school census returns forms (Department of Education and Skills (DES2 (formally DES1), 2012) exemplify this. Schools must furnish numbers of Traveller pupils 'for statistical and support allocation purposes' (identification requires parental/student consent). The instructions for primary schools cite the Equal Status Act (Government of Ireland, 2004) definition of Travellers, but I could find no such conceptual frame in the second-level forms. In one, the heading is 'Traveller Support'; elsewhere two data items are classified as 'sensitive': possession of a medical card, and membership of 'the Travelling community'. On the data form on participants in part-time courses, specified headings are unemployment, disability, Traveller, the elderly and others. The intent is to monitor needs and equality of access, but the framing of diversity is flawed. Travellers are implicitly constructed as innately needing support; inadequate conceptualization intersects at the school level with 'common-sense' assumptions.

A second problem is that the data thus gathered, and data on learners' countries of birth or nationalities which are also gathered, are not made public. Given the gaps in understanding at the policy level, it cannot be assumed that inclusion means empowerment (Levinson, 2008). As Traveller organizations frequently argue, ethnic profiling is essential to providing, and to evaluating, the need for and provision of targeted support services within an inclusive context. These data should be published (observing data protection requirements) so that Traveller parents, the wider Traveller community and Traveller organizations can function as informed education partners.

Perhaps the fractures in the data collection instruments are evidence of bureaucratic lag – the instruments had not been revised to comply with the new vision. The result is that these poorly conceptualized instruments and perceptions are in place to link up with more recent policy, where something of a U-turn in the direction of neo-liberalism has occurred. The government report on Traveller and Roma integration states:

> The core principle of the report is one of inclusion with an emphasis on equality and diversity and the adoption of an intercultural approach. The principle of 'individual educational need' rather than 'Traveller identity' will underpin future actions including allocation of resources. (Government of Ireland, 2011, p. 7)

The first sentence reflects the broader spirit of earlier intercultural policy, but this is contradicted in the individualized focus asserted in the second sentence (which is a reprise, with quoted phrases, of the core principle laid down in the 2006 strategy). Identity is taking a back seat.

The economic focus in a neo-liberal framework (Bryan, 2009; Lentin, 2007) is evident in the wider domain of the new Intercultural Education Strategy (DES2 and Office of the Minister for Integration, 2010). Cultural diversity gets frequent but nominal mention. The emphasis is on cohesion, and on equality of access and attainment for students of all backgrounds. Anti-racism is promoted, in the service of social cohesion; the economy, not a vision of a knowledgeably diverse society, is the driver.

Inclusion and identity in policy

The boom over, the discourse of ethnic, religious and 'racial' diversity is being more loudly challenged by a neo-liberal, economically driven discourse of inclusion, as exemplified in European Union texts. The Irish government's framework for social partnership, 2006–2015 (Department of the Taoiseach, 2006) reflects this, in its vision of Ireland as 'a dynamic, internationalized, and participatory society and economy with a strong commitment to social justice, where economic development is environmentally sustainable and is internationally competitive' (2006, p. 10). 'Culture' is discussed in the sense of work culture, and the arts and culture (the term 'multicultural' is used once, without explanation, in relation to housing). Planned initiatives will target children at risk of multiple disadvantage from poverty and social exclusion, including children of migrant and Traveller communities, and vulnerable families. Plans for enhancing participation in third-level education also target the disadvantaged, Travellers, ethnic minorities and students with a disability (2006, p. 57).

State policy has powerfully driven a broad societal process whereby Travellers and immigrant ethnic minorities are channelled into disadvantaged areas. People with disabilities are also socio-economically marginalized. That is mirrored in education policy, where diversity is persistently sandwiched between disadvantage and disability. To insist that this cluster be disaggregated is not to repudiate or denigrate any one of the three social sectors thus labelled, but to assert that the situation and issues are distinct for each, and that conflating them allows leakage so that any one sector carries a double or triple stigma, and undermines the possibility for fine-tuned responses. The focus on gaps in Travellers' participation and performance in education is one outcome of this blurring; I argue that unless collective identity is placed centre stage, fostered and valued, needs and difficulties cannot be addressed effectively, in explicit but not exclusionary support strategies.

Concluding comment

In policy regarding diversity in education or in society, the trajectory – from monochrome to rainbow, to cohesion-for-efficiency – is very clear in texts regarding Travellers and Roma in education. Travellers and the education system currently face many challenges, issues and barriers; some are old and seemingly intractable, some are emerging in a newly multicultural and recession-stricken Ireland. The power imbalance and racism that have informed historic sedentary–nomadic relations continue to inform current system relations with Travellers and Roma. At the core of a dialogical engagement between system and people lies the need for policies and programmes informed by a deep and rich understanding of this historic and current reality. The balance of power lies with the system, the education providers; the balance of insight lies with Travellers and Roma. Each can challenge and educate the other, and work together to envision and build a just future for all.

Notes

1   Gender differentials, though outside the scope of this discussion, warrant comment. In all sectors, enrolments, retention and progression rates are higher for female than for male Travellers. This is common in education but there are culture-specific factors involved for Travellers and Roma. Modernization has brought occupational and identity issues for the men; women are recognized as leading community development (Liégeois, 2007). Traveller organizations are developing innovative strategies to engage with gender-related issues.

Further reading

Danaher, Patrick A., Kenny, Máirín, and Remy Leder, Judith (eds). (2009), *Traveller, Nomadic, and Migrant Education*. New York: Routledge (Research in Education).
This book also addresses the interface between formal education systems, and populations generally seen as mobile, and marginalized on that account. The very slight overlap between that publication and this hints at the range of peoples in these margins, and the wide gaps between them and the institutions purporting to serve them.

Gouwens, Judith A. (2001), *Migrant Education: A Reference Handbook.* Santa Barbara, CA: ABC-CLIO Inc. (Contemporary Education Issues Series).

The author dedicated this book 'to migrant educators throughout the United States who believe in the tremendous potential of migrant children and youth ... ' The migrant people's voices are central in this handbook, which documents a little-known area of inequity in US society and its education system.

McCann, May, Ó Síocháiné, Séamás, and Ruane, Joseph (eds).. (1994), *Irish Travellers: Culture & Ethnicity.* Belfst: Queen's University Belfast, Institute of Irish Studies.

This is an important collection of papers given at an anthropology conference in 1993. It opens up new approaches to issues of culture, identity and discrimination, in the case of Travellers in Ireland.

McVeigh, Robbie. (1999), 'Theorising sedentarism: The rots of anti-nomadism', in T. Acton (ed.), *Gypsy Politics and Traveller Identity.* Hatfield, UK: University of Hartfordshire Press.

Robbie McVeigh turns to history, including the work of the fourteenth-century Muslim scholar Ibn Khaldun to interrogate this ancient social fissure.

References

All Ireland Traveller Health Study Team (AITHST), School of Public Health, University College Dublin. (2010), *Our Geels All Ireland Traveller Health Study.* Dublin: Department of Health and Children.

Barry, J., Herity, B., and Solan, J. (1989), *The Travellers Health Status Study: Vital Statistics of Travelling People (1987).* Dublin: Health Research Board.

Bhreatnach, A. (2006), 'Chapter one. Fair days and doorsteps: Encounters between Travellers and settled people in twentieth-century Ireland', in C. Bhreatnach and A. Bhreatnach (eds), *Portraying Irish Travellers: Histories and Representations.* Newcastle upon Tyne, UK: Cambridge Scholars Publishing, pp. 1–16.

Binchy, A. (1994), 'Travellers' language: A sociolinguistic perspective', in M. McCann, S. Ó Síocháin, and J. Ruane (eds), *Irish Travellers: Culture and Ethnicity.* Belfast: Institute of Irish Studies, Queens University of Belfast, pp 134–153.

Blood of the Travellers. (2011), Two-part television documentary series. Scratch Films for RTÉ with the support of the Broadcasting Authority of Ireland, 22 and 29 May 2011.

Bryan, A. (2009), 'The intersectionality of nationalism and multiculturalism in the Irish curriculum: Teaching against racism?', *Race Ethnicity and Education,* 12, (3), 297–317.

Central Statistics Office (CSO). (2012), *Census 2011.* Retrieved from http://www.cso.ie/en/census/census2011reports/.

Collins, M. (1994), 'The sub-culture of poverty – A response to McCarthy', in M. McCann, S. Ó Síocháin, and J. Ruane (eds), *Irish Travellers: Culture and Ethnicity.* Belfast: Institute of Irish Studies, Queen's University, pp. 130–132.

Commission on Itinerancy. (1963), *Report on the Conditions of Itinerants.* Dublin: Stationery Office.

Commissioner for Human Rights (CHR). (2012), *Human Rights of Roma and Travellers in Europe.* Strasbourg: Council of Europe.

Council of Europe. (1994), *Framework Convention for the Protection of National Minorities.* Strasbourg: Council of Europe.

Dáil Eireann. (2008), *Dáil Éireann Debate*,Vol. 670, (2), p. 139. Retrieved from http://oireachtasdebates. oireachtas.ie/debates%20authoring/debateswebpack.nsf/takes/dail2008121000139?opendocument.

———. (2011), *Dáil Éireann Debate*, Vol. 681, (4), p. 397 & Vol. 734, (4), p. 59. Retrieved from http:// oireachtasdebates.oireachtas.ie/debates%20authoring/debateswebpack.nsf/yearlist?readform&chamber=dail.

Darmody, M., Smyth, E., and McCoy, S. (2012), *School Sector Variation among Primary Schools in Ireland*. Dublin: ESRI and Educate Together.

Deleuze, G. and Guattari, F., (1987), *A Thousand Plateaus: Capitalism and Schizophrenia*, trans. Brian Massumi. Minneapolis: University of Minnesota Press.

Department of Education. (1970), *Education Facilities for the Children of Itinerants*. Dublin: Stationery Office.

Department of Education and Science (DES1). (2002a), *Guidelines on Traveller Education in Primary Schools*. Dublin: Stationery Office.

———. (2002b), *Guidelines on Traveller Education in Second-Level Schools*. Dublin: Stationery Office.

———. (2006), *Report and Recommendations for a Traveller Education Strategy*. Dublin: Stationery Office.

———. (2008), 'Youthreach and Senior Traveller Training Centre Programmes Funded by the Department of Education and Science', *Value for Money Review*. Retrieved from http://www. education.ie/en/Publications/Value-For-Money-Reviews/vfm_review_youthreach_sttc_ programmes.pdf.

Department of Education and Skills. (2012), *School Returns*. Webpage for primary and postprimary schools. Retrieved from http://www.education.ie/en/Schools-Colleges/Services/Returns/.

——— and the Office of the Minister for Integration. (2010), *Intercultural Education Strategy 2010– 2015. Executive Summary*. Retrieved from http://www.into.ie/ROI/Publications/OtherPublications/ OtherPublicationsDownloads/Intercultural_education_strategy.pdf.

Department of the Taoiseach. (2006), *Towards 2016 Ten-Year Framework Social Partnership Agreement 2006–2015*. Dublin: Stationery Office.

Devine, D. (2005), 'Welcome to the Celtic Tiger? Teacher responses to immigration and increasing ethnic diversity in Irish schools', *International Studies in Sociology of Education*, 15, (1), 49–70.

Devine, D., Kenny, M. and Mac Neela, E. (2008), 'Naming the "other": Children's construction and experience of racisms in Irish primary schools', *Race Ethnicity and Education*, 11, (4), 369–385.

European Commission (EU). (2009), Council Conclusions of 12 May 2009 on a Strategic Framework for European Cooperation in Education and Training ('ET 2020') (2009/C 119/02). Retrieved from http://ec.europa.eu/education/lifelong-learning-policy/framework_en.htm.

European Union. (2000), Charter of Fundamental Rights of the European Union (2000/C 364/01). Retrieved from http://www.europarl.europa.eu/charter/pdf/text_en.pdf.

European Union Agency for Fundamental Rights. (2012), The Situation of Roma in 11 EU Member States. Survey Results at a Glance. Retrieved from http://fra.europa.eu/sites/default/files/fra_ uploads/2099-FRA-2012-Roma-at-a-glance_EN.pdf.

Fanning, B. (2002), *Racism and Social Change in the Republic of Ireland*. Manchester: Manchester University Press.

Free Legal Aid Centres. (2004), *Guide to the Habitual Residence Condition*. Dublin: FLAC.

Government of Ireland. (2004), Consolidated Text of the Equal Status Acts 2000 to 2004. Retrieved from http://www.justice.ie/en/JELR/EqualStatusActsConsldtd_00_04.pdf/Files/EqualStatusActsConsldtd_00_04.pdf.

——. (2006), *Report of the High Level Group on Traveller Issues*. March, 2006. Retrieved from http://www.justice.ie/en/JELR/HLGReport.pdf/Files/HLGReport.pdf.

——. (2011), *Ireland's National Traveller/Roma Integration Strategy*. Retrieved from http://ec.europa.eu/justice/discrimination/roma/national-strategies/index_en.htm.

Hansen, A. (2004), 'Exhibiting vagrancy, 1851: Victorian London and the "Vagabond Savage"', *Literary London: Interdisciplinary Studies in the Representation of London*, 2, (2). Retrieved from http://www.literarylondon.org/london-journal/september2004/hansen.html.

Helleiner, J. (2000), *Irish Travellers: Racism and the Politics of Culture*. Toronto: University of Toronto Press.

Higher Education Authority (HEA). (2012), *Higher Education: Key Facts and Figures 2010/11*. Dublin: HEA.

Hourigan, N. and Campbell, M. (2010), *The TEACH Report: Traveller Education and Adults: Crisis, Challenge and Change*. Athlone: National Association of Travellers' Centres.

Irish Times Online. (2013), 'Travellers must be accorded their own ethnic status', *Brigid Quilligan*. Retrieved from http://www.irishtimes.com/newspaper/opinion/2013/0206/1224329705900.html.

Kenny, M. (1997), *The Routes of Resistance: Travellers and Second Level Schooling*. Aldershot: Ashgate Publishing.

Kenny, M. and Mac Neela, E. (2005), *Assimilation Policies and Outcomes: Travellers' Experience*. Dublin: Pavee Point Publications.

Lentin, R. (2007), 'Ireland: Racial state and crisis racism', *Ethnic and Racial Studies*, 30, (4), 61–27.

Lentin, R. and McVeigh, R. (2006), *After Optimism? Ireland, Racism and Globalisation*. Dublin: Metro Eireann Publications. Retrieved from http://www.tara.tcd.ie/bitstream/2262/25156/1/after%20optimism.pdf.

Levinson, M. P. (2008), 'Issues of empowerment and disempowerment: Gypsy children at home and school', *Citizenship Teaching and Learning*, 4, (2), 70–77.

Liégeois, J.-P. (2007), *Roma in Europe*. Strasbourg: Council of Europe Publishing.

Mac Éinrí, P. (2002), 'Cultural identity and political transformation', *The Irish Association Annual Conference*, 11–12 October 2002. Cork: Irish Centre for Migration Studies. Retrieved from http://migration.ucc.ie/irishassociationpme.htm.

Mac Gréine, P. (1932), 'Irish Tinkers or "Travellers"', *Béaloideas*, 3, 170–186.

Macpherson. (1999), *The Stephen Lawrence Inquiry: Report of an Inquiry by Sir William Macpherson of Cluny*. London: The Stationery Office.

McDonagh, M. (1994), 'Nomadism in Irish Travellers' Identity', in M. McCann, S. Ó Síocháin, and J. Ruane (eds), *Irish Travellers: Culture and Ethnicity*. Belfast: Institute of Irish Studies, Queen's University.

McVeigh, R. (1997), 'Theorising sedentarism: The roots of anti-nomadism', in T. A. Acton (ed), *Gypsy Politics and Traveller Identity*. Hatfield, UK: University of Hertfordshire Press, pp. 7–25.

Munnelly, T. (1975), 'The singing tradition of Irish Travellers', *Folk Music Journal*, 3, (1), 3–30.

National Council for Curriculum and Assessment (NCCA). (2005), *Intercultural Education in the Primary School. Guidelines for Schools*. Dublin: NCCA.

———. (2006), *Intercultural Education in the Post-Primary School*. Dublin: NCCA.

Ní Laodhóg, N. and Collins, D. (1995), 'Pavee pipers and players', in N. Ní Laodhóg (ed), *A Heritage Ahead: Cultural Action and Travellers*. Dublin: Pavee Point Publications.

O'Connell, J. (1994), *Reach Out. Report by the DTEDG on the Poverty 3 Programme, 1990–1994*. Dublin: Pavee Point Publications.

Okely, J. (1983), *The Traveller Gypsies*. Dublin: Cambridge University Press.

Pavee Point Travellers Centre. (2005), *Travellers and Education*. Dublin: Pavee Point Publications.

———. (2011), *Towards a National Traveller and Roma Integration Strategy 2020*. Dublin: Pavee Point. Retrieved from http://paveepoint.ie/sitenua/wp-content/uploads/2011/10/Towards-National-Traveller-Roma-Strategy_20.09.11.pdf.

———. (2013), Roma. Pavee Point programmes information page. Retrieved from http://www.paveepoint.ie/what-we-do/programmes/roma/.

Potter, J. and Wetherell, M. (1989), *Discourse and Social Psychology*. London: Sage Publications.

Trumpener, K. (1992), 'The time of the Gypsies: A "people without history" in the narratives of the West', *Critical Inquiry, (Identities)*, 18, (4), 843–884.

Education as Cultural Conflict: Gypsies and Travellers in Southern England

2

Juliet McCaffery

Introduction

Conflict and culture frame any analysis or discussion of the education of Gypsies and Travellers. Street (1995) argues that no education is neutral; all education is ideological. Over thirty years ago, Worrall stated that education is a site of cultural conflict between Gypsies and the dominant settled community:

> Education within this context of often acute social conflict cannot but reflect and take account of the broader social tensions, [it will tend]…to either further undermine the Travellers' morale, and above all their possibilities of retaining their economic integrity, or…to enhance the Gypsies' power to remain their own masters. There is no such thing as a 'neutral' education. (Worrall, 1979, p. 3)

This social and cultural conflict continues. Prejudice and exclusion are still manifested at personal, organizational and institutional levels.

The United Nations (UN) document on safe and just societies relates to the situation of Gypsies and Travellers:

> Social exclusion can be described as the opposite of social integration and as the process by which systematic neglect, oppression or discrimination against people exists in social institutions, whether government, organisations, communities or households … in conspicuous as well as veiled forms. (UN, 2007, p. 30)

The UN document continues by stressing the importance of a community's freedom to assert its identity and have the opportunity to represent itself. It also states that education is an important lever for enhancing social cohesion: 'Schools and other educational institutions help provide the context within which students learn the appropriate behaviours' (UN, 2007, p. 38).

My research in the South of England revealed a concern among many Gypsies and Travellers that formal education would result in their children's assimilation into the dominant community and consequently the loss of their own culture and identity. Though there are excellent exceptions, in the majority of schools Gypsy and Traveller culture is not reflected in the curriculum and few teachers understand or have received any cultural training. As a result, many Gypsy and Traveller parents are reluctant to send their children to school, where they face many difficulties, and many parents withdraw them at puberty.

The dominant discourses of both education and development perceive literacy as the ability to read and write text, and as essential to economic success, self-esteem and status. The formal education system is an integral component of the nation state. The curriculum determines what children should know, how they should behave and what they should think. Education is considered necessary for the well-being of individuals, the prosperity of the community and the economy of the nation. Most communities value formal education and perceive it as beneficial, but some minorities, including Gypsies and Travellers, view it with suspicion. Though many Gypsies and Travellers now believe that their children should learn to read and write and send them to school for this purpose, there is a real fear that success at school will involve incorporation into mainstream society and result in the loss of their culture. Gypsies and Travellers in Southern England reflect this tension.

Gypsies' and Travellers' attendance and levels of educational achievement are the lowest of any minority group in England. Until the 1980s, Gypsies and Travellers in England had very few educational opportunities and, as a result, many of those over 40 are not able to read and write or have very limited reading skills. Many do not believe that the ability to read and write would enhance their self-esteem, status or income. However, many do feel they lack the language and discourse of formally educated people as they 'do not know the words' to interact effectively with public officials and bureaucratic systems, so the issue is not just textual literacy but, more broadly, 'discourse' including both spoken and written communication.

Any consideration of the education of Gypsies and Travellers is conducted against a background of extreme prejudice towards them. The burning in 2003 of a cardboard caravan with images of women and children inside on the Guy Fawkes bonfire at Firle, East Sussex, and the destruction in 2011 of the unauthorized encampment at Dale Farm, Essex, at an estimated cost of £22 million (Sawyer and Ljunggren, 2011) are outcomes of the derogatory remarks made by the general public, extreme criticism by some elected councillors and MPs, and a consistently negative press (Bhopal and Myers, 2008; Coxhead, 2007; McCaffery, 2012; McVeigh, 1997; Ni Shuinear, 1994).

In this chapter I briefly outline my research methods, describe the Gypsy and Traveller communities in Southern England, their attitudes to schooling and the barriers and challenges they face. I conclude by suggesting that while formal education might bring advantages to Gypsies and Travellers, educational institutions must become more responsive and culturally aware if the advantages are to be realized.

Research methods and access

I became interested in Gypsies' and Travellers' perceptions of education and their attitudes to literacy after teaching adults in England and elsewhere for many years. My research, as part of a PhD during the 2000s, was qualitative and constructivist. I undertook face-to-face interviews with 32 Gypsies and Travellers, which are best described as informal conversations, and which, in some instances, were held over a period of time. I have attempted to represent the Gypsies' and Travellers' views accurately, but inevitably my own experiences affect my interpretation.

I used a range of ethnographic-style tools and collected 'whatever data was available' (Hammersley and Atkinson, 1995, p. 1). This included a range of material in the public domain – minutes of meetings, notes of conferences and seminars, publications, newspaper articles, news reports, videos and television programmes. I attended forums, conferences, national council meetings and a police advisory group. I also drew on information from three surveys of 138 Gypsies' and Travellers' use of statutory and voluntary services, including education and, like Okely (1983), also 'relied on unstructured and random information from a wide range of Travellers'. I have some knowledge of the Irish experience to set against experience in England, as I also visited three literacy classes for Travellers in the Republic of Ireland and talked to several Travellers individually.

Undertaking research in the Gypsy and Traveller community as a *Gaujo*, a non-Gypsy, is problematic. Levinson (2008) provides a detailed account of the barriers he had to overcome to gain access. At a conference held in London in October 2004, a Gypsy commented, 'They come, ask us questions and then go away and build a career on the answers'. Another stated that 'An academic makes up a myth, which is then reproduced by all the others'. It is possible that secrecy and suspicion of researchers and a desire to keep 'under the radar' are factors in the persistence of Gypsy and Traveller culture. Perhaps they were willing to talk to me because I was already involved in the community and not a total stranger. I hope that by providing help and assistance when requested, I gave something back in return.

Romani Gypsies and Irish Travellers in England

The size of the Gypsy and Traveller population in England is not known. The 2011 Census was the first to include Gypsies and Travellers as a separate category, but the figure of 57,680 for England and Wales (0.01–2 per cent of the population) is a significant under-representation, as is 14,542 for the South East. Sadly, many are afraid that self-identification may lead to victimization, loss of work and, as in some countries, removal. Informal estimates range from 300,000 to 400,000, out of whom 25,000 are known to have no secure stopping place or site. Additionally, the Commission for Racial Equality estimated that between 270,000 and 360,000 Gypsies and Travellers live in bricks and mortar (Commission for Racial Equality, 2006).

Gypsies and Travellers in the British Isles comprise six groups: Romani Gypsies, Welsh Gypsies, Scottish Gypsies, Irish Travellers, Roma and New Age Travellers, each with different histories, cultural traditions and languages. The broad narrative is that Romanies moved westwards from northern India over a thousand years ago, or possibly several hundred years earlier. While this narrative is generally accepted, aspects are now contested and different theories have arisen as to the reasons for the migration, the routes taken and the level of integration and intermarriage with the population of the countries through which they travelled (Acton and Mundy, 1997; Bhopal and Myers, 2008; Hancock, 2002, 2008; Kenrick, 1998; Matras et al., 2000; Okely, 1983).

English Romanies

English Romanies arrived in England at the beginning of the sixteenth century. Gypsies in England are known as 'Romanichals' or 'Romani Gypsies', while their Welsh equivalents are known as 'Kale'. 'Romanichals' are usually referred to as 'Gypsies', a term derived from 'Egyptians' as they were thought to have come from Egypt. Estimates of the number of English Romanies vary from 120,000 to 300,000 (Bowers, n.d.). Nomenclature is an issue. The term 'Gypsy/Traveller' implies travelling and many no longer travel. I prefer the descriptor 'English Romanies', but 'Gypsies' is the descriptor in common use and in official documents. In this chapter when used alone, 'Gypsies' refers to English Gypsies (Romani Gypsies/Romanichals) and 'Travellers' refers to Irish Travellers. Some English Romanies also refer to themselves as 'Travellers' and 'Romani Travellers'. Settled Gypsies sometimes describe themselves as of Romani heritage. Physically the majority of English Gypsies are indistinguishable from the general population. English Gypsies comprise the majority of the Gypsy and Traveller community in Sussex; some Irish Travellers also live on the sites and a significant number travel to the area.

English Romani Gypsies spoke the Romani language until the nineteenth century, when it was replaced by English and Angloromani, which combines the syntax and grammar of English with the Romani lexicon. All English Romanies also speak English. There are many Romani dialects; the dialect spoken in England is known as *Poggadi Jib*, or 'broken language' because it largely consists of Romani verbs and nouns but uses many English words. As Bowers (n.d.) states:

> It is a very effective way of retaining a language and excluding people from outside the culture who you don't want to understand what you are saying. For example: 'If Mande rokkered the poggadi jib tutti wouldn't jin what mande was pukkering'.[1]

Irish Travellers

Irish Travellers are a minority in Southern England, but the percentage within the Gypsy-Traveller group is not separately identified. According to the 2003 Census there were 24,000 Travellers in the Republic of Ireland, 2,000 in Northern Ireland and an estimated 1,500 Irish Travellers in England, Scotland and Wales (Kenrick and Clark, 1999). While Irish Travellers may be of Romani origin, this is contested by some (Binchy, 2000; Kenrick, 1998; Ni Shuinear, 1994; Okely, 1983; Worrall, 1979). They may be of pre-Celtic origin. Irish Travellers, like others from the Irish Republic, came to England at various times in the nineteenth century, and also after the Second World War (Kenrick and Clark, 1999). Those born in England frequently retain strong Irish accents though they may never have been to Ireland. Travellers living there also regularly come over to England to find work. Irish Travellers speak Gammon or Cant, which has no connection to Romani. It also uses English words but mixes these with ancient Gaelic words.

Culture and society

Though the populations are small, the culture of both English Romanies and Irish Travellers is very strong, possibly because for centuries they have chosen to remain apart from the majority despite some intermarriage. If a Gypsy or Traveller takes a *Gaujo* or 'non-Gypsy' spouse, they are accepted but remain *Gaujo*; the children of such marriages are considered Gypsies or Travellers (Okely, 1983).

The culture of English Romanies and Irish Travellers is highly gendered. Men are responsible for supporting the family financially and women for the home and family. Traditionally women dress modestly[2] and abstain from sex until marriage. Early marriage is the norm. Romani culture is built upon strict codes of cleanliness learnt over centuries of life on the road. The trailers in which many Romanies and Travellers live are spotless and must be kept clean like the inner body. Concepts such as *mokadi* and *mahrime* place strict guidelines, for example, on what objects can be washed in bowls. Romani Gypsies view *Gaujos* as unclean because of the way they live. Gypsies and Travellers rarely let animals inside their homes, because they believe them to be dirty and carriers of disease. Death and childbirth are considered polluting and preferably should occur in hospital, not in the home. Lavatories and baths should not be shared with *Gaujos*.

Both English Gypsies and Irish Travellers prefer to be self-employed. Traditionally Gypsies in Southern England followed the harvest from Kent to Cornwall, stopping in farmers' fields while working. With the mechanization of agriculture and the increase in foreign workers, this traditional source of income has ceased. Many Gypsies in the South still live close to these routes and identify with this geographical area. Hop picking in Kent was another traditional source of income and is often spoken of nostalgically.

Current occupations among both communities include tarmacking, clearing driveways, gardening, small nurseries, tree cutting, horse dealing and 'cold calling'. Some work alone; others have small firms and employ staff. Some travel for work throughout the year, others travel only in the summer months or when work is available. Very few living on private or public sites are employed in the formal sector, but some settled in housing work for a variety of employers, rarely revealing their cultural heritage. Women traditionally made paper and wooden flowers which they sold along with 'lucky' heather. I have interviewed and also talked informally to many Gypsy and Traveller women but did not meet any women living on local authority sites who worked outside the home, but some of those living on private sites or in housing did so.

Neither personal nor business communications rely on text. Though some now have bank accounts, transactions, even significant ones for cars or horses, are often paid in cash. New laws restricting the amount of cash that can be carried without proof of the source have caused some concern. Large horse fairs such as those at Appleby and Stowe and smaller ones such as Horsemorden on the Kent–Sussex border provide the opportunity for the exchange of news and general information. Weddings and funerals are important social occasions as was shown by the television series in 2012.

The culture is clan based. I was informed that in England the Gypsy population comprises eight extended families. When meeting for the first time Gypsies exchange genealogical information to locate common relatives. Traditionally disputes are settled internally, sometimes violently, though recently the police in some forces are called upon more than previously. Bare-knuckle boxing and horse trotting are among the leisure pursuits, though famous entertainers, artists, musicians and footballers suggest a variety of interests within the communities.

There are cultural and religious differences between English Gypsies and Irish Travellers and the two groups tend to keep apart. Evangelical and Baptist missionaries such as 'Gypsies for Christ' have been active among English Romanies; Irish Travellers are predominantly Catholic.

Tensions

Though many are now settled, travelling is still part of the heritage and affects their children's education as well as causing tension with the settled community. With an insufficient number of sites, unauthorized encampments are common and result in tension and social conflict with the settled community. English Gypsies prefer to live and travel in small family units whereas Irish Travellers tend to travel in large convoys for safety reasons. The large convoys cause greater antagonism with the settled population and English Gypsies feel these impacts negatively on their acceptance by the settled community.

The 1959 Highways Act stated that living on, or hawking goods, by the roadside was an offence. In June 1985, the Battle of the Beanfield, when police attempted to stop a large convoy of New Age Travellers moving towards Stonehenge for the summer solstice celebrations, led to the Criminal Justice and Public Order Act, which made unauthorized encampments illegal (Clark, 1997).

In 1968, the Caravan Sites Act placed a duty on councils to provide sites for Gypsies and Travellers, but many local authorities simply ignored the directive. Others complied and in 2006, 75 per cent were on local authority or private sites (Commission for Racial Equality, 2006). Gypsies and Travellers were recommended to make their own provision and many bought land but were then refused planning permission. Ninety per cent of Gypsy and Traveller planning applications were initially rejected (Advisory Council for the Education of Romany and Other Travellers (ACERT) and Wilson, 1997). Appeals frequently failed. In March 2005, a leading Gypsy campaigner and his extended family were evicted after losing an eight-year legal battle to remain on land he owned.[3]

In 2006, the tensions and costs of eviction led the government to undertake an Accommodation Needs Survey. The figures published in the Partial Review of the Regional Spatial Strategy (South East England Regional Assembly, 2009) indicate the need (Table 2.1).

Table 2.1 Regional accommodation needs

District authorized	Pitches in January 2006	Additional pitches required 2006–2011
East of England	1,782	1,237
South East of England	1,868	1,064

Source: South East England Regional Assembly (2009, p. 9).

The Accommodation Needs Assessment also identified targets for individual authorities and in some authorities the assessment included the need for transit sites (Table 2.2).

Table 2.2 Accommodation needs for selected authority areas

	2006 baseline	Additional permanent pitches required	Transit sites required
Brighton and Hove	0	13	2
East Sussex	43	55	
West Sussex	173	177	25
Dorset	407	430–440	

Source: South East England Regional Assembly (2009, pp. 9–11).

Caravan counts are undertaken biannually and show the number of caravans on public and private authorized and unauthorized sites, including sites on land which Gypsies and Travellers own, but for which they have not received planning permission. The count only counts caravans, not people. The July 2011 caravan count showed that the highest number of both authorized and unauthorized public and private pitches was in the South East and East of England and that 21 per cent of Gypsy and Traveller caravans were on unauthorized land (see Figure 2.1).

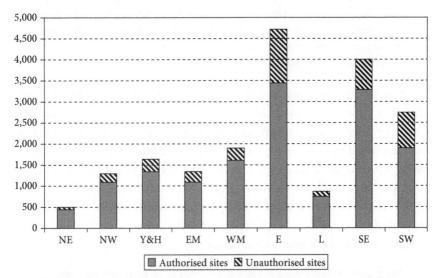

Figure 2.1 Regional breakdown of Gypsy and Traveller caravans (July 2011 count)

Source: DCLG. Housing Statistical Release 17 November 2011, p. 5.

The count in July 2012 showed a slight improvement in the number of sites, but 16 per cent of caravans were on unauthorized land (Communities and Local Government, 2012).

Experience of education

The education of Gypsies and Travellers in England is a complex issue on which there is comparatively little literature. Much of the information on schooling is contained in government reports. The limited amount of academic analysis suggests that the education of Gypsies and Travellers is not yet in the mainstream of research (Worrall, 1979) and 'has been under theorised in the past' (Levinson, 2007, p. 19). There is no analysis of Gypsies' and Travellers' experience of adult and non-formal education.

In 1902, the English Education Act extended compulsory schooling to the whole population of England and Wales. In 1908, the Children's Act required children of nomadic parents to attend for 200 half-day sessions (Kenrick and Clark, 1999; Waterson, 1997). This has now changed and Code T below states how the law applies to the general group of 'Travellers': (Roma, English and Welsh Gypsies, Irish and Scottish Travellers), Showmen (fairground people), Circus People, Bargees (occupational boat dwellers) and New Travellers.

> To help ensure continuity of education for Traveller children it is expected that the child should attend school elsewhere when their family is travelling and be dual registered at that school and the main school. Children from these groups whose families do not travel are expected to register at a school and attend as normal. (Department for Education (DfE), 2012)

The first serious attempts to include Gypsy and Traveller children in the education system were made in the 1960s following the establishment of a school for Travellers in Dublin. The first Gypsy Caravan School in England was established by volunteers in the summer of 1967. This initiative and the setting up of other schools for Gypsies and Travellers led to a number of developments in both the voluntary and statutory sectors (Kenrick and Clark, 1999). Progress was slow and for many Gypsies and Travellers schooling was not part of their childhood experience, as the following examples indicate:

Gary[4], an English Romani, commented:

> We travelled all over the place, England and Scotland, on the road in the sixties ... and seventies. I never went to school ... it's not easy. I'm embarrassed about it now, before it didn't matter. (interview of May 2009)

Siobhan, an Irish Traveller, also had very limited schooling:

> I went to school for about six months and that was it, because we went from one place to another. We were constantly moving, constantly moving, from Ireland to England, from England to Ireland, from Ireland to France, to Germany. We was constantly on the trot somewhere. I suppose for the older generation, education wasn't important. (interview of January 2009)

Kenrick and Clark (1999, p. 167) point out that 'since … most councils put their efforts into moving Gypsy families out of their area, there was little enthusiasm for organising education for them'. Working life started at an early age for older Gypsies and Travellers; working alongside their fathers was the expected norm. An Irish Traveller commented: 'I left school at seven, had to go to work. I was working at 7. I was shoeing horses when I was 10' (interview at Dale Farm, April 2008).

Table 2.3 summarizes the literacy levels of those I interviewed, 5 of whom were Irish Travellers and 27 English Gypsies.

Table 2.3 Summary of interviewees' reading levels

Approximation to national adult reading levels	Estimated reading ability	Count
Level 3 or above	Fluent readers	5
Level 2	Good readers	3
Level 1	Reasonable readers	8
Entry level 1	Very limited readers	7
Below entry level	Below entry level	9
Total		**32**

The table shows that, according to formal educational measures, 16 interviewees (50 per cent) had minimal literacy skills. Five could sign their name and write a few words; nine could not sign their name. Sixty-four per cent of the men had low or very low literacy skills compared to 36 per cent of the women. The 'reasonable' readers used a variety of strategies to understand the information presented, but could not read word for word and had very poor writing skills. Three had a level of literacy above the General Certificate of Secondary Education (GCSE) level and two of these were women. The three fluent readers had all completed secondary school and two had been to university. The eight good readers had secure accommodation; five out of the eight lived in houses or flats and three on permanent sites. Only one person interviewed travelled throughout the year. Most of those who had some reading skills were the younger people or those who had attended school, if only for a limited time.

There were exceptions. An older English Gypsy had been taught to read in the army. Despite a travelling lifestyle, Doris, now aged 50 and living on a permanent site in West Sussex, was a competent reader. She commented: 'Granny said we loved school. We would sneak off and go to school... I love reading. I like reading books' (interview of April 2009).

Whether they could read or not, all those I interviewed had sent their children to primary school. As Bernie said 'We made a point of it; they went to school' (interview of August 2008). Harriet was equally forceful: 'I sent my son to the local school and he did very well... made sure my children could read' (interview of February 2009). When education was discussed on sites and at conferences, almost all who spoke had sent their children to primary school, but achievement levels remain very low.

Achievement levels in England

In England, despite a directive of the Department for Children, Schools and Families (DCSF) that schools should record Gypsy/Roma and Irish Traveller ethnicity in the Annual School Census, information on the enrolment and achievement of Gypsy and Traveller children of school age is limited. The DCSF specifically stated that statistics, such as those in Table 2.4, should be treated with caution.

Table 2.4 Achievements at GCSE and equivalent for pupils at the end of Key Stage 4 by pupil characteristics, 2010/2011

Ethnic/ cultural group	Number of eligible pupils	% 5+ A*-C grades	% 5+ A*-C grades inc. English & maths	% 5+ A*-G grades	% 5+ A*-G grades inc. English & maths	% A*-C in English and maths
Gypsy/Roma	595	31.4	10.8	59.2	50.4	11.1
Traveller of Irish Heritage	137	35.0	17.5	55.5	48.2	18.2
White and Black Caribbean	6,444	75.6	49.1	93.2	91.8	49.6
White British	464,056	80.1	58.0	95.0	93.8	58.5

Source: Department for Education (2011).

The only other group with a GCSE percentage pass rate (in the third column) of less than 50 per cent were White and Black Caribbean pupils. The 2011/2012 results showed that the position had not changed.

The tables also showed a high number of Gypsy/Roma and Irish Traveller children in the SEN categories, in School Action Plus, and attending Special Schools despite the national programme to raise achievement launched in 2006 (DFES, 2006).

Challenges: Attendance and exclusions

Attendance rates of Gypsy and Traveller children are below the national average. National data published by the DCSF (2008b) showed the average absence rate of Gypsy/Roma pupils was approximately three times that of all pupils, while for Irish Traveller pupils the absence rate was four times the national average. Attendance declines as Gypsy and Traveller children moved up the school. In 2008, a third of Gypsy/Roma pupils and less than half the Travellers of Irish Heritage recorded at Key Stage 1, were recorded at GCSE and equivalent levels (DCSF, 2008b).

The DfE (2010) report found that 20 per cent of Gypsy, Roma and Traveller pupils failed to transfer from primary to secondary school. The Irish Traveller Movement (ITM) in Britain reported that of those who transferred successfully to secondary school, more than 50 per cent of Gypsies and 62 per cent of Irish Travellers dropped out, or were excluded, before the statutory leaving age (Moore and Brindley, 2012).

There is some evidence that local authorities do not always place as high a priority on the attendance of Gypsy and Traveller children as on that of other children and that there is a higher level of 'informal' exclusions and 'part-time learning'. Derrington and Kendall (2004) noted that patterns of 'medical' absences, which in some cases coincided with bullying episodes, were not always investigated or analysed by schools.

The most common reasons given for the exclusion of Gypsy pupils were physical aggression towards peers and verbal abuse towards staff. According to the DFES (2006), Irish Travellers are often excluded for persistent disruptive behaviour. Some teachers who attended diversity training in 2009 admitted they found Gypsy and Traveller children difficult. The rate of permanent exclusion in 2007/2008 was highest for Gypsy/Roma, at 0.56 per cent of the school population, and Travellers of Irish heritage, at 0.53 per cent of the school population (Wilkins et al., 2010).

The situation in Sussex resembled the national picture. In January 2010, there were 257 school aged children from English Gypsy and Irish Traveller families in West Sussex and 200 in East Sussex. In both authorities, the majority were English Gypsies with strong local connections. The actual number of children was probably higher, as some under-reporting was likely (Office for Public Management (OPM), 2010) (Table 2.5).

Table 2.5 Number of Irish Traveller and Gypsy/Roma pupils attending schools maintained by East Sussex, West Sussex and Brighton and Hove LEAs, 2008/2009 and 2009/2010 (final data)

Local authority	Number of pupils in maintained primary schools				Number of pupils in maintained secondary schools			
	Traveller of Irish Heritage		Gypsy/Roma		Traveller of Irish Heritage		Gypsy/Roma	
	2008/ 2009	2009/ 2010	2008/ 2009	2009/ 2010	2008/ 2009	2009/ 2010	2008/ 2009	2009/ 2010
Brighton and Hove	x	12	0	0	x	x	x	x
East Sussex	9	6	93	103	6	x	72	83
West Sussex	22	21	134	128	10	8	93	100

x = less than five pupils.
Source: Data and Statistics Division, Department for Education and Science, 2010.

The table excludes pupils who were dually registered. However, the statistics provided by the manager of the Traveller Education Service (TES) to Brighton and Hove Scrutiny Panel in 2009 showed that a greater number of children had attended the previous year.

Levels of the achievement of Gypsy and Traveller children at local level were hard to obtain as they were omitted due to 'low not statistically significant numbers, and reasons of confidentiality'.[5] However, my ten-year-long request for a report on Traveller Education was finally granted and in 2009 a report was presented to the Brighton and Hove Scrutiny Committee. The report showed patterns of attendance and achievement as in Table 2.6 and that, between them, four students had gained six GCSEs, though below C grade.

Table 2.6 Gypsy /Roma and Irish Traveller children attending schools in Brighton and Hove 2007/2008

	Primary	Secondary	Total
Pupils enrolled in schools, all/part 2007/2008	33	16	49
Schools with Traveller pupils	13	7	20
Highly mobile children resorting to the area with whom TES engaged but who did not attend any school	17	9	26

Source: Report to Brighton and Hove Children, Schools and Family (CSF) Scrutiny Panel: 28 January 2009.

Shortage of sites

Between September 2007 and August 2008 there were a total of sixty unauthorized encampments in 30 locations in Brighton and Hove. The report stated that approximately 50 per cent of the children at some point engaged in 'appropriate education'. Of the 49 attending school, 33 attended primary school with an attendance rate of 80 per cent and 16 attended secondary school with an attendance rate of 76 per cent. The statistics the following year were similar. Weekly information on the evictions and movement of Travellers provided to Brighton and Hove councillors did not include the impact on schooling.

However, the Brighton and Hove Annual TES Report for 2007–2008 noted that the shorter the time unauthorized encampments were tolerated, the greater the difficulty children experienced accessing schools. With relatively short or insecure stopping places, many of those travelling felt there was no point in sending their children to school when they were about to be moved on. Carol, an English Gypsy, said:

> It is very difficult, very hard for us, getting our kids an education when we have nowhere to live, and may be evicted, very hard for our kids. (interview of March 2009)

The constant evictions cause considerable stress as well as lack of achievement. Kate, for example, reported:

> I have a daughter of thirteen who is bed wetting. She went to school one day. She had to move from there when we left [the] transit site; she went back [to a different school] today. She can hardly read at all. (interview of January 2009)

The family want to stay in the area as they have local connections but there are no permanent pitches. They were moved five times in nine months. The impact of evictions on school attendance is a sensitive issue. When education was discussed at the Scrutiny Committee, a council education officer quickly interrupted saying: 'We are here to discuss education; it should not be political' (Brighton and Hove CSF Scrutiny Committee).

It is therefore surprising that the literature does not place more emphasis on the impact of evictions. No statistics correlating numbers leaving school with enforced evictions are available. Despite the government's aim to increase Gypsy and Traveller school attendance, the policies in England fail to acknowledge sufficiently the shortage of permanent sites and the impact of evictions on children's education (Derrington and Kendall, 2004; Jordan, 2001; Marks, 2004).

Undoubtedly, there are issues around school capacity when Gypsy and Traveller families suddenly arrive in the area and schools receive no financial support if the children are not in attendance in January when school numbers are calculated. Office for Standards in Education (OFSTED) has suggested strategies for minimizing disruption, including the transfer of school records, IT and distance learning, but, though very positive, these only mitigate the situation to a certain extent (Wilkins et al., 2009). In 2012, some authorities gave schools a pupil premium for Traveller children but others did not.

School atmosphere

There were clear preferences for schools. One parent said his daughter would not attend the local secondary school but would eventually go to a neighbouring college as 'They do all kinds of things there' (interview of February 2009). One young man compared two schools: one he considered 'awful', but in another the presence of a large number of other Gypsies 'made it more relaxed'. An OFSTED inspection recognized that higher than average attendance of Gypsy and Travellers pupils at some secondary schools affected staff expectations and achievement levels. An understanding of the heritage and culture and a policy of listening to parents encouraged a good atmosphere and positive relationships between the school and Gypsy and Traveller pupils (DCSF, 2008b).

At a conference organized by the ITM in September 2007, delegates reported that relations with teachers were poor in many schools and parents found it difficult to talk to them (*ITM conference: September 2007*). Another conference participant was also very critical: 'A lot of the teachers are so racist. You put down you're a Gypsy and it follows you all through your school life'.

A TES teacher supported their comments:

> The schools won't talk to me or the Travellers. They often send a letter home which the parents can't read. So the parents say the school is not talking to them, so they won't talk to the school. (interview of March 2008)

One parent was pleased with the atmosphere in a different school: 'Lovely people, good attendance, place to stay, part of society we thought'. Then the situation changed. The parent continued:

> There were fifty kids in the school and the locals took their kids out of that school. That was their choice obviously, but that was pure racism, not correct as far as I can see. (statement at ITM conference, September 2007)

Bullying

Bullying was mentioned over and over again. The Irish Traveller Movement of Britain (2010) report on economic and social inclusion for Gypsies and Travellers found that 55 per cent of the sample of 95 interviewees experienced bullying and discrimination in education and racist bullying acted as a barrier to participation in school, often causing parents to remove their children. Racist bullying in general might be monitored by the school, but racist bullying towards Gypsies and Travellers was not often separately identified.

The DCSF encourages voluntary self-declared ethnicity as it is a 'human right for the world to respect you for who you really are' (DCSF, 2008a). However, self-identification can be problematic. When Jack, a young Gypsy from West Sussex, was asked about the reaction if he self-identified, he replied emphatically: 'Oh the bullying got much worse, much worse' (interview of July 2009). Revealing your identity or having your identity revealed could be not only unpleasant but dangerous, as Siobhan, an Irish Traveller from Kent, recounted:

> My Red was in hospital. This is what happened to him. I want this published. When he was small he really enjoyed school and everyone knew him. When he went to big school, he just kept quiet. One day a teacher was talking about culture and said to him. 'Tell us about your culture'. Red said, 'What? Mine is the same as yours'. The teacher says, 'No it isn't, you're a Traveller. Tell us about your culture'. Then in the playground he was really beaten up; his head bashed and bleeding and everything … When we got there he was lying on a bench all on his own and bleeding. He was unconscious. We called an ambulance and rushed him to hospital. It was awful to see him lying there with tubes in him. When he see me he just said, 'Hi Nan'. It broke my heart to hear it … In fact the teacher really liked him.
>
> The head teacher had done nothing. He had to go to a meeting. Just thought it was boys in the playground … He did apologise when he learnt how serious it was. But I want this known. (interview of April 2009)

This incident was the result of a well-intentioned teacher being apparently unaware of how other students would react to the knowledge that Red was a Traveller; but Red had known.

There are some encouraging developments. An English Gypsy is on the governing body of a Community High School in East Sussex and several Gypsies and Travellers work as teaching assistants, though they do not necessarily reveal their ethnic identity. A teacher in Kent has compiled a large index of resources to be used by teachers wishing to incorporate aspects of Traveller culture into the literacy hour.

There are examples of success in education. A young Irish woman is now at law school; a young man is training to become a teacher; a young man finished school successfully and is now working for a large company; another attends college and is training to be farrier. Yet another attended a private school, went on to university and achieved a first-class degree. However, these are exceptions.

Cultural issues

Harvey, one of the few who has been to university, expressed contradictory feelings about education:

> I've been a success [but] when I look at my cousins ... the boys want to work with their Dads. [My brother] can go into my Dad's business and earn £300 a day and drive up to the school in a Porsche. The kids don't need education and the teachers don't understand it. I don't need to read and write and my brothers will take over the business, which will be there for many years. You don't need to read and write to cut a tree down. (interview of August 2009)

Literacy is considered by many adult Gypsies and Travellers as irrelevant to their ability to earn a living, but views are changing. Many now think it is important that their children learn to read and write, but consider other subjects irrelevant. Martha, for example, said:

> I think all this other stuff, like the biology and all that sort of stuff is neither here nor there to be honest with you, for Travelling people, especially for the people on the road, it's not that important. (interview of March 2009)

Doris, who was literate herself and who had sent her children to primary but not to secondary school, agreed:

> I don't like what goes on there. They get to know too much ... I've got an 11 year old granddaughter and her parents won't let her go to secondary school. The teacher says it is a pity because she is very clever and could be a journalist. (interview of April 2009)

Although parents can request that their children are withdrawn from sex education, it seems that cultural traditions at puberty are not always understood by schools. Jamie said:

> [The teachers] haven't taken into account our sexual orientation, sex education which is … done … in the home … Our children are separated at puberty or around twelve or thirteen years of age. When you've got male and female in a classroom being taught sex education, we feel this is promoting [a promiscuous way of life] – and it goes totally against what we believe. We have asked for our children to be excluded from sex education and they will not do it … [Teachers] feel that Gypsies who are in housing are not Gypsies and so they get excluded from school when they refuse to attend sex education. (interview of August 2009)

Anecdotal evidence from the TES suggests that the barriers Gypsy and Traveller children experience have led to opting for Education Otherwise/ Elective Home Education (EHE), especially in the secondary phase. OFSTED (2003, p. 5) commented adversely on the overall adequacy, suitability and quality of home education. Ivatts (2004, 2006) and Badman (2009) suggest that EHE is used as a device to avoid school attendance without legal penalty.

Pre- and post-school education

This chapter has focused on formal school education but pre- and post-school education is also important. The TES makes great efforts to stimulate very young children by distributing packs of books provided by government funding to all preschool children. All three authorities in Sussex run play buses for preschool children which visit permanent, transit and unauthorized sites. The service is very much appreciated by both children and adults. Some Gypsies and Travellers now attend local pre-school playgroups.

In contrast and despite very low literacy levels, my research suggested that Gypsies and Travellers over school age appear to be invisible to the education services in the South (McCaffery, 2012). This absence of educational opportunities targeted at Gypsies and Travellers needs to be addressed at both local and national level. The very few short-term projects here and the experience in Ireland suggest that if there is political will, suitable programmes can be provided for adults.

Cultural conflict

According to Sen, the difficulties Gypsies and Travellers experience in accessing and benefiting from formal education denies them 'the opportunity to take part in crucial decisions regarding public affairs which is a clear limitation of their freedoms in a democratic society' (Sen, 1999, p. 16). In contrast to Sen, Bernstein, in his postscript to *Class, Codes and Control*, states that:

> The school functions ... as an instrument of social control regulating the behaviour
> of [the working class] ... , their emotional sensitivities ... and their modes of social
> relationship to what is considered acceptable to a section of society to which
> pupils often feel they do not belong. (Bernstein, 1971, p. 259)

Many Gypsies and Travellers reject the culture of mainstream society and perceive that the aims of formal education include socialization, citizenship and possible assimilation. Bourdieu (1991) argues that education is about maintaining control by those in power; others suggest its purpose is to suppress the culture of minorities.

Though the Human Rights Act accepts the right to a 'nomadic way of life', experience elsewhere in the world shows that when minorities and nomadic people lose their traditional culture, their societies experience serious difficulties and possible disintegration (Dyer, 2006; Le Roux, 1999). Kratli and Dyer (2006) point out that 'Policy on education for nomads was linked often explicitly with the perceived need to encourage nomads to sedentarise'. Kratli (2000) states that education was usually intended to transform pastoralists into something else and those involved – policy makers, local officials and teachers – generally believed that they had to be 'saved' from their way of life. This resonates with the angry rejection by Martin, an Irish Traveller, of the motives of a voluntary sector worker as 'wanting to save us from ourselves' (interview of 2009).

Many Gypsies and Travellers fear that participation in education beyond the basics of reading and writing risks their children adopting the values and lifestyle of the settled community and losing their identity. Bowers (2004, p. 13) terms this 'Gorgification'. Many see schooling as associated with 'the erosion of more important knowledge gained at home' (Levinson, 2007, p. 24). The practical process of working alongside their fathers enables young men to gain the knowledge and skills required to earn a living, which is very different from the abstract learning required in school (Gee, 1996; Heath, 1983; Lankshear, 1997).

Levinson (2007, p. 32) states the antagonism to education more strongly:

> Formal (school based) literacy was still viewed by many ... as being potentially
> divisive, its very use signifying a degree of assimilation. At the extreme end ... there
> persisted a mistrust of the written word itself, a *gadjo* code, both a symbol and
> potential weapon of an antagonistic external world.

Hancock (2000) and Levinson (2007) suggest that a conscious rejection of literacy may act to reinforce group cohesion, cultural identity and pride and that for some Gypsies and Travellers retaining a non-literate tradition has become institutionalized, 'serving as a means of sustaining non-acculturation'. Similar views are expressed by the Salish, native Indians living on the west coast of Canada, who view White Canadian educators as the enemy (Marker, 2012).

Huffman (2010), however, also working with Native American Indians, suggests that schools could strengthen cultural identity and encourage cultural preservation. He terms this 'transcultural theory'. Transcultural theory resonates with the concept of bi-discoursivity, learning the language of the dominant in school and yet retaining the 'primary' language or dialect of home and community (Gee, 1996).

While many Gypsies and Travellers now want their children to learn to read and write, many remain suspicious of formal education. Jamie, an English Traveller, considered education 'the weapon of the enemy' (interview of August 2009), but one which could be useful. Some Gypsies and Travellers like Sally and Bill (interview of January 2013) see formal education and literacy competence as the route to effective engagement and participation in decision-making processes.

Gypsies' and Travellers' views on education and literacy are complex and contradictory and, like those in other minority cultures, they face difficult choices. Though successive governments have introduced positive education policies, a greater consistency across departments resulting in a real effort to develop both permanent and transit sites and a modification of the current planning laws to allow more private sites would improve Gypsies' and Travellers' access to education.

This and a greater emphasis on the contribution of Gypsies and Travellers to the economy and culture of England coupled with cultural training for teachers and the provision of appropriate educational materials might reduce conflict with the settled community and enable Gypsies and Travellers to retain their culture and achieve their full educational potential.

Notes

1 'If I spoke the broken language you wouldn't understand what I was saying'.
2 Though, as the TV programme 'My Big Fat Gypsy Wedding' showed, this appears to be changing (ITV 4. February 25, 2012).
3 This was highlighted in Kilroy-Silke's 'Week with the Gypsies' (Channel 4, April 2005).

4 All names of informants used here are pseudonyms.
5 Telephone conversation with a Department for Education statistician, 12 May 2011.

Further reading

Bhopal and Myers. (2008), *Insiders, Outsiders and Others*. Hertford: University of Hertfordshire Press.

Derrington, C. and Kendall, S. (2004), *Gypsy Traveller Students in Secondary Schools*. Stoke-on-Trent: Trentham Books.

Nabi, R., Rogers, A. and Street, B. (2009), *Hidden Literacies*. Bury St Edmunds: Uppingham Press.

References

Acton, T. and Mundy, G. (eds). (1997), *Romani Culture and Gypsy Identity*. Hertford: University of Hertfordshire Press.

Advisory Council for the Education of Romany and Other Travellers (ACERT) and Wilson M. (1997), *Directory of Planning Policies for Gypsy Site Provision*. Bristol: Policy Press.

Badman, G. (2009), *Report to the Secretary of State on the Review of Elective Home Education in England*. London: Department for Children, Schools and Families. Retrieved from http://www.education. gov.uk/publications/.../HC-610_Letter.pdf on 4 July 2009.

Bernstein, B. (1971), *Class, Codes and Control*. Vol. 1. London: Routledge.

Bhopal, K. and Myers, M. (2008), *Insiders, Outsiders and Others*. Hertford: University of Hertfordshire Press.

Binchy, A. (2000), 'Shelta/Gammon in Dublin societies', in T. Acton and M. Dalphinis (eds), *Language, Blacks and Gypsies*. London: Whiting and Birch, pp. 128–132.

Bourdieu, P. (1991), *Language and Symbolic Power*. Oxford: Polity Press.

Bowers, J. (2004), *Prejudice and Pride: The Experience of Young Travellers*. Ipswich: The Ormiston Children and Families Trust.

———. (n.d.), *Gypsies and Travellers: Their Lifestyle, History and Culture*. Retrieved from http:// www.travellerstimes.org.uk/downloads/lifestyle_history_and_culture_24052010111520.pdf on 3 January 2013.

Clark, C. (1997), 'New age Travellers: Identity, sedentarism and social security', in T. Acton (ed.), *Gypsy Politics and Traveller Identity*. Hertford: Hertfordshire University Press, pp. 125–141.

Commission for Racial Equality. (2006), *Common Ground: Equality, Good Race Relations and Sites for Gypsies and Irish Travellers*. Retrieved from 83.137.212.42/sitearchive/cre/about/gtinquiry.html on 3 October 2009.

Communities and Local Government. (2012), *Count of Gypsy and Traveller Caravans on 28 January 2012*. Geographical and Statistical Evidence Division for Communities and Local Government.

Coxhead, J. (2007), *The Last Bastion of Racism*. London: Trentham Books.

Department for Children, Schools and Families (DCSF). (July 2008a), *The Gypsy, Roma and Traveller Achievement Programme*. Retrieved from http://www.dcsf.gov.uk/research/data/uploadfiles/DCSF-RR077.pdf on 23 August 2009.

———. (2008b), *The Inclusion of Gypsy Roma and Traveller Children and Young People*. London: Author. Retrieved from http://www.dcsf.gov.uk/research/data/uploadfiles/DCSF-RR077.pdf on 23 August 2009.

Department for Education (DfE). (2010), *Improving the outcomes for Gypsy, Roma and Traveller Pupils: Final Report*. Retrieved from http://www.gov.uk/government/publications/improving-the-outcomes-for-gypsy-roma-and-traveller-pupils-final-report on 11 November 2012.

———. (2011), *GCSE and Equivalent Attainment by Pupil Characteristics in England, 2010/11*. London: DfE.

———. (2012), *Advice on School Education*. Retrieved from http://media.education.gov.uk/assets/files/pdf/a/advice%20on%20school%20attendance%20-%20final%20cleared%20v2-march22.pdf. on 8 April 2013.

Department for Education and Skills (DFES). (2006), *Ethnicity and Education: The Evidence on Ethnic Minority Pupils*. Department for Education and Science Research Topic, Paper RTP01-05. Retrieved from http://www.education.gov.uk/publications/.../DFES-0208-2006.pdf on 12 November 2009.

———. (2006), *Further Education: Raising Skills, Improving Life Chances*. Retrieved from http://www.dfes.gov.uk/furthereducation on 14 November 2009.

Derrington, C. and Kendall, S. (2004), *Gypsy Traveller Students in Secondary School*. Stoke on Trent, UK: Trentham.

Dyer, C., (ed.). (2006), *The Education of Nomadic Peoples: Current Issues, Future Prospects*. Oxford: Berghahn Books.

Gee, J. (1996), *Social Linguistics and Literacies*. 2nd ed. London: Taylor and Francis.

Hammersley, M. and Atkinson, P. (1995), *Ethnography: Principles in Practice*. London: Routledge.

Hancock, I. (2000), 'Standardisation and ethnic defence in non-literate societies', in T. Acton and M. Dalphinis (eds), *Language, Blacks and Gypsies*. London: Whiting and Birch, pp. 3–8.

———. (2002), *We are the Romani People*. Hertford: University of Hertfordshire Press.

———. (2008), 'Romani origins and Romani identity: A reassessment of the arguments', in *Roma Memorial Issue*. Chandigarh, India: Roma Publications, pp. 39–45.

Heath, S. B. (1983), *Ways with Words: Language, Life and Work in Communities and Classrooms*. Cambridge: Cambridge University Press.

Huffman, T. (2010), *Native American Educators: Perceptions on Academic Achievement among Reservation Students: An Examination of Transcultural Theory*. Paper Presented at the Annual Conference of the British Association for International and Comparative Education, Cambridge.

Ivatts, A. (2004), *Breaking Down Prejudice, Supporting Inclusion*. Presentation at Advisory Council for the Education of Romany and Other Travellers Conference, 'Working Together: Raising the Educational Achievement of Gypsy and Traveller Children and Young People', London.

———. (2006), *The Situation Regarding the Current Policy, Provision and Practice in Elective Home Education for Gypsy, Roma and Traveller Children*. Research Report, Department for Children, Schools and Families. Retrieved from http://www.multiverse.ac.uk on 7 February 2007.

Jordan, E. (2001), 'Exclusion of Travellers in state schools', *Educational Research*, 43, (2), 117–132.

Kenrick, D. (1998), 'The Travellers of Ireland', *Patron Web Journal*. Retrieved from http://www.geocities.com/~Patrin/ on 2 January 2008.

Kenrick, D. and Clark, C. (1999), *Moving On: The Gypsies and Travellers of Britain*. Hertford: University of Hertfordshire Press.

Kratli, S. (2000), 'The bias behind nomadic education', *UNESCO Courier*, October. Retrieved from http://findarticles.com/p/articles/mi_m1310/is_2000_Oct/ on 4 June 2010.

Kratli, S. with Dyer, C. (2006), 'Education and development for Nomads: The issues and the evidence', in C. Dyer (ed.), *The Education of Nomadic Peoples: Current Issues, Future Prospects*. Oxford: Berghahn Books, pp. 8–34.

Lankshear, C. (1997), *Changing Literacies*. Oxford: Oxford University Press.

Le Roux, W. (1999), *Torn Apart: San Children as Change Agents in a Process of Acculturation*. Shakwe, Botswana: Kuru Development Trust.

Levinson, M. (2007), 'Literacy in English Gypsy communities: Cultural capital manifested as negative assets', *American Educational Research Journal*, 44, (1), 5–39.

——. (2008), 'Researching groups that are hidden and/or marginalised', *Research Intelligence, Comment, British Educational Research Association*, 2, (4), 16–18.

McCaffery, J. (2012), *Access, Agency, Assimilation: Literacy among Gypsies and Travellers in Southern England*. Stuttgart: Lambert Academic Publishers. University of Sussex. http://sro.sussex.ac.uk/38614

McVeigh, R. (1997), 'Theorising sedentarianism: The roots of anti nomadism', in T. Acton (ed.), *Gypsy Politics and Traveller Identity*. Hatfield: University of Hertfordshire Press, pp. 7–25.

Marker, M. (2012), *Coast Salish Youth and Resistance to Multicultural Education: Transnational Identities and the Re-inscription of Indigenous Cognitive Identities*. Paper Presented at Annual Conference of the British Association for International and Comparative Education, Cambridge.

Marks, K. (2004), *Traveller Education: Changing Times, Changing Technologies*. Stoke on Trent: Trentham Books.

Matras, Y., Bakker, P., Hibschmannova, M., Kalinin, V., Kenrick, D., Kyuchukov, H., and Soravia, G. (eds). (2000), *What is the Romani language?* Hertford: University of Hertfordshire Press.

Moore, M. and Brindley, M. (2012), *Gypsies and Travellers Shadow Report*. Retrieved from http://www.irishtraveller.org.uk/wp-content/uploads/2010/12/ITMB-Submission-to-CLG-Select-Committee-inquiry-into-Localism.pdf on 3 January 2013.

Ni Shuinear, S. (1994), 'Irish Travellers, ethnicity and the origins question', in M. McCann, S. O' Siochain, and J. Ruane (eds), *Irish Travellers, Culture and Ethnicity*. Belfast: Institute of Irish Studies, Queen's University, pp. 54–77.

Office for Public Management (OPM). (2010), *Health and Social Care Needs of Gypsies and Travellers in West Sussex: Report to NHS West Sussex County Council*. London: OPM. Retrieved from http://rcn.org/development/practice/socialinclusion/gypsy_and_traveller_communities on 5 December 2012.

Office for Standards in Education (OFSTED). (2003), *Provision and Support for Traveller Pupils*. London: Her Majesty's Stationery Office.

Okely, J. (1983), *The Traveller Gypsies*. Cambridge: Cambridge University Press.

Sawer, P. and Ljunggren, H. (2011, October 2), 'The £22 million cost of evicting the Dale Farm travellers', *Daily Telegraph*. Retrieved from http://www.telegraph.co.uk/news/uknews/law-and-order/8800962/The-22-million-cost-of-evicting-the-Dale-Farm-travellers.html on 3 January 2013.

Sen, A. (1999), *Democracy as Freedom*. Oxford: Oxford University Press.

South East England Regional Assembly. (2009), *Partial Review of the Regional Spatial Strategy for the South East: Provision for Gypsies, Travellers and Showpeople*. Guildford: South East England Partnership Board.

Street, B. V. (1995), *Social Literacies: Critical Approaches to Literacy in Development, Ethnography and Education*. London: Longman.

Townsend, M. (16 November, 2003), *A Burning Issue in the Village*. London: The Observer Newspaper.

United Nations (UN). (2007), *Towards a Stable, Safe and Just Society for All*. New York: United Nations.

Waterson, M. (1997), 'I want more green leaves for my children', in T. Acton and G. Mundy (eds), *Romani Culture and Gypsy Identity*. Hertford: Hertfordshire University Press, pp. 129–151.

Wilkins, A., Derrington, C., and Foster, B. (2009), *Improving the Outcomes for Gypsy, Roma and Traveller Pupils-Literature Review, Research Report No. DCSF-RR077*. London: Department for Children, Schools and Families. Retrieved from http://www.nfer.ac.uk/publications/TGR01/ on 3 March 2011.

Wilkins, A., Derrington, C., White, R., Martin, K., Foster, B., Kinder, K., and Ruff, S. (2010), *Gypsy, Roman and Traveller Pupils: Final Report. DFE-RR043*. London: Department for Education. Retrieved from https://www.education.gov.uk/publications/standard/publicationDetail/Page1/ on 8 April 2013.

Worrall, D. (1979), *Gypsy Education: A Study of Provision in England and Wales*. Walsall: Walsall Council for Community Relations.

A Case Study of Educational Experiences of Gypsies and Travellers[1] in the East Riding of Yorkshire, UK

Judith Smith and Helen Worrell

This chapter will offer a professional perspective of and insight into the educational experiences of Gypsies and Travellers in the East Riding of Yorkshire from the 1970s to the present day. It will include reference to the legislative framework in relation to education and accommodation, including impact. The complexities of identity in the wider social context will also be noted as significant factors in the success and failure of Gypsies' and Travellers' educational experiences. The history of Traveller education will be referenced in regard to input and association, exampling several case studies, of varying degrees of success. The chapter concludes with an overview of the impact of and challenges faced by the East Riding Gypsy and Traveller communities and those working with them. It is hoped this will demonstrate that a strong, multi-agency and collaborative approach supports and promotes interaction at all levels. Although respect and appreciation is given to the wealth of research and theory surrounding education, practical efforts for engagement, attainment, identity and integration, and the value and importance of these in shaping policy and practice, must be commended. As professionals working with the Gypsy and Traveller community at an operational level, we hope the case studies speak for themselves.

The Gypsy and Traveller communities in the East Riding

A brief history of the Gypsy and Traveller families and communities in the East Riding of Yorkshire sees a historical pattern of migration along the banks of the Humber estuary (Ivatts, 1971). As in many areas of the country, this mainly came about because of socio-economic necessity. Not only would Gypsies and Travellers meet up to share celebrations as well as to support one another at times of need but many families would follow the agricultural calendar of employment opportunities. Within the Humber region this mainly involved strawberry and potato picking as well as the more localized general farm work passed on through generations of Gypsies and Travellers and farmers (Ivatts, 1971). The annual events of Hull Fair and Seamer Fair also contribute to movement into the region, with the East Riding being a regular stop-off point for Appleby Fair. They attract Gypsies and Travellers from West Yorkshire, North Yorkshire, Cambridgeshire and sporadic groups of Irish families also passing through during the course of the year (Figure 3.1).

Regular routes in the area took in Bridlington on the coast, various spots on the Hull and Cottingham boundary, venturing further afield to York and Doncaster for family connections. Many unofficial stopping places were well established by the 1960s, some more tolerated by local settled communities than others. At this point in time, 40 per cent of the Gypsy and Traveller population in the region was in horse-drawn wagons.

The East Riding of Yorkshire Councils' Gypsy and Traveller Accommodation Needs Assessment of 2008 notes the long-standing role played by Gypsies and Travellers in society and how prejudice, discrimination and legislative changes have increasingly marginalized this distinctive ethnic group.

Figure 3.1 Appleby Horse Fair 2012.
Photograph courtesy of Nick Holroyd–Doveton.

The East Riding Gypsy and Traveller population has a mix of very traditional and non-traditional cultural beliefs and values, and this can be seen across the generations. Family life is clearly paramount and life cycle events are valued highly. Gypsy and Traveller funerals are well-known and respected events within the East Riding both for Gypsies and Travellers and for others. Traditional values could be seen to be barriers towards secondary and post-sixteen education opportunities, such as cultural expectations around gender roles. Evidence of this can be seen in one family where leniency around choice of college, transport, social activities and employment in general was given to a son, whereas the daughter was only allowed to gain her qualifications in school and then had restrictions placed on the above-mentioned choices. For example, she was not allowed to use public transport alone, to access wider opportunities. However, the daughter within these restrictions still found employment in the school nursery provision, which also supported her professional development. Traveller girls often have to provide childcare for younger siblings, as well as engage in wider family responsibilities. Males are expected to engage in activities such as animal husbandry, horses and dogs being prevalent, with trading, breeding and racing as prime activities. Annually, a small number of male family members of different generations make the trip with traditional bow top wagons and horses from the East Riding to Appleby. This journey takes a long-established route over three weeks. In the past, the whole family made the journey by wagon, now the women and other children will generally stay at home but drive to meet up at certain points to replenish supplies and still have time together. It is hoped these examples can be seen to support the importance of informal learning passed on by family members over generations. One observable cultural shift with respect to relationships is that there are more couples living together and more single parents. This is in line with the national picture.

Much of the East Riding falls into the 50 per cent least deprived Lower Layer Super Output Areas (LSOAs) in England (East Riding of Yorkshire Council, 2012a),[2] but there are nine LSOAs in the authority that are among the 10 per cent most deprived nationally for overall multiple deprivation. These areas are in Bridlington, Goole and South East Holderness. The East Riding total population is said to be growing generally, with the number of retirees increasing the most and predicted to be 40.4 per cent by 2030. The 15–19 population has declined by 3.6 per cent between 2010 and 2013. There is outward migration of young adults for education and employment and 45 per cent of residents travel outside the area for work. There is lower-than-average Black Minority ethnic population, but this is forecast to continue rising from 7 per cent in 2009. The migrant worker populations have seen a significant increase over the last 3–4 years (East Riding of Yorkshire Council, 2012b) and recognized within this are Eastern European Roma. Migrants seem to be particularly settling in Goole, Bridlington, Beverley and Driffield; many use English as an additional language. The Minority Ethnic Traveller Attainment Service (METAS) has identified 56 languages in use throughout the East Riding thorough their data collection, based on Pupil Level Annual School Census information.

Developments of the later twentieth century

The passing of the Caravan Sites Act (Her Majesty's Government, 1968) brought about a significant shift in the living patterns of Gypsy and Traveller people that would reverberate throughout every aspect of their lives:

An Act to restrict the eviction from caravan sites of occupiers of caravans and make other provision for the benefit of such occupiers; to secure the establishment of such sites by local authorities for the use of gypsies and other persons of nomadic habit … (Her Majesty's Government, 1968)

This put the responsibility on each local authority to provide adequate spaces and facilities for the travelling population. Theoretically, it was believed it would facilitate better integration into a more settled way of life as well as wider opportunities for consistent employment, as the agricultural industry was becoming more mechanized and thus needed fewer workers. Likewise changes to licensing legislation (Her Majesty's Government, n.d.) affected door-to-door selling and collecting and therefore again limited economic opportunity. This is evident in the East Riding, where unemployment is high, although some Gypsies and Travellers are self-employed and successfully running small businesses in agricultural machinery and engineering, landscaping, horticultural services, scrap metal recycling and dog breeding. There is also some employment within service industries such as social and child care.

A more static lifestyle could also potentially facilitate better access to consistent state education. This echoes and reinforces the 1944 Education Act, which requires Local Education Authorities to ensure that there are 'sufficient schools' for primary and secondary education (Her Majesty's Government, 1944, Clause 8).

While the long-drawn-out process of establishing suitable land, gaining planning permission and overcoming various obstacles to actually building the three permanent sites within the East Riding took place throughout the 1970s and 1980s, there were various attempts to initiate some volunteer-led educational experiences for local Gypsy and Traveller children. A good example of education as a humanitarian response on a localized scale was a Gypsy summer school project in 1971, held in three places within the East Riding, as part of a national scheme, organized by the National Gypsy Council (Ivatts, 1971). The project was deemed a success: not only did it introduce the children to a more informal way of education, on site and using hands-on exploratory methods, but it also afforded the opportunity of the tentative establishment of relationships between staff and adults from the Gypsy and Traveller community. This in turn generated reciprocal cultural awareness. As a consequence, the East Riding was among the first authorities to develop a dedicated Traveller Education Service.

By the mid-1990s three permanent sites had been established: Woodhill Way and Eppleworth quarry at Cottingham and Woldgate at Bridlington (Yorkshire Post, 1993). The former two are on the outskirts of one of Britain's largest villages, potentially seen as affluent and predominantly middle class, with the majority of its inhabitants potentially coming from the skilled and professional sectors of the employment market. All three could be seen as isolated from local amenities from the outset. Given the placing of the sites, it is little wonder that integration with the settled communities has not been seen as a smooth transition, with reciprocal fears and misapprehension on both sides.

The current situation

Table 3.1 below gives the estimated figures for Gypsies and Travellers in the area. It should be noted that the housed population is scattered through both small rural villages and larger conurbations. Consequently, issues of isolation

Table 3.1 Gypsy and Traveller population based in East Riding

Type of accommodation	Families/households (based on 1 pitch/ house = 1 household)	Individuals	Derivation
Socially rented sites	55	184	Based on number of pitches currently occupied inclusive of actual number of individuals as recorded by the local authority.
Bricks and mortar	66[17]	264	Number of families estimated to live in the area multiplied by average household size from the survey (4)
Unauthorised developments	2[18]	10	Number of families estimated to live in the area multiplied by average household size from the survey (4)
Private authorised	6	18	There are two sites in the area with a combined pitch capacity of 6 pitches but it is unknown how many are accommodated on these, if any. Assume household size equals that of socially rented sites (3)
Unauthorised encampments which accommodate ER residents (not transient community)	2	8	Based on information provided by Enforcement officers. The number of individuals concerned is an estimate.
Travelling Showpeople	1	4	Estimate
Total	132	488	

Source: East Riding of Yorkshire Council, 2012b.

and identity are significant. Many families have been split across the various types of accommodation provision. Geographically, this means for some families they are living in different authorities. Large periods of time are spent together predominantly on the sites.

The changes in law and therefore the lifestyle for Gypsies and Travellers have included changes in their ways of education. Throughout the East Riding there are now three community groups on permanent sites, totalling 65 pitches (East Riding of Yorkshire Council, 2012b), with 30-year long connections to local schools. These have been supported from within the schools and with extra local authority provision and increasingly through extension into and by the local settled communities. Despite the permanent sites, it is believed there is still not enough allocation for all the East Riding Gypsies or Travellers, especially when taking into account the still transient nature of many, through either family, work and social necessity or lack of permanent provision. This local situation reflects the national picture. Notably there are difficulties in identifying the correct population figure because of Gypsies' and Travellers' reasoned reluctance to state their background and therefore be identified. Bhopal and Myers cite Taylor as contending that, within the contemporary politics of multiculturalism, it has become expected to demand recognition. He argues that the recognition of culture is vital to recognition of identity:

> The thesis is that our identity is partly shaped by recognition or its absence, often by the misrecognition of others, and so a person or group of people can suffer real damage, real distortion if the people or society around them mirror back to them a confining or demeaning or contemptible picture of themselves. Non recognition or misrecognition can inflict harm; can be a form of oppression, imprisoning someone in a false, distorted, and reduced mode of being. (Bhopal and Myers, 2008)

This has wider implications in respect of health, education, employment and accommodation. The last decade particularly has seen a shift towards Gypsies' and Travellers' accepting changes in their accommodation within the region, becoming housed in order to be able to access facilities such as health and education. This has had varying amounts of success with many older Gypsies and Travellers who grew up on the road and who are struggling to adapt to a completely opposing and restrictive way of life, some still finding sympathetic landowners and small village communities willing to accept their presence in the area and thus helping to support a nomadic lifestyle. The additional impact of the Criminal Justice and Public Order Act of 1994 (Her Majesty's Government, 1994), with a shift of emphasis from provision to trespass and a link with anti-social behaviour, needs to be mentioned here. Notably the East Riding Local Authority is sensitive to the impact that this has on the Gypsy and Traveller community, and are cognizant of this with respect to the eviction process.

While there is still a strong culture of informal learning inherent within Gypsy and Traveller families, their valuing the importance of wider educational opportunities is evident. In relation to education and training, METAS' current figures of participation are 45 in secondary education, 80 in primary education, 16 in Elective Home Education, five in Local Authority Alternative Provisions and 60 in post-16 education. These Traveller pupils are split across the 13 secondary and 122 primary schools within the East Riding of Yorkshire. A further breakdown shows that in the secondary sector 11 schools hold Gypsy and/or Traveller pupils on the roll, four being within the vicinity of the authorized sites, and 28 primary schools have Traveller pupils on the roll, with six also being near authorized sites.

Whether it is formally in state provision or more informally as in distance learning, educational resources can be provided by base schools for travelling times, or, with the advent of improving digital information technology applications, direct online links with base schools can be maintained.

As certain data is already collated through the school census, the ability to utilize the variety of professional relationships with children and families, which may also already be established to greater and lesser degree in education, is seen to be a prime area to research with regard to the Gypsy and Traveller communities:

> This reflects a number of factors, not least the widely held assumption that the single best means to improving the life chances of individuals from deprived backgrounds is through the education system. Improved educational opportunities at a young age have the greatest impact on ensuring future attainment. (Bhopal and Myers, 2008)

It follows therefore that one arena where there is potential to open up more opportunity for a deeper understanding between the variant cultures is local education provision. As it is incumbent on local authorities to provide equal education prospects for all children within their borders, as well as the responsibility of parents and carers to advance each child's life chances through ensuring uptake of appropriate provision, education would appear to be the ideal setting for an opening of communication and relations.

Long-term input and impact

Acknowledgement should be made of the wider picture with regard to identity, misconception and expectations and their impact as a long-term historical thread through educational experience. This is evident in perceptions of levels of Gypsy and Traveller parents' and children's engagement, for example, low attendance at parents' evenings. It is important to achieve an understanding of the intersection of different communities inside and outside the school and the wider impacts of society beyond the school gates. All impact on the level of engagement and potential for positive dialogue.

We cannot conceptualize the position of Gypsy and Traveller culture in the same way as well-known examples of oppression such as slavery, the Afro-Caribbean experience or the Jewish Holocaust. These do not resemble the Gypsy and Traveller historical experience (Derrington, 2007). But the document 'Understanding and appreciating Muslim diversity towards better engagement', while coming from a religious base, is a good model for all ethnic diversity, emphasizing its promotion to develop broader understanding (Institute of Community Cohesion, 2008).

The conceptual dissonance between Gypsies and Travellers and others who do not share the same value base feeds disengaged dialogue starting from hostile vantage points:

> The fixidity of prejudice is different to any other immigrant experience. Stereotypes of Gypsy and Travellers are more hostile whereas many understandings of 'otherness' are reconciled within a shared set of understanding about prejudices. It is not enough to simply understand different cultures to promote a more equitable world, but more beneficial to have willingness to enter into dialogue between these understandings. Gypsy and Travellers are not understood as ordinary neighbours or part of wide tapestry of diverse communities: they remain subject to enormous hostility and the intention is harmful not harmonious. Absolute misrecognition of Gypsy and Traveller culture needs to be understood from both Gypsy and Traveller and non Gypsy, Traveller perspectives'. (Bhopal and Myers, 2008, p. 72)

In 1990, the four local authority areas, Hull, East Yorkshire, North Lincolnshire and North East Lincolnshire, that made up the county of Humberside agreed to finance jointly a local Traveller Education Service (TES). This team consisted of several teaching assistants, an access and welfare officer, administrative staff, a service manager and several teachers, all deployed throughout varying schools across the whole of the Humberside area to facilitate access to, and integration in, formal education for all children from Gypsy and Travelling families.

The work of Traveller Education Services has frequently been commended, and particularly so by Her Majesty's Inspectors of schools, for the quality and sustainability of the professional activities in relation to the support for Gypsy, Roma and Traveller students and their schools, and the development of trusting relationships with the families. These positive assessments have been well founded on evidence (Danaher et al., 2007).

In 2006, following the disbanding of Humberside as a unitary authority, the three remaining councils – Hull, North Lincolnshire and East Yorkshire – opted to make individual provision and split the existing TES team. The East Riding Council expanded the remit to become the Minority Ethnic and Traveller Attainment Service (METAS), maintaining a service manager, two teachers, an access and welfare officer, a family learning officer and three outreach support officers to continue and move forward the positive relations and work with local Gypsy and Traveller and settled communities as well as schools and other professional services forged during the previous sixteen years.

For many Gypsies and Travellers education is valued, but this may not be a formal school-based version. There is often a perception of loss of identity and fear of exposure to other experiences; this is possibly fuelled by questioning the general relevance of curriculum material and by lack of consultation and engagement with the families and the wider community.

Trans-generational experience may restrict and lead to self-exclusion and maladaptive behaviours, but perceptions and assumptions may not be true to lived experience across the generations. METAS interviews which took place in 2009 with different families across the East Riding support this; older generations stated that they had experienced bullying, racism and exclusion as regular occurrences and serious barriers. Younger generations stated that such things were still happening, but they felt school staff and pupils were in general supportive and understanding, which made a substantial difference from their parents' experiences. However, they still considered these types of incidents were significant. Notably, these experiences were different generations' experiences of the same educational settings.

Case study examples

Bridlington – an informal education

A 52-year-old woman who has lived in the East Riding all her life spent her childhood living on the roadside around the region, working on farms potato picking, with no formal education. On becoming a mother she moved onto the Bridlington site, and then into housing. The children attended school from primary through to secondary; there have been times when this has been problematic for all the family. One son now works in full-time employment; the other is still of statutory school age and on an alternative learning package. She has regularly expressed her sense of loss of lifestyle, but values the opportunity the children have had through continuous education. She has made attempts to engage in adult education, but this has been regularly put on hold because of the children's needs. She was encouraged to join in the "skills for life" sessions and has succeeded in 100 per cent attendance. Her younger son also attends some sessions as part of his educational plan. Over the past year she has become a reader and is gaining confidence in her writing skills.

This example shows the importance of awareness of acceptance of different lived experiences. Her CV shows that her main working life was as a child, and her main educational life has been as an adult, a reverse of the expected sequence. She has recently led a session independently, providing resources for discussion around the history of wagons and trailers in the East Riding. Family members were recognized in the materials and an impromptu opportunity for sharing personal, local history of lived experience was created and enjoyed.

Bridlington – skills for life: A more formal education

The second example is an East Riding partnership project, organized in association with Adult Education, METAS, Hidden Voices, MIND and the Youth and Careers Services. The project was initiated to address the under-representation of Gypsies and Travellers in adult learning and to promote the development and sustainability of new businesses, bringing together members of the Gypsy and Traveller community and local arts and crafts people. The project had a targeted engagement approach. Adult education has a clear diversity strategy, particularly with regard to addressing economic disadvantage and digital exclusion. The project has engaged 53 Gypsy and Traveller learners across the East Riding with a mixed skills base from milestone pre-entry skills for life, literacy and numeracy to National Vocational Qualification (NVQ) Level Two. In a representative sample of the Bridlington group, one learner began learning, mentoring and training until family circumstances forced him to leave the area; three are currently improving English and Mathematics, three families are involved in family learning and one learner wishes to undertake Level Two NVQ in care. Activities have included family history research, lace making, jewellery, painting and creative writing, numeracy and literacy and information and communication technology, with the development of a blog and website for the group. Collaborative opportunities involved participating with Hull Gypsies and Travellers with a 'Cooking pot' event of the kind described by Cunningham:

> COOKING POT
> Coming together of all walks of life
> One purpose to open people's eyes to gypsy times by
> Opening the doors to this wonderful event
> Kushti food is thoroughly enjoyed by lady and gent
> Inspiration is being received in the main hall
> Nothing ventured nothing gained I hear somebody call
> Gorgio I am referred as by a friendly gypsy
> Photographs she points out show me plenty of history
> Oh how I reflect on what life could be like being a traveller
> Travelling home I visualise thoughts and ponder (Cunningham, 2012)

Another part of the programme was to join Gypsies, Roma and Travellers from across the East Riding together on Celebration Day, using dance as a focus (Figures 3.2 and 3.3).

The project has had flexibility in delivery and style; various locations have been used, from Adult Education facilities to community venues. Outreach work has been integral to sustainability, giving partners the opportunity to be less formal and more responsive to individual needs. An opportunity for awareness-raising for partners and learners has been positive and informal in nature with the chance to have lived experience exposure, and a general broadening of understanding has emerged. There has been significant impact on confidence building of all participants, staff and community members. The sessions are developed collaboratively, so everyone is given an opportunity to contribute ideas and skills. Tutors who were known to community members were brought into the project on request.

Figure 3.2 Activity during Gypsy Roma Traveller History Month, 2012
Photograph courtesy of Lindsey Jones.

Figure 3.3 Roma flag made from traditional paper flowers
Photograph courtesy of Helen Worrell.

Further outcomes were the promotion of offering a forum for discussion and mediation to reduce tensions, and promote health and well-being with the involvement of MIND (a mental health charity). Specific mental health issues could be discussed and MIND group participants have become learners too. The forum could be offered in support for families if required. Discussion also took place with the Gypsy Liaison team involved in the management and transition to the new site; in effect the sessions also impacted on community cohesion.

During the initial stages of the project, the move of families onto the new site in Bridlington affected the level of regular attendance, so flexible attendance occurred and was accepted as necessary. It also highlighted the different perspectives with regard to continuous attendance and engagement. The wider diverse interpretation of 'skills for life' and the value of education outside formal settings now has a much broader meaning for all those involved. The Adult Education staff involved in the project stated they appreciated that the small successes are the building blocks and not the main achievements. They foster the informal relationships from which to build and sustain learning capacity.

Significantly, the flexible approach, providing blended learning opportunities, engaging families as well as individual participants, and delivering a variety of sessions in different locations, all supported sustainability and positive outcomes and encouraged the opportunity for personal growth for all. The value of shared, lived experience was very real during the course of this project. The future of the project is funding dependent, but we are currently able to continue with creative partnership working. The Gypsies and Travellers involved are enthusiastic to develop a community-based enterprise scheme, possibly involving producing goods for local farmers' markets, becoming more involved in awareness opportunities and tendering for the maintenance contract on the site. All have continued to attend whenever possible and have carried on with engaging in further learning on an informal basis.

Additional outcomes are being realized through the opportunity to take practical training to the sites. By using a whole family approach, barriers relating to trust and to transport to the training venues, which are genuine concerns for parents whose children are accessing post-16 provision across the East Riding, are being alleviated.

Cottingham – 'mums and tots', an informal education

Subsequent to the advent of a new service provided by the local authority in 2006, not only did the METAS remit extend to other ethnic minorities but also more community work was officially undertaken, particularly through the role of the family learning officer. On the back of this, an opportunity to advance further support and awareness across boundaries became apparent in the shape of a pre-school group. As a very family-orientated society, culturally Travellers share responsibility for child rearing, from older siblings to members of the extended family and neighbours who live in close proximity. Therefore, there is always a babysitter handy, someone to watch a child while the mother attends to other chores for the family, from cooking, cleaning and shopping to visits to other more distant family members where it may not be practical to take such a large family group, Traveller families of ten or more children not being uncommon historically. Gypsy and Traveller children in the Cottingham area had been attending the same local primary and secondary schools regularly, with increasing consistency, for over two decades.

With the dedicated support from Traveller Education for the children, families and schools, it had become an accepted 'given' by this time, to more and more Travellers, that state education was not only a legal requirement, but could also be seen as a useful and enhancing right to which their children, as much as any other, are entitled. The generation of 'young mums' that were in the area at the time had all accessed the full education system, starting during their own childhood by participation in a weekly mums and tots group run by a TES teacher and Teaching Assistant, working with adult education and the local youth service. The TES provision extended to regular outreach sessions on site and roadside with the use of a play bus. The same cohort went on to complete primary and secondary education, passing several subjects in the General Certificate of Secondary Education (GCSE) and some attending college courses. As the first generation in this area to complete this system, they had the opportunity to witness for themselves the extent of further opportunity that formal education could bring them, and consequently they wanted this for their own children.

METAS worked with this group again as Young Parents and together sourced funding and a venue to provide a Mother and Toddler Group. The weekly group met in the local church hall, providing an open-door informal play session and venue close to other local amenities, notably the local primary school. 'Dads' also became involved in the group and helped with the moving and setting up of equipment. At this point in time the *Every Child Matters* agenda (Department of Education and Skills (DfES), 2004) was rolled out and the government directive for Children's Centres came into force. We invited the staff of the Children's Centre to the group as the Centre was being built and began partnership working on the sites. The local library provided Bookstart packs and delivered story sessions; a local specialist music play team also visited. Family days to visit local places of the parents' choice were provided. The group moved to the Children's Centre and parents had the opportunity to access the wider scope of sessions and services offered by the Centre.

This collaborative approach has given a wealth of opportunity. Extended family members and relatives from outside the East Riding also access the Children's Centre sessions and services, notably the Health Visitor. Three of the women are now volunteer workers at the Children's Centre; one is considering a career in Social Care and another has learnt sign language skills. All have completed safeguarding training and have access to staff training opportunities. This has also led to development of an additional women's drop-in session and we have had a request from the male family members to run a drop-in for them with a basic skills element. Fortnightly drop-in sessions are part of the outreach programme and partnerships with METAS. Children Centre staff, Health Visitors and the Police Community liaison officers are available on the sites. The coffee morning/parent drop-in at the primary school has also been attended by several Gypsy and Traveller parents.

All the above groups and sessions were open to all users at the Children's Centre, school and Church Hall and were not segregated. This has been problematic and great care and sensitivity is used to ensure that these groups are not exclusive. The Children's Centre is a critical venue in respect of access and exposure for Gypsy and Traveller and non-Gypsy and -Traveller users. Through the Gypsy and Traveller women volunteers, we have taken invaluable steps to shift misperceptions on all sides; this is evidence of attention to the importance of the notion 'to actively promote a sense of belonging' (Institute of Community Cohesion, 2008). The volunteers, METAS and Centre staff took time to share experiences and perceptions. One volunteer expressed her concern at the thought that everyone would see her Gypsy and Traveller identity first and be hostile to her helping in play sessions.

Cottingham – TES/METAS support with local schools as formal education

Traditionally, Traveller Education Services had mainly an in-school focus, with some home–school liaison undertaken as and when necessary, more so through the welfare officer role but also by teaching and non-teaching staff within the team. This proved invaluable for enabling the foundations for long-term, positive relationships to be built between the Travellers and the team, leading to productive connections for both parties, and also with schools and eventually other interested and relevant organizations. The children were supported well in schools but also witnessed the aforementioned bonding as becoming an acceptable asset to Travellers' lives.

Previously and particularly during the 1980s, individual schools employed their own support staff to facilitate better chances for Traveller children to integrate into and achieve within the system. In 1990, when Humberside formed the local Traveller Education Service, individual staff in schools, working with Traveller children, were assigned to the TES team and became a unit independent of the schools and answerable to the Local Authority directly. TES staff worked with school staff to seek ways to help the children feel welcomed into and part of what was affectively a completely different way of being to that previously enjoyed. Children who had previously had the freedom to run and play, interact or not, at will, now had the restrictions of set times and rules that had little relevance to their home lives and expected futures. TES and school staff had to work in very small steps to accommodate the emotional, psychological, social and physical needs of young children who were expected to suddenly transform and perform in circumstances unlike any previously experienced.

Secure and safe environments were provided in the primary school for the Traveller children to escape from the often overwhelming expectations daily school life thrust on them. This was provided in the form of a nurturing and less formal setting in the TES teacher's classroom. While Traveller children were a part of the whole school and each a member of a particular class group, they were also afforded some leeway in the provision of small group work and individual educational and pastoral sessions in the TES room. When in class the children were as often as possible and/or necessary supported, again in groups or individually by a TES assistant, in much in the same way as school Teaching Assistants would support children with special educational needs.

While prejudice and racial bullying is not unknown in primary schools, the smaller setting enables a stronger community ethos and incidents are believed to increase on transition to the secondary level, this often leading to an increase in levels of self-exclusion and maladaptive behaviour (Derrington, 2007). One Traveller boy had consistently good attendance, behaviour, academic participation and peer group integration at the primary level. On transfer to a secondary school, he suffered and was witness to regular racial abuse, often perceived in school as low level, such as name-calling, peers' refusal to sit near, participate with, talk to or acknowledge him. This culminated in a full-on physical assault involving medical and police intervention. Despite a positive early attitude to education, these experiences over time led to him becoming more and more disengaged and 'treading water' to get through the school system, as opposed to engaging and participating fully to have the opportunity to reach his potential.

Gypsies and Travellers have the highest level of fixed-term and permanent exclusions and lowest attendance profile of any ethnic minority or group of free-school-meal pupils. The complexities of legislation, curriculum content and disparity of provision all contribute to the wider impact of engagement. Changes in government, legislation, policies and funding all must be considered as significant in the shifting educational landscape.

Both multicultural and assimilation models (Cherti and McNeil, 2012) have become evident in the curriculum particularly with respect to citizenship education. While these may be seen to be positive and proactive ways forward, they are not without problems. Introducing aspects of cultural diversity without sensitivity can cause discomfiture and possible identification or labelling of individuals who may just wish to blend in. Additional criticism suggests that these models potentially contribute to fragmented societies and parallel living. Multiculturalism's preference for defining communities as fixed rather than fluid misses the complexities of patterns of identity. On the other hand, the assimilative approach focuses on a shared sense of citizenship and national identity. Focusing on specific events as opposed to embedding core material throughout the curriculum can complicate the experiences of pupils in school by highlighting differences. Gypsy Roma Traveller History Month (GRTHM) has also shown how difficult it can be in practice to facilitate the inclusion of culturally specific events without being exclusive.

During the 2012 GRTHM celebrations in a local secondary school, two METAS workers only had the capacity to involve a small number of pupils, therefore limiting the working group to Gypsy and Traveller pupils, in the weeks leading up to the main event when all planning and preparation work was done. On several occasions, pupils and members of the school staff asked why only Gypsy and Travellers were allowed out of lessons. The perception was that the Gypsy and Traveller pupils were just getting a special treat as opposed to engaging in extra work. The main event, however, was embedded in a wider local community annual celebration day and therefore was completely open as a public event. Peers and school staff members were invited to participate in the activities as well as enjoy the performance by the 'Gypsy

Figure 3.4 Model horse built for the GRTHM celebration of 2011

Girl Crew' – five local Traveller girls who entertained the community with their interpretation of modern dance.

In contrast, GRTHM in 2011 involved a whole school approach; this was possible because it was in a primary school setting, giving easier opportunity for interaction with a wider cohort of pupils. Over a week, two METAS workers led the design and building of a life-size wire and papier-mâché horse, to reflect the importance of the horse in Gypsy and Traveller culture. This was conducted in an outside play area which enabled all pupils, staff, parents and other visitors to participate and engage in discussion around the activity (Figure 3.4).

Conclusion

Cherti and McNeil cite Rogers and Brubaker as asserting, 'Groups are internally diverse and the process of integration into the mainstream is far more subtle, we should not assume people have simple identities which are formed by the groups outsiders associate them with' (Cherti and McNeil, 2012).

The challenges faced by Gypsies and Travellers are complex. Trying to tease out individual or specific causes is in itself problematic because of the interconnected nature of health, accommodation, marginalization, isolation, socio-cultural disparity, misconceptions and expectations, all of which impact on educational experiences. The history of Traveller education support nationally illustrates that, even where educational providers and other services have long-term, established relationships with Gypsy and Traveller families, there are still common threads perpetuating barriers to attainment and achievement. This is mirrored on a local level in the examples put forward. Success is evident in the journey for the young mothers and toddlers, and perhaps less so in the historic persistence of disengagement at secondary school level. Time, resources and consistently sustained relationships are crucial to increasing the possibility of positive outcomes for all. The influence of legislative changes must also be recognized as a force affecting outcomes. But, above all, the voices of Gypsy and Travellers must be heard:

> It is really important that Travellers are heard, their voices are heard, their experiences as much for their own future generations as for our understanding of these different cultures because they are different. (Danaher et al., 2007)

Acknowledgements

We wish to thank the Gypsy and Traveller community of the East Riding of Yorkshire, East Riding of Yorkshire Council, and all partnership services and organizations. We also thank Arthur Ivatts, OBE, for his vision and inspiration.

Notes

1 For the purposes of this chapter, the term 'Gypsy and Traveller' will be used to refer to all groups of nomadic tradition across the East Riding, including Show People, Irish Travellers and New Age Travellers.
2 Lower Layer Super Output Areas (LSOAs) are local geographical units used in England to record certain social and economic statistics.

Further reading

Bhopal, K. (2004), 'Gypsy Travellers and education: Changing needs and changing perceptions', *British Journal of Educational Studies*, 52, (1), 47–64.

Derrington, C. and Kendall, S. (2004), *Gypsy Traveller Students in Secondary Schools*. Staffordshire: Trentham Books.

References

Bhopal, K. and Myers, M. (2008), *Insiders, Outsiders and Others. Gypsies and Identity*. Hatfield: University of Hertfordshire.

Danaher, P. A. Coombes, P., and Kiddle, C. (2007), *Teaching Traveller Children. Maximising Learning Outcomes*. Stoke on Trent: Trentham books.

Department of Education and Skills (DfES). (2004), *Every Child Matters*. Nottingham: DfES. Retrieved form   http://www.education.gov.uk/publications/standard/publicationDetail/Page1/DfES/1081/2004.

Derrington, C. (2007), *Fight, Flight and Playing White: An Examination of Coping Strategies Adopted by Gypsy and Traveller Adolescents in English Secondary Schools*.

East Riding of Yorkshire Council. (2012a), *14–19 Education and Skills Plan 2013–2014*.

———. (2012b), *Gypsy and Traveller Need Assessment*. Manchester: Salford University.

Her Majesty's Government. (1871), *Pedlar's Certificate and Street Trader's Licence*. London: Her Majesty's Stationery Office. Retrieved from http://www.legislation.gov.uk/ukpga/Vict/34-35/96.

———. (1944), *Education Act 1944*. London: Her Majesty's Stationery Office.

———. (1968), *Caravan Sites Act 1968*. London: Her Majesty's Stationery Office. Retrieved from http://www.legislation.gov.uk/ukpga/1968/52/contents.

———. (1994), *Criminal Justice and Public Order Act 1994*. London: Her Majesty's Stationery Office. Retrieved from http://www.legislation.gov.uk/ukpga/1994/33/contents.

Institute of Community Cohesion. (2008), *Community Revitalization in the United States and the United Kingdom*. Coventry: Centre for Social Relations, Coventry University. Retrieved form http://resources.cohesioninstitute.org.uk/Publications/Documents/Document/DownloadDocumentsFile.aspx?recordId=14&file=PDFversion.

Ivatts, A. (1971), *Report on the Hull and East Riding Gypsy Summer School Project*. Great Britain. National Gypsy Education Council.

Padfield, P. (2006), *Learning at a Distance Supported by ICT for Gypsy and Traveller Young People's Views*. Edinburgh: Scottish Executive Educational Department.

Robinson, M. and Martin, K. (2008), *Approaches to Working with Children, Young People and Families for Traveller, Irish Traveller, Gypsy, Roma and Show People Communities. A Literature Review*. Slough: National Foundation for Educational Research.

Yorkshire, Post. (1993), 'Official camp will ease gipsy problem in town', *Yorkshire Post*, 26 October.

Multi-Dimensional Sámi Education: Towards Culture-Sensitive Policies

4

Pigga Keskitalo, Satu Uusiautti and
Kaarina Määttä

Chapter Outline

Introduction

The content of indigenous education is constructed by the attempts of research and professional practice to meet the challenges of the present situation that are due to historical processes, and to work for the future of indigenous peoples. In this chapter, we explore the Sámi schooling context as an example of indigenous education. We will present culture-sensitive Sámi education as an effort to combine the traditional Sámi upbringing and the educational needs of the modern Sámi community.

According to current estimates, the Sámi language was born, at the latest, during the second millennium BC, which also gave birth to Sámi culture (Aikio, 2012). The reason for the separation of the language from Finnish was subsequent cultural changes. The Sámi language is thought to be intrusive in its present territory and the background of the Sámi people is genetically a European one (Aikio, 2004).

The Sámi have mostly represented a hunter-gatherer culture, and the Sámi lifestyle was based on multiple livelihoods for thousands of years. The Sámi's livelihoods also included fishing in seas and lakes, bird hunting and berry picking. The forest Sámi society was well organized: the basic units, *siida*, comprised families or lineages and the network of these units covered the whole of northern Fennoscandia. Small-scale reindeer herding may have been practised for millennia, but large-scale reindeer herding did not start until the sixteenth and seventeenth centuries (Lehtola, 2013).

The Sámi livelihoods have traditionally been connected to nature. At present, only a minority of the Sámi get their livelihood from reindeer herding (Sametinget, 2007/2008a). Instead, they are most likely to combine livelihoods such as small-scale agriculture and tourism (Sametinget, 2007/2008b). Moreover, the Sámi work in service trade, for municipalities and the state and in the private sector as a result of modern life. Today, they are part of the globalizing world and its various cultural flows and blends: 'people are no longer bound to certain places, and their lives have become non-local' (Seurujärvi-Kari, 2012, p. 147). Social and economic changes influenced the Sámi's areas of settlement, habitat and traditional lifestyle (Ruong, 1971). The traditional Sámi lifestyle was modified by new elements, such as paid work. On the other hand, the Sámi's migration to urban centres and recent global changes have resulted in new social identities: Irja Seurujärvi-Kari (2010) calls the result 'postmodern nomads'.

The present situation of the Sámi is regionally varied and complex, especially owing to cultural and historical differences. The Sámi live in four countries: Norway (50,000–65,000 people), Sweden (15,000–20,000), Finland (10,000) and Russia (2,000). The estimations of the total number of Sámi people vary between 50,000 and 100,000 depending on the method of assessment. Likewise Sámi education is influenced by the varied educational systems of these four countries. In addition, the Sámi's history includes a long period of assimilationist policy in each country inhabited by the Sámi. The Sámi have had to face an assimilation process for many centuries, initiated by the Christian church and continued by the school (Lehtola, 1997). Power relations also affect the role of indigenous people in relation to the nation state and society, and the social and economic situation.

The Sámi languages belong to the Finno-Ugric family of languages. At the moment, nine Sámi languages are left. All of them are endangered. North-

Sámi is spoken in Norway, Sweden and Finland. Lule, Ume, Pite and Southern Sámi are spoken in Norway and Sweden. Skolt Sámi is spoken in Finland and Russia, and it was spoken also in Norway in the Neiden area. Kildin and Ter Sámi are spoken in Russia. Furthermore, Inari Sámi is spoken only in Finland. The Sámi languages were secured by law in Finland and in Norway in 1992. In Sweden, the law on using Sámi when dealing with authorities and courts took effect in 2004 (Vuolab-Lohi, 2007). The Sámi languages are in need of special measures to maintain their vitality (Rasmussen, 2012; Taipale, 2012).

Our findings in this chapter are based on our various studies on Sámi education (e.g. Keskitalo, 2010; Keskitalo and Määttä, 2011; Keskitalo et al., 2013).[1] We are aware of the many ethical demands on indigenous research and the challenges of securing the Sámi's position and voices in the research on Sámi pedagogy and education in a way that is just, valuable and productive.

The history of assimilation from the viewpoint of Sámi education

The common history of the Christian church and the Sámi is filled with tensions (Kylli, 2005).The church played a major role in oppression and assimilation pressures targeted at the Sámi. The church's contacts with the Sámi were extensive.

In Norway the Christian church arrived at the Lofoten Islands as early as 1110 AD (The Royal House of Norway, 2009). The missionary era in the Sámi region of Norway started in 1717 and lasted until 1880. The assimilation period was long: it lasted from the 1800s until the end of the 1960s. In the 1980s, emphasis on bilingualism started to gain ground in schooling, and finally, in 1990, Sámi became an official language in the administrative district of the Sámi in Norway. The 'Sámi school' and curriculum were established in 1997.

In Sweden, the history of Sámi education started in 1612 when Sámi men were educated in Uppsala (Wiklund, 1922). Various missionary schools were responsible for teaching until the establishment of a mandatory elementary school system in 1842. At the same time, the missionary schools funded by welfare organizations continued to operate among the Sámi people alongside state schools (Henrysson, 1992). The Sámi had segregated 'nomadic schools' from the beginning of the twentieth century and 'Sámi schools' starting from 1977 (Welle-Strand and Askheim, 2011).

In Russia, the Sámi were under the influence of Christianity starting from the twelfth century. As part of a general expansion of the Russian empire, from the sixteenth century onwards missionaries were sent to the far reaches of the empire. During the regime of the Soviet Union, there was no Sámi.education. In the period 1930–1970, displacements of the Sámi by the Soviet Union caused considerable changes in the Sámi's life. The industrialization and militarization of the Soviet Union overruled the needs of indigenous peoples (Alleman, 2013). Today, in the Kola Peninsula, the teaching of the Kildin Sámi language occurs to varying degrees and is limited to primary school education in the rural locality of Lovozero (Rantala, 2005).

The Christian church arrived in Utsjoki area, the North of Finland, in 1673. From the 1750s until the 1980s, the Sámi was only an 'assisting language'. In 1979, the first Sámi-speaking classes were introduced in Finland (Lassila, 2001). Finland does not have any separate Sámi curriculum or Sámi school but municipal schools at Sámi core areas that have Sámi-speaking and Finnish-speaking classes based on demand.

In sum, the present state borders that divide Sámi regions were defined between the middle of the eighteenth century and the Second World War. In each country with a Sámi population, the assimilation policy has been pursued, in a written political or in a more hidden form, and as a result of these nationalist endeavours, a large-scale language shift has taken place (Seurujärvi-Kari, 2012). Furthermore, the Second World War had ruinous effects on Sámi education and language. The war's legacy (except in Sweden) left the Sámi without education in any language for several years, which negatively affected their literacy rates and ability to transfer their language to future generations (Anaya, 2011).

Wherever the Sámi resided, their populations were subjected – through education and other means – to pressures of assimilation. The Sámi were forced to give up their native language, or at least to start using the dominant language, and to change their values and lifestyle. The history of assimilation affects the Sámi to some extent even today. Thus, many Sámi's contact with traditional livelihoods disappeared because of school and boarding house arrangements. Eventually, some Sámi children grew away from their own culture, language and costume tradition (Rasmus, 2008). A distinct, large-scale re-awakening of the Sámi identity did not take place until the 1960s, after certain societal and political processes among the Sámi people. The Sámi school culture was and still is moulded according to premises brought from outside the Sámi culture.

The present situation of Sámi education

Sámi education in four countries

Of the countries with a Sámi population, Norway has developed Sámi education the most. In the Sámi administrative district of Norway, the Sámi have a special comprehensive school that follows a Sámi curriculum with emphasis on the idea of an inclusive and intercultural school. Overall, large-scale language revitalization has already been possible in Norway for a longer period of time, as in the course of the 1970s the strategy was to revitalize Sámi culture (Kalstad, 2012). The aspiration is to increase the number of active Sámi speakers. Currently, three types of Sámi schools and models for using and studying the Sámi language exist in Norway: (1) Norwegian-speaking schools where the Sámi language is studied as a subject, (2) Sámi-speaking schools and (3) bilingual schools with Sámi and bilingual classes. Where classes are composed of native Sámi-speaking pupils and those who have passive knowledge of the Sámi language when they start school, teaching in the Sámi language can be compared to language immersion, as instruction has to be adjusted to resemble an immersion course because of the pupils' various linguistic backgrounds. Schools in the Sámi administrative district follow the Sámi curriculum and the Norwegian school system works separately elsewhere in the country.

In Sweden, the Sámi School Board was established in 1981 and directs Sámi school education (Welle-Strand and Askheim, 2011). The 'Sámi school' is a school form equivalent to elementary school grades 1–6 but designed and profiled by the need for education that utilizes and develops the Sámi language and culture. The Sámi school is functioning in Karesuando, Kiruna, Gällivare, Jokkmokk and Tärnaby (Sameskolstyrelsen, 2013). The Sámi curriculum was launched in 2011 (Skolverket, 2011).

In Finland, Sámi education is organized so that schools follow the national Finnish curriculum and Sámi children study together with Finnish children in the same schools. Separate Sámi classes are arranged in the official Sámi domicile area. In practice, this can mean anything between 51 and 100 per cent class teaching in the Sámi language. Otherwise, pupils get Sámi-language teaching as a foreign language, if they wish. Sámi children are taught the Sámi language for two hours a week outside the Sámi domicile area. Yet, about 75 per cent of Sámi-speaking children below ten years of age live outside traditional area and lack proper support and strong pedagogy for their native language (Aikio-Puoskari, 2005).

The present situation in Finland is dangerous for the future of the Sámi language. In contrast, the national language is secure because its position in society, media and education is strong. In Nordic countries the speakers of minority and indigenous languages are usually bilingual, having a mastery of a mainstream or national language in addition to their mother tongue. What is emphasized here is that, if the model of indigenous children's schooling does not follow the goal of multilingualism and give the instruction in their native languages to a sufficient level, the pedagogical model of language teaching can be considered weak or culturally unsupportive (Skutnabb-Kangas and Dunbar, 2010).

In Russia, there has been Sámi education for Grades 1–6, but the continuation of teaching has been uncertain (Rantala, 2005). The 1993 Constitution of Russia did include protection of indigenous peoples. As Article 69 states: 'The Russian Federation shall guarantee the rights of the indigenous small peoples according to the universally recognized principles and norms of international law and international treaties and agreements of the Russian Federation' (Russian Federation, 1993). The new controversial law on education officially recognizes the right to education in languages of Russia's ethnic minorities, but does not make it mandatory or completely guarantee such education (Nilsen, 2013). Therefore, the educational situation of the Sámi people is still challenging.

The values of the mainstream school and Sámi values in curricula

Teaching is organized with varying success in countries with Sámi populations, owing to the educational history, societal differences and political situation. Official Sámi schools are functioning in Sweden and Norway. They are on the borderline: they are Sámi Schools but they are controlled by majority school culture and doctrines. They are also a result of the national and nationalistic history of the educational system. In general, the situation of Sámi-language teaching and Sámi-medium teaching is challenging. Although teachers do remarkably important work, their time is taken up with sociolinguistic and power questions, leaving little time and resources for developmental work at the school level. This refers to the development both of instruction and of the language itself. Such development may be hindered by the school culture, as it is such a powerful machine and there are few large-scale progressive efforts to break the existing practices. Giving up strict pedagogical models appears impossible, even if leaning on Sámi thinking would be beneficial and make Sámi-language learning and teaching meaningful. Children's language proficiency is influenced by different issues in their background. All in all, language planning is needed to make teaching more successful in the indigenous peoples' context: the position of the indigenous language and a culture-based approach should be adopted at the core of teaching and language planning.

According to our interpretations, there are many different challenges in Sámi-language teaching. These challenges originate in the sociological state of the Sámi language and culture, combined with the harsh background of a history of assimilation. Additionally, the asymmetric power relations affect schooling. It means that self-determination in indigenous education is only realized at a limited level, as the Sámi have in general only the role of providers of information to the state instead of active and independent organizers of education. A new exception to this is, however, the Sámi University, which organizes Sámi teacher training in accordance with its own programme.

In the case of basic education in Finland, the national core curriculum includes many important premises for successful Sámi education: the values on which the Finnish educational system is based cover human rights, equality, democracy, natural diversity, maintenance of environmental viability and tolerance for and intercultural understanding. The task of basic education is to promote communality, responsibility and respect for individual rights and freedom. Furthermore, the National Core Curriculum emphasizes the Finnish culture, which has developed in interaction between indigenous, Nordic and European cultures. Culture-specific features have to be considered in teaching, along with languages pertaining to national and local levels, including Sámi. Municipalities can mould the national curriculum according to the local and school-specific interests. The local curriculum will specify the local values on which teaching is based in its content and everyday practices (Finnish National Board of Education, 2004). However, to put teaching into practice according to these values is not a simple matter.

The gatekeeper phenomenon

In addition to the challenges introduced by pupils' heterogeneous language needs, parents, teachers and the system function as gatekeepers for teaching the Sámi language and determine whether the revitalization of pupils' Sámi language is enabled or not. While some parents' attitudes towards language revitalization are positive, other parents do not have time, or lack the skills, to support children in this aspect of learning because of their own insufficient knowledge of the Sámi language. Indeed, the divergence of pupils' backgrounds was described in the interviews among Sámi teachers: some parents supported pupils' schoolwork, while other families needed support from school. In addition to cultural factors, the reason is partly the assimilation of the Sámi, as some of the parents have lost their language and even their cultural identity.

Some parents are, however, more conscious and expect much of the school. This attitude demonstrates the change in values: education and 'Sáminess' are considered more and more valuable. Many expectations and much value-related pressure are aimed at the school. Hence the goal of the schools is, on the one hand, to maintain the traditional Sámi upbringing and, on the other hand, to bring back nature as the children's learning environment in a broader sense. Schools have to decolonize their practices, families and pupils (see Smith, 2012) and create transformative solutions for indigenous schooling (Smith, 2011, p. 24).

Means of strengthening Sámi pedagogy

In every country inhabited by the Sámi people, there are four key ideas about the means of strengthening Sámi education:

(1) Positive attitudes and resources

Positive attitudes towards Sámi pedagogy are considered a salient factor in the realization of Sámi education. Sámi pedagogy should be appreciated by the school community and also in the wider society. Certain practical means could promote positive attitudes, too. 'Sáminess' could be brought out in a positive manner in school practice and plans.

(2) A Sámi curriculum and the Sámi language

It is essential to create and implement a Sámi curriculum where the Sámi language has a central role. The curriculum cannot just be an application of the national curriculum, as it still is in Finland, for example, but it should be based on interculturalism and Sámi premises. The core principle of curriculum design should be equality and parity: Sámi children should have the same rights to an education that is based on their own culture as other children have.

(3) Culture-sensitive teaching arrangements

It is important to overcome stereotypical conceptions or prejudices concerning Sámi children's background or future. Traditional livelihoods are often pursued as part of compound livelihoods, for example, together with tourism and other service industry. The proportion of traditional livelihoods in revenue and the workforce is not very large but the cultural meaning is significant. They are not just livelihoods or professions but parts of a unique lifestyle. Some of the Sámi still earn their living through traditional livelihoods but a considerable proportion of the Sámi work in modern professions (Saami Parliament, 2008). Still, the old myths seem to hinder development also in the Sámi's own cultural context. At the same time, the Sámi conception of time, place and knowledge necessitates a breakaway from mainstream teaching practices. The Sámi group is small and, therefore, new practices should be developed to make teaching more integrated and stable. It would be important to try new approaches—a sort of pedagogical revolution.

(4) The Sámi School that is genuinely based on the Sámi language and culture

According to our understanding, in functional Sámi schools everyone would speak the Sámi language and their language proficiency would be furthered through constant usage. This school would be everyone's school and not a 'lonely island'. The school would support local intercultural society, Sámi families and stronger family-co-operation. The school would support the Sámi's traditional pedagogical practices and transmit traditions from one generation to another.

Togetherness, trust, appreciation and responsibility for various school tasks would enhance pupils' positive self-image and be based on the Sámi story-telling tradition. Consequently, school premises and the physical environment would be moulded to represent the locality and the Sámi culture. The connection with nature should be preserved and thus nature education, 'night schools' and cultural projects would support the understanding of nature.

Conversely, everyone should share knowledge and understanding about the objectives and goals of the school and education and all this would result in the well-being of local society, the Sámi culture and Sámi children. For example, according to the most recent research, there are already individual teachers in Norway who are following the ideas of intercultural and inclusive school (Hirvonen, 2004). Personnel might be aware of the multidimensional priorities, even if the school itself does not sufficiently support the goals in practice or general agreements about common goals have not been reached yet.

Discussion

The basics of Sámi pedagogy

Traditional Sámi upbringing is based on holism. It means that it is concerned with the humanitarian, moral, emotional, physical, psychological, cognitive and spiritual dimensions of a developing child (see Banks, 2006). In this model, the indigenous culture and local society will co-operate closely when aiming at developing children's cultural identities. A holistic way of thinking in education seeks to encompass and integrate multiple layers of meaning and experience rather than defining human possibilities narrowly (Miller, 2000). This includes educational ideas of, for example, common responsibility, co-operative learning and learning according to children's conditions. A child learns through trying and making mistakes, and according to his or her own pace and conditions. The approach also includes the non-authoritarian adult, negotiation and guidance on how to think and cope by oneself even in demanding circumstances (Balto, 1997). Humane manners are the goal. Sámi parents use informal techniques. For example, they teach children by telling stories aimed to warn about scary or dangerous things. The Sámi way of thinking is child-centred: the aim is to increase the children's abilities to cope in demanding conditions, through self-evaluation and independent thinking skills.

Sámi pedagogy should be applied at school on a large scale. The Sámi world-view and Sámi values and culture should occupy a central position in teaching and in the curriculum. From the point of view of Sámi culture and interculturalism, enculturation at school is a real challenge: How can we make sure that the curriculum and its implementation initiate pupils into Sámi and local culture? How can Sámi education be enhanced and what kinds of pedagogical methods and thinking are needed to strengthen Sámi culture in multiple contexts?

In the present situation, there is the need for further developing a distinct Sámi pedagogy because the Sámi already have distinct school curricula in Sweden and Norway, and, in addition, Sámi-speaking teaching is established in Finnish Sámi municipalities. Sámi pedagogy covers Sámi-speaking teaching and teaching that happens in Sámi language and culture. When extended, it could also cover teaching that takes place in multi-ethnic local communities with a Sámi population. Sámi pedagogy is based on general principles of education and the principles of traditional Sámi knowledge and upbringing. They form an entity that can be called Sámi pedagogy, *Sámi pedagogihkka*.

Pedagogy refers to the way of practising teaching and its underpinning educational principles. Sámi pedagogy is based on the values of the Sámi community and the nation state in combination. The objectives and practices of these two systems direct Sámi pedagogy.

Asta Balto points out that learning happens through teaching and experience. Her thoughts reflect reformed pedagogical ideas about learning and teaching. Basically, in indigenous communities, experiential learning has a larger role than in the modern systems of formal education. Nowadays learning in schools takes place mostly through structured, information-oriented settings (Balto, 2003). According to Jan Henry Keskitalo (1999), when it comes to schooling, Sámi values can be summed up by saying that the school is for the local community society and that the school and the society should collaborate. The Sámi family, connection with the natural environment and special features of traditional upbringing should be considered at school. The traditional upbringing involves the integration of the individual in the local Sámi community.

Developmental suggestions for Sámi education

Recent publications have brought out epistemological questions about research on indigenous peoples as well as special questions about child-rearing and education (e.g. Kuokkanen, 2000; Smith, 2005). Studies on indigenous peoples' teaching and education around the world seem to elicit information that is relevant to Sámi education as well (see Darnell and Hoëm, 1996; Lipka and Mohatt, 1998). According to Rauna Kuokkanen (2000), indigenous peoples' education necessitates paradigmatic change that alters assumptions about learning and methods of acquiring information towards the holistic approach that is typical of indigenous peoples. This requires the context where the cultural and linguistic reality at school is taken into consideration.

Language is one of the significant factors in schooling. Therefore, teaching in indigenous languages should be guaranteed in primary education, so that strong models of language education with aims of multilingualism are used (see also Skutnabb-Kangas and Dunbar, 2010, p. 44). Furthermore, it is important to promote positive attitudes towards indigenous peoples among other populations. Naturally, it is a matter of economic investments, too: the organization of Sámi education should be financially supported, even when provided outside the Sámi domicile area.

In order to be effective, Sámi education needs a curriculum, teaching premises and arrangements, and an extended range of Sámi learning materials.

The Sámi themselves have to be active and highlight the necessity of strengthening their own culture within school practices. Thus, their own history and knowledge about the modern Sámi community and Sámi handicrafts (*duodji*), art, music and the story-telling tradition (*máinnasteapmi*) have a central role. The connection with the natural environment, the coexistence of the human being with nature and traditional livelihoods, is important. It means that reindeer pasturage, fishing waters, small-scale agriculture, picking culture and handicrafts are considered a part of cultural knowledge. It is a question of building up cultural capital via schools (see Yosso, 2006). Pupils should be provided with positive experiences related to their own culture through play, story-telling, action and participation. Teaching should be adjusted to the yearly cycle of the local Sámi community, traditional seasonal work and changes that take place in nature (Rasmus, 2004).

The central task of the school is to support the Sámi pupils' identity: the school must provide chances to the development of a healthy self-esteem so that the Sámi pupils can have their Sámi identity whilst also playing a part in the wider national community. National interests are secured nowadays by national curriculum requirements, even in Sweden and Norway.

Conclusion

Our chapter shows that many things should still change to bring about the reform of Sámi education. Is this kind of a change possible? The school system is affected by world-wide economic, political and social forces: schools have become places where teachers and pupils are controlled, supervised, compared and considered accountable for their actions (Youdell, 2011). Education is one of the most powerful state structures that instil and renew dominant ideologies. Education and child-rearing have conscious and unconscious influence on us. Education does not teach just practical skills, such as reading and mathematics, but instils societal moral rules, norms and culture (Hier, 2003).

Consequently, it is possible to be aware of different perspectives and to challenge mainstream interpretations and ideologies. Indeed, rarely heard viewpoints in the field of education and child-rearing, such as those of the Sámi, are among those that deserve more attention. If we become informed about these issues, we are aware of the kinds of appreciations, practices, models, hidden effects, resources and social relationships that are included in daily schooling. At its best, such awareness leads to critical discussion and enables us to see new perspectives.

The macro level of education should be developed so that authentic Sámi education could be realized. In Finland, curriculum reform work is going on, and it will be finished in 2016. In Norway and Sweden, Sámi curricula have already been introduced. How should Sámi education be realized—through integration or segregation? Will the Sámi have their own curriculum also in Finland or will the Finnish curriculum be radically changed, so that it would support better the varied needs of the local communities of the Sámi domicile area and elsewhere in the country? It is hoped that Russia also will respond to the current demanding situation of Sámi teaching.

The ideal school is the one where cultural sensitivity and policies are recognized and acknowledged and which strengthens the cultural identity of its members. Further, premises are open, accessible and welcome to everyone. It is a place where everyone listens, hears, discusses; where teachers have the time and interest to understand pupils' ideas, thoughts, experiences, feelings, fantasies and hopes; where mutual trust between various generations and genders is present; where the conception of knowledge and knowing has new forms; and where experiential and communal learning are given space (cf. Youdell, 2011).

Note

1   We represent collaboration of indigenous and non-indigenous researchers. Associate Professor Dr Keskitalo is a Sámi woman, teacher and researcher who works at the Sámi University College, in Kautokeino, Norway, in the field of teacher training. Adjunct Professor Dr Uusiautti works as a specialist at the University of Lapland and has lately focused on questions of well-being at school and caring teacherhood. Professor Dr Kaarina Määttä from the University of Lapland has supervised Dr Keskitalo's and Dr Uusiautti's doctoral theses, and is also the scientific leader of our research project. The purpose of our research group is to increase knowledge about the educational practices of an indigenous people, in countries populated by the Sámi and internationally.

Further reading

Keskitalo, Pigga, Määttä, Kaarina, and Uusiautti, Satu. (2013), *Sámi Education*. Frankfurt am Main: Peter Lang.

Kuokkanen, Rauna. (2007), *Reshaping the University. Responsibility, Indigenous Epistemes and the Logic of the Gift*. Vancouver, BC: University of British Columbia Press.

Olthuis, Marja-Liisa, Kivelä, Suvi, and Skutnabb-Kangas, T. (2013), *Revitalising Indigenous Languages. How to Recreate a Lost Generation*. Bristol: Multilingual Matters.

References

Aikio, A.(2004), 'An essay on substrate studies and the origin of Saami', in I. Hyvärinen, P. Kallio, and J. Korhonen (eds), *Etymologie, Entlehnungen und Entwicklungen: Festschrift für Jorma Koivulehto zum 70. Geburtstag.* Helsinki: Finno-Ugric Association, pp. 5–34.

——. (2012), 'An essay on Saami ethnolinguistic prehistory', in R. Grünthal and P. Kallio (eds), *A Linguistic Map of Prehistoric Northern Europe.* Helsinki: Finno-Ugric Association, pp. 63–117.

Aikio-Puoskari, U. (2005), *The Education of the Sámi in the Comprehensive Schooling of Three Nordic Countries: Norway, Finland and Sweden. (Gáldu čála 2/2005.)* Guovdageaidnu: Resource Centre for the Rights of Indigenous Peoples.

Anaya, J. (2011), *Report of the Special Rapporteur on the Situation of Human Rights and Fundamental Freedoms of Indigenous People.* Geneva: United Nations.

Alleman, L. (2013), *The Sámi of the Kola Peninsula: About the Life of an Ethnic Minority in the Soviet Union.* Tromsø: University of Tromsø.

Balto, A. (1997), *Samisk barneoppdragelse i endring* [Sámi Childrearing in Change]. Oslo: Ad Notam Gyldendal.

——. (2003), 'Muitalusat Sámis. Árbevirolaš bajásgeassima nana bealit' [Stories in Sámi Land. The Strengths of Traditional Education], in E. Hætta Eriksen (ed.), *Árvvut. Árvo Vierhtie. Samiske verdier* [The Sámi Values]. Karasjok: Davvi Girji, pp. 9–16.

Banks, J. (2006), *Cultural Diversity and Education. Foundations, Curriculum, and Teaching.* 5th ed. Boston, MA: Pearson Education.

Darnell, F. and Hoëm, A. (1996), *Taken to Extremes: Education in the Far North.* Oslo: Scandinavian University Press.

Finnish National Board of Education. (2004), *Perusopetuksen opetussuunnitelman perusteet 2004* [National Core Curriculum for Basic Education 2004]. Helsinki: National Board of Education.

Henrysson, S. (1992), 'Saami education in Sweden in the 1900s', in R. Kvisti (ed.), *Readings in Saami History, Culture and Language, III.* Umeå: Umeå universitet, pp. 103–110.

Hier, S. P. (2003), 'Probing the surveillant assemblage: On the dialects of surveillance practices as processes of social control', *Surveillance and Society*, 1, (3), 399–411.

Hirvonen, V. (2004), *Saami Culture and School. Sámi Teachers and the Realization of the Sámi School. An Evaluation Study of Reform 97.* Translated by K. Anttonen. Kárášjohka: ČálliidLágádus.

Kalstad, J. K. (2012), 'Norgga sámepolitihkka 1970-logus – ođastemiin nanosmahttit sámevuođa' [Norwegian Sami policy in the 1970s – strengthening "Saminess" through renewal], *Sámi dieđalaš áigečála*, 2, 85–111.

Keskitalo, J. H. (1999), *Čálusráidu O97 Sámi oktavuođas. Temágihpa 1: Sámi oahppoplánat – Sámi skuvla? Skriftserie til l97 samisk. Temahefte 1: Et samisk læreplanverk – en samisk skole?* [Series to Curriculum Sámi. Thematic Writing 1: Sámi Curriculum – Sámi School?]. Guovdageaidnu: Sámi oahpahusráđđi – Samisk utdanningsråd.

Keskitalo, P. (2010), *Saamelaiskoulun kulttuurisensitiivisyyttä etsimässä kasvatusantropologian keinoin* [Seeking the Cultural Sensitivity of Sámi School through Educational Anthropology]. (Dieđut 1/2010). Guovdageaidnu: Sámi University College.

Keskitalo, P. and Määttä, K. (2011), *Sami pedagogihka iešvuođat /Saamelaispedagogiikan perusteet/The Basics of Sámi Pedagogy/Grunderna i samisk pedagogik/Основы саамской педк*. Rovaniemi: Lapland University Press.

Keskitalo, P., Määttä, K., and Uusiautti, S. (2013), *Sámi Education*. Frankfurt am Main: Peter Lang Publishing.

Kuokkanen, R. (2000), 'Towards an "indigenous paradigm" from a Sami perspective', *Canadian Journal of Native Studies*, 20, (2), 411–436.

Kylli, R. (2005), *Kirkon ja saamelaisten kohtaaminen Utsjoella ja Inarissa 1742–1886* [The Church and the Sámi Encounter in Inari and Utsjoki during 1742–1886]. Oulu: Historical Association of the North-Finland.

Lassila, J. (2001), *Lapin koulutushistoria – Kirkollinen alkuopetus, kansa-, perus-ja oppikoulut. Osa 1* [The Educational History of Lapland – Christian Elementary Education, Folk, Basic, and Secondary Schools. Part 1]. Oulu: University of Oulu.

Lehtola, V.-P. (1997), *Saamelaiset. Historia, yhteiskunta, taide* [The Sámi People. History, Society and the Arts]. Inari: Kustannus Puntsi.

———. (2013), *Monikasvoinen Saamenmaa* [Multifaceted Sámi Land]. Kautokeino: Gáldu. Retrieved from http://www.galdu.org/web/index.php?sladja=25&vuolitsladja=11&giella1=spa.

Lipka, G., Mohatt, V., and the Ciulistet Group (eds). (1998), *Transforming the Culture of Schools. Yup'ik Eskimo Examples*. Mahwah: Lawrence Erlbaum Associates.

Miller, R. (2000), 'A brief introduction to holistic education', in *The Encyclopaedia of Informal Education*. London: YMCA George Williams College. Retrieved from http://infed.org/mobi/a-brief-introduction-to-holistic-education/.

Nilsen, T. (2013), 'New law discriminates indigenous languages', *Barents Observer*, 3 January. Retrieved from http://barentsobserver.com/en/society/2013/01/new-law-discriminates-indigenous-languages-03-01.

Rantala, L. (2005), 'Venäjän saamelaisten oikeudellinen asema' [The legal position of the Russian Sámi people], in C.Smith, H.Danelius, M.Niemivuo, I.-L.Pavall, M.Scheinin, M.Åhren, J. B.Henriksen, and H. J.Hyvärinen (eds), *Pohjoismainen saamelaissopimus: Suomalais-norjalais-ruotsalais-saamelaisen asiantuntijatyöryhmän 27. lokakuuta 2005 luovuttama luonnos* [The Nordic Sámi Convention: Report of the Finnish-Norwegian-Swedish-Sámi Expert Group, 27 Oct 2005]. Helsinki: Ministry of Justice, pp. 251–261. Retrieved from http://www.regjeringen.no/upload/AID/temadokumenter/sami/sami_samskonvensjonen_finsk_H-2183%20F.pdf.

Rasmus, E.-L. (2004), *Saamelaisen identiteetin merkitys Utsjoen nuorille. Kasvatusantropologinen tutkimus saamelaisten maailmankuvasta ja identiteetistä* [The Significance of the Sámi Identity to the Youth of Utsjoki. An Educational-Anthropological Study of the Sámi's Worldview and Identity]. Rovaniemi: University of Lapland, Master's thesis.

Rasmus, M. (2008), *Bággu vuolgit, bággu birget. Sámemánáid ceavzinstrategiijat Suoma álbmotskuvlla ásodagain 1950–1960 –logus* [Must Go, Must adjust. Sámi Children's Coping Strategies in the Finnish Boarding Schools in the 1950s and 1960s]. Oulu: Giellagas Institute.

Rasmussen, T. (2012), 'Sámegielaid ealáskahttin ja hehttehusat Suomas' [The revitalization of Sámi languages and obstacles in Finland], in P. Keskitalo and K. Määttä (eds), *Ulbmilin sámi pedagogihka ollašuhttin* [The Realization of Sámi Pedagogy as the Goal]. Rovaniemi: Lapland University Press, pp. 71–92.

The Royal House of Norway. (2009), *Riikačoakkáldat* [State Collection]. Oslo: The Royal House of Norway. Retrieved from http://www.kongehuset.no/artikkel.html?tid=75701&sek=74946.

Ruong, I. (1971), *Samerna* [The Sámi People]. Stockholm: Bokförlaget Aldus/Bonniers.

The Russian Federation. (1993), *The Constitution of the Russian Federation*. Adopted at National Voting on 12 December 1993. Russia: The Russian Federation. Retrieved from http://www.constitution.ru/en/10003000-01.htm.

Saami Parliament. (2008), *Saamelaisten kulttuuri-itsehallinto opetustoimessa. Saamelaiskäräjien perusopetusta ja lukiokoulutusta koskevat koulutuspoliittiset tavoitteet* [The Sámi's Cultural Self-government in Education. Educational Political Goals of the Saami Parliament Regarding Basic and High School Education]. Inari: Sámi Parliament. Retrieved from http://www.samediggi.fi/vanha/oktavuohta/kulttuuri-itsehallinto.doc.

Sameskolstyrelsen. (2013), *Sameskolstyrelsen* [Sámi School Board]. Jokkmokk: Sameskolstyrelsen. Retrieved from http://www.sameskolstyrelsen.se/.

Sametinget. (2007/2008a), *Ealáhusáššit* [Livelihoods]. Kiruna: Sametinget. Retrieved from http://sametinget.dev.imcode.com/2847.

——. (2007/2008b), *Sámit Ruotas* [The Sámi in Sweden]. Kiruna: Sametinget. Retrieved from http://sametinget.dev.imcode.com/2870.

Seurujärvi-Kari, I. (2010), '"Nubbi" sápmelašvuođas - ođđalágan identitehtat' [Otherness in Sámihood – New Identities], *Sámi dieđalaš áigečála*, 2010/1, 71–95.

——. (2012), *Ale jáskkot eatnigiella. Alkuperäiskansaliikkeen ja saamen kielen merkitys saamelaisten identiteetille* [Don't Keep Silent Your Mother-tongue. The Importance of the Indigenous People's Movement and the Sámi Language to the Sámi Identity]. Helsinki: University of Helsinki.

Skolverket. (2011), *Läroplan för sameskolan, förskoleklassen och fritidshemmet 2011* [Curriculum for Sámi School, Pre-school Education, and Boarding Schools]. Stockholm: Fritzes.

Skutnabb-Kangas, T. and Dunbar, R. (2010), 'Indigenous children's education as linguistic genocide and a crime against humanity? Global view', Gáldu Čála. *Journal of Indigenous Peoples Rights*, 1, 1–128. Retrieved from http://www.afn.ca/uploads/files/education2/indigenouschildrenseducation.pdf.

Smith, G. H. (2011), *Transforming Education: Maori Struggle for Higher Education. 'Manu-Ao' Presentation*. Wellington: Te Whare Wānanga o Awanuiārangi: Indigenous-University. Retrieved from http://www.manu-ao.ac.nz/massey/fms/manu-ao/documents/Graham%20Smith%20Powerpoint.pdf.

Smith, L. T. (2005), 'Building a research agenda for indigenous epistemologies and education', *Anthropology and Education Quarterly*, 36, (1), 93–95.

——. (2012), *Decolonizing Methodologies: Research and Indigenous Peoples*. 2nd ed. New York, NY: Zed Book.

Taipale, R. (2012), *Utsjoen saamenkielisten nuorten kielenkäyttö* [The Language Usage of Sámi-Speaking Young People in Utsjoki]. Utsjoki: Sámi Siida ry. and Ovttas! Project.

Vuolab-Lohi, K. (2007), *Pohjoissaamen kielen tilanne sekä kehittämistarpeet* [The Situation of Northern Sámi Language and the Need for Development]. Inari: Sámi Parliament. Retrieved from http://www.kotus.fi/files/742/pohjoisSelvitys.pdf.

Welle-Strand, A. and Askheim, S. (2011), *Skole og utdanning i Sverige* [School and Education in Sweden]. Oslo: Store Norske Leksikon. Retrieved from http://snl.no/Skole_og_utdanning_i_Sverige.

Wiklund, K. B. (1922), *ABC-bok på lapska (Stockholm 1619): med en efterskrift om de svenska lapparnas skolundervisning i äldsta tid* [ABC Book in Lappish (Stockholm 1619): with a Post Script about the Swedish Lapps Education in the Old Days]. Stockholm. Faksimileupplagor af äldre svenska tryck.

Youdell, D. (2011), *School Trouble. Identity, Power and Politics In Education*. London: Routledge.

Yosso, T. J. (2006), *Critical Race Counterstories along the Chicana/Chicano Educational Pipeline*. New York, NY: Routledge.

Roma/Traveller Inclusion in Europe: Why Informal Education is Winning

5

Christine O'Hanlon

The concept of the term 'indigenous', that is, being native by birth or origin, proves controversial generally—and especially in Europe at the present time. Europe is undergoing profound change as many new European Union (EU) countries are attempting to build democratic institutions and adjust to mixed economies. Europe was at war twice in the twentieth century and since 1945 has successfully been rebuilding its identity. The EU allows the free movement of people, goods, capital and services. The right to free movement granted to all EU citizens represents a unique experiment in the contemporary history of global migration systems. To date, however, the integration of mobile EU citizens as a specific target group has not been widely discussed, either at EU or national levels, and EU-level integration policies focus on the integration of legally residing third-country nationals. The free movement of workers in the EU has led to continuing waves of migration to and from different countries, although not all the migrants are EU citizens.

Europe has not been officially colonized by an imperial force in recent centuries, consequently the vast majority of Europeans can be considered to be settled and 'indigenous'. Since its formation, the EU has defined its own rules for education, commerce and capital, and the 'official' languages for legislation in Brussels and for use in educational situations. However, thousands of different ethnic minorities exist together with their traditional cultures and languages and are recognized as indigenous peoples. One of these groups, for example, is the Saami (see Chapter 4). The Roma, however, are more recent itinerant people who have travelled from Asia, to make their home in Europe. In the distant past all European peoples originated as itinerant peoples; these were people who had to travel to survive or find work. Itinerants and migrants, known as ethnic minorities, then settled in different regions of Europe with their own specific languages and cultures. Now the diverse groups live side by side, but not always peacefully. There are currently well-established settled people who occupy a majority status in Europe and are referred to as the 'mainstream' because they lead sedentary lives and their specific language and culture dominates in particular states or countries. The politics of the country defines the policies and practices which govern each European state. However, each state in the EU shares overarching laws and statutes governing equality of opportunity, especially in education and employment.

It is important to begin by distinguishing different Traveller, itinerant and indigenous groups which are often treated as one. There are distinct Traveller groups like Occupational Traveller groups which include bargees, circus workers, fairground workers, show people, seasonal workers, temporary migrants, itinerant Gypsies, Roma, Sinti, Travellers and Sámi. The groups are defined by the fact that their occupations require an itinerant lifestyle, rather than their ethnicity. Roma gypsies may travel and work at the same time, but many are settled and live in EU countries like Romania.

The Sinti are a Roma people who live in Central Europe. They are by tradition nomadic, but today, there are only a small number of unsettled Sinti. In earlier times all these groups lived on the margins or outskirts of larger communities. The word 'Sinti' is said to come from Sind, a historical region of the Indian sub-continent, which has now been subsumed within Pakistan.

The Sinti and Roma are nomadic peoples found throughout Europe. Both groups are often referred to as Roma. Together, they are commonly referred to as Gypsies, because many Europeans thought that they were natives of Egypt. Numerous Sinti and Roma traditionally worked as craftsmen, such as blacksmiths, cobblers, tinkers, horse dealers and toolmakers. Others were performers such as musicians, circus artistes, animal trainers and dancers. The numbers of truly nomadic Gypsies are on the decline in many places throughout Europe, although sedentary Gypsies often move seasonally, depending on their occupations. These groups have been marginalized and persecuted through the ages, with education often used as a means of societal segregation. For example, in Germany under the Third Reich, Gypsies, like the Jews, were singled out by the Nazis for racial persecution and eventual annihilation. Gypsy schoolchildren who missed school were deemed delinquent and sent to special juvenile schools; those unable to speak German were sent to 'special schools' for the mentally handicapped. Finally, in March 1941, the Nazi regime excluded Gypsies totally from state schools. Fortunately, such extreme measures are a phenomenon of the past in Europe.

European countries in the twentieth century did not offer equal rights, in some respects, to all their citizens and many laws, policies and school practices were changed at the outset of the European Community, when different countries were preparing to join it, mainly for economic gain. This history is significant today because it explains why many EU countries find it difficult, even now, to erase racism totally from education and to provide unconditional support for itinerant Roma/Travelling children and their families.

The enlarged membership of the EU is now standing at 28 countries with the inclusion of Bulgaria and Romania in 2007 and of Croatia in 2013. The EU has created a process known as 'European integration', which requires co-operation between its member states as national governments allow for the harmonization of national laws. Conditions governing inclusion in the EU include a stable democratic government that respects the rule of law, with corresponding freedoms and institutions. The 1993 Copenhagen criteria require that all countries should show 'respect for human dignity, freedom, democracy, equality, the rule of law and respect for human rights, including the rights of persons belonging to minorities' (Council of Europe, 1993, Article 2).

Roma migration within Europe

The requirements just mentioned were introduced when it was clear that many Eastern Bloc countries wished to apply for membership of the EU. Many had a poor history of democratic and political practices in relation to the education of minorities, including the suppression of minority cultures and languages. Although the first priority for many countries, in joining, is to gain economic and monetary advantage, EU legislation imposes on member states a certain responsibility to provide equal access to social and educational resources, alongside EU 'rights' (O'Hanlon, 2010).

Clearly, with the accession of Eastern European countries like Romania there is a seismic shift in the numbers of Roma entering other EU countries. A west-bound Roma migration has proved unpopular in many countries and active discrimination has resulted in their expulsion in some cases (see Guardian News, 2013). Roma, like other citizens, have the right to free movement within the EU: but there have been concerns about the higher proportion of Roma living in Bulgaria and Romania than was the case with earlier accession states. There are around 2.5 million Roma living in these two countries, which is around 8 per cent of the population (Tanner, 2004, p. 69). A quarter of the 8–12 million European Roma who live in Western Europe, were forced to leave Eastern Europe and seek asylum elsewhere in recent centuries (Institute of Public Policy Research (IPPR), 2011). Yet hostile attitudes still exist, as evidenced by a MORI poll in the United Kingdom (UK) which found that the groups of immigrants that participants felt least positive about were Travellers and Gypsies (34 per cent), followed by asylum seekers (Mori Poll, 2001).

At present, the largest group of recently immigrant Roma live in Italy, where there are about 140,000, half of whom are Italian citizens. In 2008, Silvio Berlusconi (the then Italian prime minister) described illegal immigrants as 'an army of evil' and his government launched a campaign using 'extreme measures' to target Roma migrants living in nomad camps. Many camps were dismantled and thousands of immigrants were expelled from Italy.

France has at least 400,000 Roma and in recent years thousands have been arriving from Bulgaria and Romania, many of whom live in unauthorized camps. President Sarkozy in 2010 oversaw the dismantling of more than 200 settlements and 1,000 of their inhabitants have been deported to Romania and Bulgaria with French financial incentives, consisting of grants for agricultural business schemes. Subsequently, the French government has been accused of violating EU laws on human rights, by targeting an ethnic minority group.

Spain has more than 700,000 Roma, which is a well-established population, known as *gitanos*, many of whom live in Andalucia. This is the highest count outside Romania. Spain, like France, has had a recent influx of Romanian Roma, but there has been no crackdown against them. Germany has approximately 105,000 Roma who came from the former Yugoslavia, and are now long-term residents with protected status. However, in recent years thousands of Roma have also been expelled from Germany.

In the UK there are about 250,000 Roma, and many more have arrived recently from Slovakia, Romania, Poland and the Baltic States. There has been resistance to their immigration from resident communities. For example, in Belfast in 2009, about 100 Roma were forced to leave after a spate of attacks, though they were later able to return (BBC News Europe, 2010). The UK is tightening its borders, expelling illegal immigrants and failed asylum seekers, who have included Roma. Some sources claim that westward migration of Roma is slowing and in the future it is unlikely that the UK will see a renewed surge of Eastern European migrants, including Roma. As economic prospects in the home countries improve, more young people are likely to remain there (IPPR, 2006). Nevertheless evidence from various sources confirms that the Roma have been, and are still being, resisted, both at local community and at government level, in all western states in the EU (UNICEF, 2007; UNESCO and Council of Europe, 2007).

Early education

Making education systems more inclusive and available poses a challenge to many EU countries where many Roma children end up in special education or segregated schooling. However, the process of successful social inclusion begins with providing equal access to early education.

Criteria for enrolment in early education vary from country to country. For example, access may relate to the age of the child; there may be no selection criteria; or selection for state-aided provision may be on the grounds of mother's employment status, family level of poverty or the number of children in the family. Also, many countries cannot accommodate all the eligible children because of a shortage of places in early education institutions. It is normally the local authorities or the family who finance early education, although many countries provide a compulsory period of free pre-primary education. However, due to the social and economic situation of the majority of Roma, the associated costs of such things as meals, transport or extra-curricular activities are unaffordable for parents. Those countries which want to demonstrate their serious commitment to equal rights provide a quota for Roma children or low income families, family exemption from fees, Roma mediators or teaching assistants to link communities with pre-school centres, and facilitation of enrolment for all children including Roma.

Generally, in EU countries, it can be agreed that there is a lower participation of Roma in early education, compared to that of mainstream children, as well as a lower attendance rate (Zanker, 2010). Roma and many Traveller groups attach great importance to their own traditional early enculturation and prefer to raise their young children under the age of five in their own way. In addition, non-affordability of child care services due to a high degree of parent unemployment, and the failure of state provision to adapt to alternative cultures and languages, like those of the Roma, interfere with early years take-up. Parents feel distrustful of the authorities and public services and Roma children's poor skills in using the mainstream/majority language are a barrier to early education enrolment, as too, are parental illiteracy, lack of birth certificates and hostile school environments for Roma. There are links between anti-Roma prejudice exhibited by parents and teachers, early education selection procedures and a low level of awareness among education administrators and staff concerning the difficulties encountered by Roma families and children in accessing early years services. A European Monitoring Centre for Racism and Xenophobia (EUMC, 2006) report draws attention to the 'lack of pre-school education', this level of education being crucial for the assimilation of school norms and expected behavioural patterns and also for developing proficiency in language. There appears to be a perpetual lack of premises and space for providing appropriate early years services for Roma and Travellers throughout the EU.

Access to pre-school education can bridge the gap in basic knowledge and skills commonly occurring when Roma children enrol in first year compulsory schooling. Early education is seen as an effective way to combat the most negative and pervasive aspect of the schooling of Roma children, that of being channelled into special schools and classes (for children with special educational needs). Access to pre-school can also reduce drop-out rates, and contribute towards the successful mainstreaming of Roma children at all stages of education. Yet Roma/Traveller families throughout Europe still choose to 'home educate' their children. The greatest problem for early years education of these children is that, although educational opportunities vary across countries and regions, access to education is still in general unsatisfactory because of endemic societal discrimination and prejudice.

Threats to culture

Minority groups worldwide cherish their languages and cultures and resent any 'mainstream' attacks on their way of life, which can only be countered through the enculturation of their own children. Taking children away from families in the early years weakens their influence and eventually leads to the disintegration of minority cultures' traditions and foundations.

Many organizations, such as the UN, UNESCO and the Organisation for Security and Cooperation in Europe (OSCE), now want to change the low participation of Roma in early education by conducting awareness raising campaigns and developing policies for the effective integration of Roma into mainstream education. Some suggestions have been to sensitize the authorities responsible for providing early education services to the rights of all children to develop their full potential, to ensure the involvement of Roma parents and to strengthen ties between them and their local communities. Also, plans include the strengthening of educators' abilities and skills through pre and in-service training, to work in diverse multicultural settings and to create supportive learning environments for Roma children.

The present selection criteria, used throughout Europe, that have an indirect discriminatory effect on Roma need to be reconsidered and alternative documentation used, rather than the currently accepted birth and health certificates, compulsory vaccinations, etc. There are too many obstacles in the way of the full acceptance of what formal government offers for Roma/ Travellers. Although what is provided is offered in good faith, this may not be the way to approach the situation. It is important to look at the situation from another perspective, especially the Roma perspective, to resolve this low early education take-up and suspicion of authority.

General education

Reports from all over Europe show evidence of consistent shortfalls in the educational attainment of Roma/Travellers when compared to the mainstream. Reports document that these groups drop out of formal education at high rates and their literacy levels remain low. It appears that an itinerant lifestyle interferes with formal educational practice throughout the EU (Advisory Committee on the Framework Convention for the Protection of National Minorities, 2006).

In the UK the Plowden Report (Central Advisory Council for Education, 1967) was concerned about the education of the Roma/Traveller children, and contended that they were 'probably the most severely deprived children in the country'. It acknowledged that the majority did not go to school, because they self-excluded themselves through '*their way of life* and their lack of education from entering *normal* occupations as a consequence of their continual travelling' (p. 160, emphasis added). Roma/Traveller children were seen to exclude themselves because they were born into a lifestyle that made it difficult for them to do otherwise. The normative view is that, for access to schooling, specific home and lifestyle conditions need to be met for a successful outcome, and that this principle applies throughout Europe. This implies that Roma need to change rather than school systems adapting to their needs.

At present, in the UK, the government states that it aims to enable every child to fulfil his or her potential. On 4 April 2012, the UK Department for Education published a ministerial working group report containing measures designed to improve outcomes for the Gypsy, Roma and Traveller communities. The Department states that 'Gypsy/Roma pupils and pupils of Irish Traveller heritage (GRT) are among the lowest-achieving groups at every Key Stage of education, although individual GRT pupils can and do achieve very well' (Department for Education (DFE), 2012). The underperformance of GRT pupils is seen to be due to a combination of factors, including financial deprivation, low levels of parental literacy and low aspiration for their children's academic achievement, poor attendance and bullying. The Department further notes that there is a strong link between deprivation and underachievement and in primary schools, with 43.2 per cent of all pupils registered as either Gypsy, Roma or Irish Traveller currently eligible for free school meals. This figure rises to 45.3 per cent in secondary schools and 57.5 per cent in special schools. Those pupils who are eligible for free school meals benefit directly from the Pupil Premium, which is currently providing an additional £430 per pupil to help raise their attainment (DFE, 2012). Like other EU governments, the British Government is aware of the plight of Roma/Traveller pupils in schooling and repeatedly publishes documents and policies to improve the situation, alongside funded current research reports. There are estimated to be between 50,000 and 95,000 Roma in the UK at present.

Many studies have documented discrimination against Roma/Traveller communities and their limited access to education. The European Commission (EC) (2005b), for example, reports as follows:

> The situation of Roma in an enlarged European Union has become much more political and partisan, and the operational environment surrounding policy making for Roma integration remains fragile. In current systems there is a lack of capacity, understanding and professional expertise to deal effectively with the complex and multi-dimensional nature of the problem. (p. 15)

Also, the perpetuation of segregated schooling, the over-representation of Roma/Travellers in special school facilities and the denial of educational rights to them results in only a small proportion reaching secondary education (Kjaerum, 2013).

Eastern and Southern Europe

Specific Eastern and Southern European countries show a greater neglect of Roma/Traveller educational rights than the North-Western states of the EU. In the Former Yugoslav Republic of Macedonia (FYROM), it was reported that, out of a total of 8,000 Roma children enrolled in primary schools, fewer than 700 completed their primary education (FYROM, 2007). The discrimination that exists in Croatia, the Czech Republic, the FYROM and Slovakia has become a matter of international concern. Research by Gimenez (2010) shows that, despite Europe-wide commitments to improve the education of the Roma, combined with regular affirmations by states regarding the priority of efforts in this respect, their practice shows great inconsistency in implementing these commitments. A survey by the United Nations Development Programme and others (2011) confirms these conclusions.

As stated previously, the internationally agreed right to education with specific reference to minorities, along with other human rights instruments (UNESCO, 2006, Chapter 9), provides guarantees for national minorities to learn their mother tongue at school or, at least, to experience schooling through their mother tongue. However, the barriers are great in Eastern Europe and, with a variety of languages and many political borders, the issue of language use in schools is always challenging. Within the FYROM, for example, teaching at the primary level is delivered in Macedonian, Albanian, Turkish or Serbian, depending on the location. Yet, throughout Europe, Roma have no access to education in their own languages, although a minority of primary schools may teach them as options. In reality, language barriers have led to the separation of pupils at both primary and secondary levels along linguistic and ethnic lines. The consequences are separate classes or institutions, and school textbooks, especially in history and literature teaching, continue to include negative Roma ethnic stereotypes (UNESCO, 2006, p. 14). In many countries including Albania, Georgia, Greece, Portugal and Russia, Roma and Travellers have been excluded from, or have dropped out of school, often because of prejudice and discrimination (European Commission against Racism and Intolerance (ECRI), 2011).

It is an issue of concern that, in EU member states like Hungary, Slovakia and the Czech Republic, Roma pupils are still placed in 'special schools'. Roma rights groups across Eastern Europe have welcomed a ruling by the European Court of Human Rights in Strasbourg, which found the Czech Republic guilty of discriminating against Roma children by placing them in special schools for children with 'Mental Handicap' (Thorpe, 2007). The Czech Republic, under international pressure, has already abolished special schools as a category, although locational segregation is still widespread. Across Eastern Europe, schools close to Roma villages inevitably have a higher proportion of Roma pupils. This often leads to non-Roma pupils being moved out by their parents, who fear a lowering of educational standards.

Special schools do not equip their pupils with employable qualifications. In the Czech Republic children at special schools are not expected to learn the alphabet, or to count to ten, until the third or fourth class: skills that are normally taught in Year One in mainstream schools. In Slovakia the certificate awarded after eight years' attendance at a special school is accepted in vocational, but not secondary schools.

In Albania, Roma children are refused admission to school because they have not been vaccinated, and many also drop out of schooling. In Greece too, many schools still refuse to register Roma children, mainly because of non-Roma parental pressure. In Portugal, Roma drop-out rates are extremely high and non-Roma parents have influenced school officials not to enrol Roma children, posting 'No Gypsies' notices near schools in the past. In Serbia, 62 per cent of Roma children have either never attended school or have dropped out, and only 9.6 per cent complete the secondary level (Council of Europe, 2012, p. 117).

Poverty prevents many Roma children from gaining access to school; lack of funds for travel, clothing and school materials is an obstacle to many. This is a particular barrier to Roma in Moldova, where half of the Roma live in such extreme poverty that they cannot afford to send their children to school. Only 57 per cent of Roma children aged 7–15 years attend school and less than half complete secondary schooling (Council of Europe, 2012, p. 118).

In Hungary, Roma children are over-represented in schemes like 'home schooling', where alternative schooling is intermittently provided for them. Hungarian courts have ruled several times in favour of Roma children who have sued the state for educational discrimination because of their placement in special schools. Yet, in Slovakia and the Czech Republic, courts have, up to now, rejected similar claims. In relation to 'inclusion' in mainstream schools, Slovakia and the Czech Republic are using financial incentives for primary schools which enrol children from 'disadvantaged' backgrounds – an oblique reference to the Roma.

Throughout Europe, not just Eastern and Southern Europe, EU member states have taken measures to reform their educational provisions, as part of their overall efforts to improve social provision for Roma. Yet there is evidence that resistance by local government and pressure from mainstream parents has resulted in slow and difficult progress. Strong negative reactions from parents have been reported in Hungary, Slovakia, Greece, Cyprus, Spain and the Czech Republic, in response to an increase in the number of Roma pupils in mainstream schools (Council of Europe, 2012, p. 118).

The significance of subsidiarity

Under the principle of subsidiarity the EU Treaty provides that the European community shall contribute to the development of quality education by supporting and supplementing the actions of member states, while fully respecting their responsibility for the content of teaching, the curriculum, and the organization and management of education systems with their cultural and linguistic diversity.

The European Commission attempts to create a system of inter-state co-operation, yet still preserving state rights with respect to the content and organization of education and training systems. This results in diverse legislation and practice, influenced by traditional educational systems that are slow to transform into a fully integrated and inclusive Europe-wide provision for young people and children.

Alongside general measures for an improvement in practices within EU states, the Commission adopted an Action Plan Against Racism in 1998: an initiative which followed the European Year Against Racism (1997). The Action Plan consisted of mainstreaming the fight against racism by involving sectors such as the employment strategy, the structural funds, education, training and youth. The European Commission has repeatedly highlighted the difficult conditions faced by Roma communities in member states and acceding countries, especially their experience of 'particularly severe forms of exclusion and discrimination in education, employment, housing, healthcare and other areas' (EC, 2005a).

Some significant legal developments affecting the Roma/Travellers are embodied in Article 13 of the Council of the EU Treaty and Directive (2000/43. EC), the Racial Equality Directive, which provides a legal reference point from which to actively address discrimination. However, transposing this directive into national legislation has still to be undertaken in some member states. When this is accomplished, there will be a strong legal framework to combat discrimination on the grounds of race or ethnic origin.

The Lisbon Agenda's stated aims were to address the education and training needs of Europe and particularly the need for social inclusion of marginalized social groups, such as Roma and Travellers, in specific states like the Czech Republic, Hungary and Slovakia. However, the Commission's 2005 report criticizes the Lisbon Agenda for inadvertently marginalizing these groups further by failing to prioritize them:

> There is a very real threat that the nature of EU Lisbon priorities in the field of education, combined with a failure to date to identify racial segregation and other forms of ethnicity-based exclusion as a threat to the realisation of the Lisbon goals, may be resulting in actions that worsen the situation of Roma, as well as others located on the margins of educational systems in Europe. (EC, 2005b, p. 17)

Although Roma and Traveller children are fast expanding groups (Save the Children, 2001, Vol. 2, p. 18), it is seen as essential to assist these groups by prioritizing the educational and vocational training needs of adult Roma and Travellers in addition to their children. The Commission's priorities also extend to parents through the insistence that Traveller/Roma parents need to be identified as an adult group for policy inclusion in the field of lifelong learning.

At present, only seven member states have agreed to include monitoring of the progress in social inclusion of Roma and Travellers in their National Action Plans. The Action Plans for European States are annual reports that provide an update on the implementation of the Lisbon Agenda to Brussels central government agencies and are therefore essential for the future evaluation of the practice of equal educational opportunities.

Socio-economic links

Roma generally experience a weak economic standing in their communities, emanating from difficult access to employment, which may be directly connected to their poor schooling. Social deprivation, segregated housing and poverty, influence directly the educational prospects and opportunities for Roma and Travellers.

In the 1990s, research in Slovakia, Hungary and Romania interpreted the marginalisation of the Roma through inter-ethnic tensions as 'cultural incompatibility', or as 'social deviation'. Cultural interpretations were due to findings which gradually replaced the emphasis on social-economic deprivation and impoverishment of the Roma population (Law, 2009). There appears to be some 'blame' on the Roma for their social behaviour and, their resistance to integration with mainstream society. Yet, it is also recognized that Roma communities have as much of a part to play in seizing the opportunities for integration and inclusion, as do majority societies and governments in providing them.

However, the education system and its effects on these Roma/Traveller groups cannot be separated from the broader context of socio-economic conditions. Government edicts on 'moving on', ownership of land, length of stay in temporary caravan parks, and general denial of equal access to social and educational resources contribute to the struggles, challenges and barriers that the groups regularly face, resulting in their further social marginalization.

Conversely, there are inevitably some tensions which arise through changing lifestyles, in parallel with mainstream economic growth, in the lives of Roma/Travellers. At the present time their lifestyles are altering, as traditional livelihoods are more difficult to maintain. Many communities, who lived according to traditional culture, now find that their young people choose alternative lifestyles and means of economic survival. These changes may involve challenging the directives in some countries, or finding a means of subsistence that is contrary to their customary practices. It is a well-known principle followed by many communities worldwide who fall on hard times.

When newsworthy Roma/Traveller activity is picked up or highlighted by the media, it is erroneously attributed to their ethnic origins, rather than to their instincts for survival, in a difficult economic climate. The Irish Traveller

Movement in Britain (ITM) submitted to the Leveson Enquiry a statement reflecting their uneasiness about the increasingly prejudicial content of press statements and conferences regarding Gypsy, Roma and Traveller criminal investigations. Though Travellers are not a large group in Britain their treatment in the media is very negative. A measure of the real ability of the media to reflect the fact that the UK is a multiracial society is its treatment of Travellers:

> Yet the print media commonly suggest to their readers, in their representations of Travellers, that this category of people routinely display certain negative characteristics not only typical of but essential to the group: that is, they represent Travellers in a stereotypical and prejudicial fashion. The relationship of the representation to the real is the same as it would be for any societal group: some Travellers are dishonest or law-breaking, some don't clean up after themselves.
> (Irish Traveller Movement, 2013)

Hostile media coverage of Gypsies and Travellers has also been acknowledged by the UN Human Rights Council in its Universal Periodic Review of the UK (2008). The Council noted 'that negative and inaccurate reporting by the media has contributed to hostile attitudes towards, in particular, Gypsies and Travellers ...'.

Another recent example is, a Guardian article (Guardian News, 2013) which outlines, how in Romania, when the industrial infrastructure was left to rot, the Roma were quick to spot the potential in scrap metal in what at the time was an unregulated market. New opportunities and changes for the Roma are described as difficult, especially the transition from poverty to relative wealth. It was reported that, like working-class lottery winners, the Roma in one small town (Buzescu) swapped their horse-drawn caravans for fast cars and gaudy, gated mansions adorned with turrets, pillars and marble floors. Parents showered their children with jewellery, flashy clothes and mini motorbikes, challenging the perception of the Roma as poor, rootless people. But behind the 'bling', homes were often sparsely furnished, many rooms were hardly used and older Roma were uneasy in their villas, preferring to use outhouses and outdoor kitchens instead.

Not all Buzescu's Roma were rich: in reality men and, increasingly, women were forced to look for work away from home. In many small towns they are absent and many Roma households contain only the old and the young – grandparents and grandchildren. Schooling was hit-and-miss: parents want sons to earn money as soon as possible, while daughters are expected to stay at home to help raise younger siblings; many are married off as teenagers (Kashinsky, 2013). Media attitudes often unwittingly display a 'them' and 'us' view that challenges the readers to examine their own perspective.

Research

The position of the Roma minority is a common focus of research in the new EU member states, but there is a need to reflect on the fact that the 'Roma' as an ethnic group is a construction of mainstream societies, whereas to the Roma the term represents a heterogeneous social group sharing various sub-identities.

There is increasing research interest in challenging the conventional use of ethnic categories through exploration of diversity within and between ethnic communities, as society is becoming more diverse due to changing patterns of migration and global access. The EC (2005b) reports:

> Although some Member States do monitor educational achievement by ethnic group, this is not yet common and achievement among Roma, Gypsy and Traveller communities is currently very low across the EU-25. This is due in large part to the segregation of Roma and majority population failure to provide adequately for Traveller children. Where Roma children are included within mainstream schools, these are often poorly provided for, or become 'ghettoised'. (p. 1)

Important gaps exist between research and policymaking. Lack of appropriate data on ethnicity, and evidence on patterns of racial and ethnic discrimination, partly inhibits the construction of anti-discrimination educational agendas. Moreover, new EU member states deal with a related problem – the lack of reliable data regarding welfare policies and their impact on Roma families.

The theme of welfare policies and, more generally, of the relations between minority groups and the welfare state is well identified in the Scandinavian context, particularly regarding the strategies of migrants coming from non-EU countries to Denmark and Sweden. But a notorious lack of evidence on segregation and education is noticeable across countries. France, for example, lacks qualitative research about schools in problematic areas with an explicit focus on the role that ethnicity plays both in external social labelling and in the operation of inter-subjective perceptions and experiences.

Despite the differences between states and their research traditions, there are common questions that are perceived as under-investigated issues. In new EU member states, it is evident that there is deficit in the research of the impact of social and education policy on new and itinerant minorities. In old EU-member states, this area has been investigated in much broader scope. However, it is obvious that the integration of minority groups and reproduction of inequalities are influenced and structured on many levels that intersect with each other. Nevertheless, there is no generally accepted and appropriate methodological perspective taking this complexity into account. Studies dedicated to migration, integration and inter-community relations in the European context would benefit from greater inter-disciplinary work. The necessity of multi-methodological, cross-national analysis is explicitly identified, because of a lack of symmetry in the categorization of ethnicity and systems of data collection and analysis across European countries (Law et al., 2009).

Roma/Traveller education and the European response

Generally, the establishment of ethnic minority rights, and multiculturalism as a normative principle, has not gained ground in the Eastern part of Europe. In Western European countries, on the other hand, there is a certain disillusionment regarding the value of diversity and a backlash in terms of tolerance. Old and deeply ingrained biases regarding immigrants have surfaced, which significantly coalesce with prejudices against Roma, the largest indigenous minority in Central and Eastern Europe. This kind of excessive concern about cultural difference, diverting attention from actual social problems, affects, in particular, radicalized minorities, like politically active Roma and Traveller groups that are now seen as a major challenge for integration. In parallel to the policy responses, stereotypes about ethnic minorities are re-introduced, largely owing to the media but also to social conditions (Guardian, 2011). Resulting images suggest that the groups portrayed are reluctant, or unable, to integrate in society, particularly the education system, or to conform to social norms in general, mainly because they are too much tied by inadequate traditions, customs and habits. Socially excluded and marginalized minorities are portrayed as backward and perverse and, therefore, impossible to manage. The structural reasons for the failure of social inclusion and anti-discrimination policies remain concealed: the blame lies on the victims. In this interpretation, the responsibility of the state consists in disciplining minorities by the adoption of tougher regulations and by the introduction of policing methods in order to control them.

In 2008, a research report commissioned by the EU claimed that only about 30–40 per cent of Roma/Traveller children attended school on a relatively regular basis, while half of them had never attended school at all. Furthermore, the report noted that illiteracy rates among the Roma/Traveller groups were very high, ranging from 50 to 100 per cent. It also concluded that there was a persistence of stereotypes, discrimination and the exclusion of the Roma, from higher education and decision-making positions, which resulted in a waste of talents and a denial of equal opportunities' (ECOTEC, 2008).

In order to tackle the persistent educational problems of the Roma/Traveller students, various policies and initiatives have been put in place by national governments and international organizations, such as the Organisation for Security and Co-operation in Europe (OSCE), the EU and the Council of Europe. The latter has worked to draw the attention of European governments to issues related to the Roma/Travellers, including their education (usually in combination with training and labour market access). It has issued various recommendations, most notably a recommendation that special classes should be provided in order to foster the integration of Roma/Traveller pupils into mainstream schooling. Recommendation 17 (2001) stressed the need to improve the economic and employment situation of Roma/Travellers in Europe. More recently, the Committee of Ministers linked these same areas by recognizing that housing and broader living conditions affect educational attainment (Council of Europe, 2001). This led to Recommendation 4 (Council of Europe, 2005), which urged member states to work towards the improvement of the housing conditions of the Roma/Travellers in Europe.

In December 2007, the Council of Europe sought to promote integration in the labour market and, in concert with the spirit of the 'European Year of Equal Opportunities for All', invited member states to work towards the prevention and tackling of discrimination inside and outside the EU labour market. Furthermore, it made specific reference to the Roma situation and appealed to member states to improve their inclusion. In the same document (Conclusion 50), the Council requested the European Commission 'to examine existing policies and instruments and to report to the Council on progress achieved before the end of June 2008' (European Parliament, 2007).

The aforementioned document has crucial implications for the Roma/ Travellers in Europe, given its aim to advance education as a means of social inclusion. More specifically, it sought to promote efficiency and equity in education and training and it invited member states 'to ensure the efficient targeting of education and training reforms and investment to improve quality and equity, particularly by focusing on pre-primary education, early intervention programmes and equitable education and training systems' (EC, 2008, p. 1).

Informal education

Roma/Travellers are naturally wary and suspicious of institutional power. They genuinely struggle to find the benefits to them of 'state' education in different countries. Traditionally, they educate their children in preparation for the perpetuation of their own lifestyle. Therefore, the majority accept only a limited amount of state-based education, that is, the basic education offered to their families, especially elementary literacy and numeracy, which can be beneficial to them in the perpetuation of their lifestyle. Consequently, primary schooling is more often better attended than secondary level. Occasionally specific individuals, who are often settled Travellers, opt for as full an education as possible, and they are among the few people who succeed in (mainstream) professional and business careers.

Informally, parents involve their families in trading and other schemes for acquiring money from an early age. Everyone who is capable, regardless of age, is included in trading and traditional work. There is no formal means of acquiring skills and practices that are passed on from generation to generation, except observation, repetition and modelling. For example, for most show and fairground people, schooling is seen as an indulgence. A child's education is at the fair, handling money, mending machines and on the road learning directions and distances between towns. A six-year-old child can change a £20 or €20 note, but may not be able to read and write. Yet, life is changing: teenagers are more likely to go to secondary school and university, but suspicion still lingers about the worth of going to school (Festing, 2013).

Traditional Roma/Traveller language is not willingly shared with *Gorgas* (outsiders) and is preserved as a means of communicating among different Traveller groups. All Roma/Traveller family members contribute to the upbringing of children. Brothers and sisters look after younger siblings, and the wider family network is seen as indistinguishable from the nuclear group as regards childcare. Traditional Roma culture continues to be strong. However, well-researched accounts of young people who escape the family's traditional ways are chronicled in newspaper and magazine articles (Ratcliffe, 2012).

The situation for Roma/Travellers is paradoxical because it appears that the state institutions are making efforts on their behalf to provide 'educational' resources, but on the other hand the Roma/Traveller groups do not want or necessarily need what is being offered to them. Provision is not negotiated with them to fit with their needs, language and culture. As a consequence, they are becoming more marginalized by the offerings of various state institutions that exist in member states. However, recognized state organizations repeatedly lament the lack of take-up by these marginalized groups and regularly commission expensive research into the reasons for low educational attainment in Roma/Traveller communities. Perhaps this excessive funding would be better spent on helping Roma to educate their own communities. It seems that the commissioning agents do not always see the contradiction faced by Roma/ Traveller communities, who feel that their lifestyle and culture are under threat and need to have their traditions and way of life recognized, respected and valued. If this happened, there might then be an increase in the take-up of educational and employment opportunities offered to them.

What the communities want is family-centred, self-directed education related to their tradition, culture and lifestyle. Yet what they get, in most countries, is a fixed curriculum with little flexibility and inappropriate curriculum content. They receive 'family unfriendly' school organization, and a school programme unsuitable for their future lifestyle, along with restrictions on clothing, homework deadlines and constraints on their freedom to travel.

Future action

In a recent report, the European Parliament recognized that the school situation of Roma in many countries had not improved adequately and it invited the European Commission to devise a comprehensive European Roma strategy to tackle their disadvantaged situation. According to the report (EC, 2008), improving the education of Roma children and young people is of paramount importance for enhancing Roma participation in the labour market, which echoes the recent recommendations to the member states by the Council of Europe discussed earlier. To this end, the updated strategic framework for European co-operation in education and training is 'an essential part of Europe's strategy to meet future challenges ... and to deliver the high levels of sustainable, knowledge-based growth and jobs that are at the heart of the Lisbon strategy' (EC, 2008, p. 3). The document is manifestly permeated by the inclusive approach that is advocated by the EU, as it stresses the role of education (and training) in enabling European citizens, 'irrespective of age, gender and socio-economic background, to acquire, update and develop, over a lifetime, both job-specific skills and the key competences' (p. 10). More importantly, though, it highlights the significance of pre-primary education and targeted support in tackling educational disadvantage, and the need for these to be combined with carefully managed inclusion in mainstream education and training.

It is also worth noting another initiative with emphasis on inclusion, namely the 'Decade of Roma Inclusion 2005–2015'. This is 'an international initiative that brings together governments, intergovernmental and non-governmental organizations, as well as Roma civil society, to accelerate progress toward improving the welfare of Roma'. At the moment it involves 11 Eastern and Southern European countries, and it has, as its remit, to 'improve the socio-economic status and social inclusion of Roma/Traveller communities within a regional framework', with a special focus on education, employment, health and housing (World Bank, 2013. Decade of Roma Inclusion 2005–2015).

However, George Soros has expressed concern about the effect of EU bureaucratic procedures on this initiative:

> The EU also needs to improve the absorption of the funds it has made available for Roma. Those who most need the money allocated under the European Social Fund and the European Regional Development Fund are least able to access it because the Commission's procedures are so unwieldy. (Soros, 2010)

Conclusion

The value of diversity is currently being debated in every EU country, although there is a widespread backlash to the values of tolerance. At the same time the rhetoric of equality is evident in social inclusion and non-discrimination interventions, yet they have failed to deliver significant reductions in inequalities and sustained political recognition of minority rights. Education has been a key battleground in which mainstream and minority claims and positions have been articulated and used in political struggles and policy debates. Beneath the politics of race and ethnicity, minority groups like, Roma/Traveller communities have drawn creatively on their cultural distinctiveness and identity to formulate distinct responses to these circumstances.

In parallel with this struggle, elite institutions in society use their power to perpetuate misconceptions about Roma/Travellers in different EU states. They continuously declare that they are offering provisions that are not taken up, without acknowledging that the educational provisions offered are not necessarily appropriate or suitable. This chapter has shown that schooling is often meagre and inappropriate and not tailored to the needs of the communities targeted. Until Roma/Travellers are given over the right to identify their own educational needs and a more democratic role in their procedures, methods and management of education, they will continue to be discounted in educational statistics and blamed for the consequences of a low level of educational attainment.

Further reading

L Járóka – European Education. (2007), – ME Sharpe.

Roma education on the agenda of the European Union.

The Roma community of Europe continues to face discrimination in a number of areas, notably education, employment, healthcare and housing. In an increasingly knowledge-based economy, education provides one of the primary tools for escaping the cycle of deprivation and poverty.

EH Orsos, K Bohn, G Fleck, and A Imre. (2001), – ERIC.

Alternative Schools and Roma Education: A Review of Alternative Secondary School Models for the Education of Roma Children in Hungary. World Bank.

Abstract: In recent years, a number of experiments have been undertaken in Hungary with alternative approaches to secondary school education for Roma children. This report examines six different institutions that have attempted to help Roma children make the idea of inclusive education a reality.

K Igarashi – Intercultural education, (2005), – Taylor & Francis.

Support programmes for Roma children: do they help or promote exclusion?

This article critically examines current education programmes for Roma primary school students in the Czech Republic and the impact of these programmes. The research described here, based on in-depth case studies, challenges popular beliefs in the general educational world.

G Kertesi and G Kézdi – Roma Education Fund. (2006), – researchgate.net.

Expected long-term budgetary benefits to Roma education in Hungary.

The vast majority of today's young Hungarian Roma drop out of the schooling system without a secondary school degree, and a negligible fraction goes to college. At the same time, the vast majority of non-Roma Hungarians completes secondary school, and 50 per cent go to special schools.

C Cahn, D Chirico, and C McDonald.. – Roma ... (1998), – opensocietyfoundations.org.

Roma in the educational systems of Central and Eastern Europe.

The Roma Education Resource Book Historical background: how did they treat Gypsy children's schooling? The relation between the Roma people and the non-Romani educational systems has historically been troubled. In the view of many Roma, school is the place where Romani children, stolen by the state, are turned into gadje (non-Roma).

References

Advisory Committee on the Framework Convention for the Protection of National Minorities (ACFC). (2006), *Commentary on Education under the Framework Convention for the Protection of National Minorities, ACFC/25 DOC (2006) 002].* Strasbourg: Council of Europe, ACFC.

BBC News. (2010), 'EU nations and Roma repatriation', *BBC News, Europe,* 17th September.

Central Advisory Council for Education (England). (1967), *Children and their Primary Schools (the Plowden Report).* London: Her Majesty's Stationery Office.

Council of Europe. (1993), *ETS no. 001 – Statute of the Council of Europe.* Retrieved from http:// conventions.coe.int/Treaty/en/Treaties/Html/001.htm.

———. (2001), *Recommendation Rec (2001) 17 on 'Improving the Economic and Employment Situation of Roma/Gypsies and Travellers in Europe'.* (Adopted by the Committee of Ministers on 27 November 2001, at the 774th meeting of the Ministers' Deputies). Strasbourg: Council of Europe.

———. (2005), *Recommendation Rec (2005) 4 of the Committee of Ministers to Member States on 'Improving the Housing Conditions of Roma and Travellers in Europe'.* (Adopted by the Committee of Ministers on 23 February 2005 at the 916th meeting of the Ministers' Deputies). Strasbourg: Council of Europe.

———. (2012), *Human Rights of Roma and Travellers in Europe.* Strasbourg: Council of Europe Publications. Retrieved from http://www.conventions.coe.int/Treaty/en/Treaties/Html/001.htm 3.

Council of the European Union. (2000), 'Council Directive 2000/43/EC of 29 June 2000 implementing the principle of equal treatment between persons irrespective of racial or ethnic origin', *Official Journal,* L 180, 19/07/2000, 0022–0026.

Department for Education (DFE). (2012), *Gypsy, Roma and Traveller Achievement.* General Article, updated 14th November 2012. Retrieved from http://www.education.gov.uk/schools/pupilsupport/ inclusionandlearnersupport/mea/improvingachievement/a0012528/gypsy,-roma-and-traveller-achievement.

ECOTEC Research and Consulting. (2008), *A Final Report to the Directorate General for Education and Culture of the European Commission.* Contract number: 2006-2300/001-001EDU-ETU. Birmingham, UK: ECOTEC.

European Commission (EC). (2005a), *Equality and Non-discrimination in an Enlarged EU.* Green Paper 1st June. Brussels: EC.

———. (2005b), *Report on The Situation of Roma in an Enlarged European Union.* Brussels: EC.

———. (2008), *Education and Training Migrant children and Education: Challenges and Opportunities for EU Education Systems.* Europa 18.06.2010, posted 3 July.

European Commission Against Racism and Intolerance (ECRI). (2011), *General Policy Recommendation no.13 on 'Combatting anti-Gypsism and Discrimination against Roma'.* Adopted 24 June. Welwyn Garden City, UK: ECRI Institute.

European Monitoring Centre on Racism and Xenophobia (EUMC). (2006), *Roma and Travellers in Public Education – Executive Summary.* Vienna: EUMC.

European Parliament. (2007), *Decision No 771/2006/EC of the European Parliament and of the Council of 17 May 2006 Establishing the European Year of Equal Opportunities for All (2007) – Towards a Just Society.* Brussels: European Parliament.

Festing, S. (2013), *Showmen: The Voice of Travelling Fair People*. Donington, Lincs: Shaun Tyas.

The Former Yugoslav Republic of Macedonia (FYROM). (2007), *The Former Yugoslav Republic of Macedonia, Progress Report*. Brussels: EC.

Gimenez, J. (2010), 'International action to prevent discrimination: The situation of the Roma community in the field of education', *European Diversity and Autonomy Papers*. Giminez J EDAP paper 03/2010.

The Guardian. (2011), 'Dale farm evictions' (editorial), *The Guardian*, 30 August.

———. (2013), 'Dale farm evictions'. Retrieved from http://www.theguardian.com/uk/dale-farm. Dale farm evictions (Dale Farm evictions 2013, www.Guardiannews).

Institute of Public Policy Research (IPPR). (2006), *EU Enlargement: Bulgaria and Romania – migration implications for the UK (Factfile)*. London: IPPR.

———. (2011), *EU Enlargement and Labour Migration (Factfile)*. London: IPPR.

Irish Traveller Movement in Britain. (2013), *Submission by the Irish Traveller Movement in Britain to the Leveson Inquiry: Gypsies and Travellers in the Press*. London: The Resource Centre.

Kashinsky, I. (2013), 'Big picture: The wealthy Roma of Buzescu', *The Guardian*, 15 February.

Kjaerum, M.. (2013), *Exclusion and Discrimination in Education; the Case of Roma in the European Union*. Speech made on 8 April at Harvard University. Brussels: European Agency for Fundamental Rights.

Law, I. (2009), 'Roma in a comparative analysis of ethnic relations', in EDUMIGROM (ed.), *Ethnicity: Comparing Inter-ethnic Relations and Categorisation*. London: Routledge, pp. 3–20.

Law, I., Nekorjak, M., Daniel, O., and Vajda, R. (2009), *Comparative Analysis of Ethnic Relations*. Budapest, Hungary: Centre for Policy Studies.

MORI Poll. (2001), Commissioned by Stonewall 'Citizenship 21: Briefing notes on Profiles and Prejudice'(2001). Retrieved from http://www.mori.com/polls/2001/stonewall-b2.shtml.

O'Hanlon C. (2010), 'Whose education? The inclusion of Gypsy/Travellers: Continuing culture and tradition through the right to choose educational opportunities to support their social and economic mobility', *Compare, A Journal of Comparative and International Education*, 40, (2), 239–255.

Ratcliffe, R. (2012), 'They need an education', *The Guardian*, 13 November, p. 12.

Save the Children. (2001), *Denied a Future*. London: Save the Children.

Soros, G. (2010), *George Soros Speech at the Second Roma Summit*. Cordoba, 8–9 April. Retrieved from http://ec.europa.eu/social/main.jsp?catId=88&langId=en&eventsId=234&furtherEvents=yes.

Tanner, A. (2004), 'The Roma of Ukraine and Belarus', in A. Tanner (ed.), *The Forgotten Minorities of Eastern Europe: The History and Today of Selected Ethnic Groups in Five Countries*. Helsinki: East-West Books.

Thorpe, N. (2007), 'Roma welcome anti-segregation ruling', *BBC News, Budapest*, 16 November.

UNESCO. (2006), *Education for All: Literacy for Life, Global Monitoring Report*. Paris: UNESCO.

UNESCO and Council of Europe. (2007), *Towards Quality Education for Roma children: Transition from early childhood to Primary education. Final Report*. Paris And Strasbourg: UNESCO and Council of Europe.

UNICEF. (2007), *Breaking the Cycle of Exclusion: Roma children*. Belgrade: UNICEF.

United Nations Development Programme. (2011), *Sustainability and Equity: A Better Future for All.* Retrieved from http://hdr.undp.org/en/reports/global/hdr2011/.

World Bank. (2013), *Roma-the Decade of Roma Inclusion 2005–2015.* Washington, DC: World Bank.

Zanker, F. (2010), 'Integration as conflict prevention: Possibilities and limitations in the experience of the OSCE high commissioner on national minorities', *Security and Human Rights*, 21, (3), 220–232.

Education and 'Orang Asli' in Malaysia: A Country Case Study

6

Hema Letchamanan and Firdaus Ramli

Chapter Outline

Introduction

The Orang Asli (OA) are the indigenous minority peoples of Peninsular Malaysia, which means 'original peoples' or 'first peoples'. There are at least 18 culturally and linguistically distinct ethnic groups of OA. The OA continue to suffer from poverty and low levels of education in Malaysia. Education for OA remains a priority for many parties concerned, including the Ministry of Education, the Department of Orang Asli Affairs, various non-governmental organizations (NGOs), individuals working with and for OA, and OA themselves. In most cases, however, OA voices are not heard. A huge gap exists in terms of access to schools and educational attainment for OA children, compared to non-OA children, in this country. Many studies in the past have reported the poor education rate of OA children in Malaysia (see, for example, Kamarulzaman and Osman, 2008; Mohd Asri, 2012).

This chapter discusses the education situation of OA children at present, details the programmes and benefits available for them and finally reviews whether all these are relevant for the children concerned, and most importantly whether these correspond to their educational needs. Perhaps it is best to begin by clarifying a few misconceptions about the OA. They no longer live a nomadic life. Traditionally, they were engaged in hunting and gathering, but there has been a drastic change in their way of life. The forest environment has changed and the government's policies favour settled farming and agriculture. In recent days, the OA are mainly involved in rubber tapping, and in tea or oil palm plantations as paid labourers and as factory workers (Nobuta, 2007). The OA comprise eighteen tribes which are categorized into three groups: Semang (or Negrito), Senoi and Proto-Malay (Nicholas, 2005). 'Orang Asli' is a Malay language phrase which means original people. Article 160 of the Constitution of Malaysia defines 'aborigines' as an aborigine of the Malay Peninsula, and makes the distinction with 'natives' in Article 161a as citizens of Sabah and Sarawak (the two states in East Malaysia) and belong to one of the races classified as indigenous by the Constitution. Therefore to avoid confusion, only the term 'Orang Asli' (OA) is used throughout this chapter. OA can be categorized into three groups according to settlement pattern: the ones who still live in remote forest areas, those in rural areas (OA settlement in villages, not integrated with other villagers) and those in townships (integrated with other communities) (Mason and Arifin, 2005). Specific examples of these would be in Ulu Tembeling and Grik (forest areas); Janda Baik, Cameron Highlands, Gombak and Tapah (OA settlement in villages); and Bukit Lanjan (a township). It is important to be clear about these geographical differences because each group possesses different characteristics, and educational needs, therefore requiring different responses to those needs.

Education programmes and challenges

All issues and affairs of OA in Malaysia are placed under the responsibility of the Department of Orang Asli Development. It serves as the centre of action on all matters relating to OA. The history of this department began with the enactment of the Perak Enactment Aboriginal Tribes Act, in December 1939, by appointing a field ethnographer who acted as Protector of Aborigines in the state. The establishment of this department at the national level began in 1954 when the Department of Orang Asli was established under the Aboriginal

People Ordinance Act. During the formation of Malaysia on 16 September 1963, the name 'Department of Aboriginal' was changed to the 'Department of Aboriginal Affairs' (JHEOA). This department's name was changed again in 2010 by the prime minister to the 'Department of Orang Asli Development'. (However, the abbreviation JHEOA continues to be used.)

In general, the function of the Department of Orang Asli Development is to protect OA and their way of life from the rapid development of civilization and exploitation outside the community as well as to provide facilities and support education, health and socio-economic development. In keeping with the change of name in 2010, its role has been broadened towards progressive and dynamic development in the OA community in line with the vision of the department. A Mind Development and Education Division was formed in this department to coordinate all programmes that are related to the education affairs of OA. The programmes under this division can be divided into two components: Education Development and Mind Development.

OA community education development is implemented through three levels, namely higher education, secondary and primary, and pre-school. For the higher education level, several initiatives have been taken by the department to improve performance by OA students. One of them is by offering scholarships to those students who have successfully obtained a place in a higher education institution to pursue a bachelor's degree or a diploma. According to statistics issued by the department in 2010, a total of 367 OA students have joined higher education institutions in the country (see Table 6.1). This number is projected to continue to increase based on performance and education assistance given by the government.

In line with rapid development in technology and communications, the government has also provided computer support to the OA students at the tertiary level to help them in their studies. In addition, the department also monitors the progress of these students through a series of discussions with

Table 6.1 OA students in higher education

No	Level	Students	Graduates
1	Matriculation/Foundation	3	3
2	Certificate	7	15
3	Diploma	130	37
4	Bachelor	226	42
	Total	367	97

Source: JAKOA Annual Report (2010).

representatives of higher education institutions to obtain information on their participation and performance level at each institution of higher learning. At the school level, the department has planned and implemented several programmes that aim to improve student performance, especially in secondary schools. The department has launched the Excellence Student Programme which focuses on student motivation and self-reliance in achieving success in the exam. In addition to motivational talks, students are also exposed to academic training. Score 'A' Programme was also conducted in order to assist students taking the exam to get an A in all subjects.

The department, aware of the high rate of student dropout in the current education system, has introduced a learner-friendly programme that aims to raise awareness among OA students to complete schooling up to the secondary level. As an incentive for them to achieve excellent results, the department also recognizes students who have obtained good results in examinations by giving awards. All these are done by the Department of Orang Asli Development to increase the motivation level of OA students to strive harder in their studies. The government is also aware of the importance of pre-school especially for OA children. A pre-school programme has been introduced to foster their interest in education as well as to help reduce the dropout problem among them. The pre-school programme is also important for a smooth transition to Primary 1, mainly because students learn to speak the Malay language and learn to read and write in pre-primary classes. However, in most cases, the children do not attend these classes, and this is reflected in their slower progress in speaking, reading and writing the Malay language in primary school (Wong and Christopher, 2012).

The government is also concerned with the development of the mind among the OA community in Malaysia. Activities have been conducted to prepare them towards excellence in achievement. In addition to academic programmes, social activities could also stimulate students' minds to achieve success in their life. Sports programmes have been organized by the department to promote healthy living among students and to identify the potential that exists in these students. One such programme is the Mind Inspire Course, held to change the perception and attitude of OA students to work hard in schools (Abdul Razaq and Zalizan, 2009).

Vocational education is an important aspect, if not the most important, for OA students. For many of them, studying and competing against other students in the mainstream education prove to be a struggle. Hence, the government recognizes the importance of vocational education for them and has organized several trainings for those who have less interest in the academic field. According to Marina et al. (2009), many OA students show interest in vocational training and express their interest to pursue upper secondary level in vocational or technical schools. Compared to formal academics, vocational skill is seen as a valuable knowledge that is related to their daily life besides helping them to earn income. The students have also been exposed to high levels of skill in such areas as automotive engine construction as a platform to produce skilled workforce among OA youth. The Skill Development Fund is maintained by the government to provide financial assistance to poor students in various vocational institutions, both private and public (Kamarulzaman and Osman, 2008).

There are several agencies such as SUHAKAM (the National Human Rights Commission of Malaysia) and the Malaysian Orang Asli Foundation that contribute to the development of education in the OA community. In the case of SUHAKAM, for instance, this organization makes efforts to close the educational achievement gap between OA and children from other communities. This is followed by the campaign launched by SUHAKAM to create awareness on the importance of education among OA parents. SUHAKAM hopes that through this programme, the OA community can contribute their views towards improving the quality of education of OA children in line with their cultural background and way of life (SUHAKAM, 2013). The Peninsular Malaysia OA Graduate Association is an organization which consists of graduate students from the OA community. It organizes many programmes to assist OA students to complete their studies both at lower and higher education levels. Many workshops and motivational talks are held to improve the OA children's performance, and to reduce the high number of dropouts (Peninsular Malaysia Orang Asli Graduate Association, 2009). This organization also introduces some of its members to the OA children as a role model in order to inspire them to enter higher education institutions. The organization has worked closely with the Ministry of Education in order to provide input to the government especially in formulating policies for OA education.

The Malaysian Orang Asli Foundation is another organization that deals with OA in Malaysia. Similar to the organization mentioned above, this NGO was formed in January 2012 with the objective of assisting OA in various areas including education. The mission of this organization is to improve and increase the standard of living among OA through education development (Malaysian Orang Asli Foundation, 2012). Several programmes have been implemented in order to achieve their mission. Interestingly, this organization has involved the national leaders and government officials in their activities in order to ensure the effectiveness of their programmes. This will help to build a positive perception among OA that the government does not neglect them in the national agenda.

According to Ikram (1997), the educational programmes managed by JHEOA were a major failure because JHEOA's field staff were not formally trained and most of them had a low level of education themselves. This led to a negative impact on the educational programmes in the OA community because all the programmes were run by JHEOA. The situation worsened because JHEOA itself had limited financial capacity to maintain all the OA schools. The Malaysian government has made an effort to overcome this problem by launching a policy that allocates special help to provide opportunities for OA to be educated on an equal footing, integrating them with the advanced section of the population and protecting their traditional beliefs (Ministry of Education, 2006). Furthermore, in 1995, the government gave the authority of governing OA schools to the Ministry of Education. Thus, under a Memorandum of Understanding (MOU) signed by the Ministry of Education and JHEOA, the ministry took over the administration of all OA schools again, a situation that continues today (Mohd Asri, 2012). The problem, however, does not end with the transferring of OA schools to the ministry. This is because the Malay teachers supplied by the ministry at the central primary schools lack knowledge of the OA culture and tradition (Asian Indigenous and Tribal Peoples Network, 2008). This may lead to conflicts between teacher and students, as happened in Gua Musang, Kelantan (MalaysiaKini, 12 December, 2012). In this situation, the teacher was criticized for not being committed to his duty because of his failure to conduct the class. The teacher, however, claimed that the OA children were not interested in learning, whereas the parents said the opposite.

The high level of dropout among OA children is also another challenge for the government in its attempts to improve OA's educational performance. Even though the number of OA children entering school increases, the dropout rate among them is still high (Mohd Asri, 2012). From the data available, it is stated that the dropout rate of OA children at the primary level was 39.1 per cent in 2008 and had significantly reduced to 29 per cent in 2010 and 26 per cent in 2011. The ministry has set a target to reduce this to 15 per cent by 2015. There are a number of factors that contribute to this problem, as highlighted by Mohd Asri (2012), such as culture, school location, poverty and pedagogy.

Therefore, it is suggested that the JHEOA and ministry cooperate with the various NGOs who are already actively working with and for the OA community in order to ensure that the number of students dropping out can be reduced in the near future.

Educational needs and responses

It is imperative to study the educational needs of any child concerned when analysing the effectiveness and relevance of education programmes implemented for them (Letchamanan, 2010, 2013). In many instances, the programmes are designed and carried out without taking into consideration what the child and the parents really desire or need. OA are unique in the sense that they are not a homogenous social group. They have diverse cultures, traditions and beliefs, which they closely uphold (Nicholas, 2006). To study the educational needs of these children and the responses to those needs, we based them against Maslow's hierarchy of needs (Maslow, 1954). Maslow's original five-stage model has been extensively used in understanding human motivation, management training and personal development. Although this theory is not without its criticisms, and has been much debated with regard to the ranking of needs and the existence of a definite hierarchy (Hofstede, 1984; Wahba and Bridwell, 1976), we believe it is still valid and relevant to apply this model in understanding and discussing the educational needs of OA children. Maslow's hierarchy of needs is used because one of the main causes of the limited transfer of students from primary to secondary education and their limited completion of schooling is thought to be their motivational level. Many factors affect their motivation to attend schooling: poverty, lack of transportation and other basic necessities, a different learning culture and a language barrier that impedes teaching and learning (Johari and Nazri, 2007; John and Sabaratnam, 13 February 2002; Karubi et al., 2011; Wong and Christopher, 2012). All these factors can be found on Maslow's hierarchy of needs and we believe that if these various needs are met, OA children will have the motivation to attend and complete schooling, and perhaps even continue and complete tertiary education.

The first, or rather the basis of Maslow's hierarchy, is biological and physiological needs which include food, water and shelter. The Ministry of Education, through its food aid programme for poor students in the country (all OA children attending included), gives free breakfast daily. In some instances, this does motivate the children to attend school. But the question that lies therein is whether the students go to school for the food or to acquire knowledge.

The second stage in Maslow's hierarchy of needs is safety. OA students have to feel safe and protected in their school environment. The distance between home and school is one of the main reasons for the high rate of absenteeism (Johari and Nazri, 2007). Although JHEOA provides transportation for these students, they have to leave as early as 5.30 am in order to reach school on time due to the distance. It is therefore questionable, in terms of commitment by the students and their parents, whether safety needs are being met (Wong and Christopher, 2012). And in some instances the transportation provided is unreliable.

Belongingness and love needs constitute the third level on the hierarchy. It is important that students feel they are part of the school culture, for them to be motivated to continue attending school as there is a higher chance of them dropping out if they could not relate themselves to the curriculum taught, the teachers or other students. Karubi et al. (2011) explain that OA children learn differently from other children, as they learn using their tribal language, arts, ritual, folklore and taboos which have neither a fixed syllabus nor a standardized timetable. Abdull et al. (2011) in examining a similar issue found that the majority of OA students have problem in reading the Malay language, which is the language of instruction in all public schools in Malaysia. Hence, there is every chance for the student to not be able to relate to what is happening in school. Given the cultural and lifestyle difference, the question then arises, is schooling relevant for these children? If so, who decides what is relevant, and not? Also, not all teachers understand these differences: a factor which could possibly lead to teaching and learning not being tailor-made to meet the needs of these children. Johari and Nazri (2007), realizing the importance of this, suggested that experienced teachers who know and understand the cultural and learning-style differences are important for improving the students' academic performance. OA students also tend to remain together and not mingle with other students (personal communication, 2012). All these factors cause the students to not feel they belong in a school environment and affect their motivation to return to school.

The fourth level in this hierarchy is esteem needs. It is important for any society to feel empowered and self-worthy. The OA community over the years has mostly remained quiet, with little visibility in public affairs. Although there is an elected senator in the parliament as a representative of this community, the OA voice is minimal when compared to other communities. The OA have not been very much involved in nation building and may, therefore, lack a sense of civic achievement. There is no legacy of education for these students and this is reflected in the learning attitude among them. In most cases, the children are not given responsibilities that could motivate them in and out of school. Only with a higher self-esteem will OA children be interested and motivated to attend and complete schooling, as they could then see beyond the day-to-day living, and prepare themselves for the future, so that they are not trapped in the vicious cycle of low-paid and insecure employment as their parents have been.

When all these aforementioned needs are met, there will be self-actualization, the final stage on the hierarchy of needs, according to Maslow. Students can then chart their personal growth and fulfilment. And that is what schools should be for these children: fulfilling. They can be motivated to learn and stay in school only if all the external factors discussed are made available for them, and most importantly in a consistent manner. Changes have to take place, and immediately that is, for there to be self-actualization by the OA students. Once this has been achieved, there is a strong possibility for the whole community to uplift themselves and be at par with the rest of the people in the country.

The way forward

SUHAKAM has used the 4A framework to examine the education issues in the OA community. This framework was developed by Katarina Tomasevski, the former UN Special Rapporteur on the right to education. Under this framework, the education system for the OA will be analysed through the four factors: Availability, Accessibility, Acceptability and Adaptability (SUHAKAM, 2009, p. 5). Availability refers to the policy of free education in the state, complete education infrastructure and the well-trained teacher in school. Accessibility is a non-discriminatory education system which allows every individual to get equal opportunity and facility. Acceptability refers to the appropriate and good quality of content in syllabus and teaching. Adaptability can be seen as the ability of the education system to adapt to the changing needs of society and contribute by challenging inequalities.

Having applied the 4A framework to OA education, it clearly indicates a multiplicity of issues surrounding OA children (SUHAKAM, 2009). The availability factor finds that, among others, poor infrastructure and equipment, and limited financial and other forms of aid, including meals, contribute to the problems in the education of OA children. Even though government, through JHEOA, has implemented many programmes as stated previously, it has still failed to support and provide for the needs of OA children to obtain a better quality of education. Similar issues occur when applying the accessibility criterion, as basic needs such as transportation and personal documents are a major roadblock for OA when trying to have access to better education.

Through the lens of acceptability, it is easy to understand the impact of having inferior school administrators and inexperienced teaching staff. Their inability to relate to the other OA serves to enhance the OA feeling of marginalization. Finally, the adaptability factor helps us to understand the factors that have led to OA being unable to adapt to the national curriculum. A closer analysis reveals that the present curriculum does not completely address the specific needs of the OA. The OA consider the environment to be an integral and contiguous aspect of their life. Any form of education which is intended to reach the OA needs to reflect a close awareness of this. This awareness has compelled the government to formulate a new curriculum, the *Kurikulum Bersepadu Untuk Murid Orang Asli dan Penan* (Integrated Curriculum for Orang Asli and Penan Students) (SUHAKAM, 2009, p. 8).

Following this study of the factors that significantly influence OA education, SUHAKAM has suggested several recommendations to improve the quality of education for OA children. First, the basic needs such as transportation, education equipment, infrastructure, financial aid, trained teacher and meals are crucial prerequisites for OA children in order to motivate them to attend school. Second, the personnel who are involved in administration or who are from the ministry will need to be sensitive towards the needs of the OA. They need to contextualize the welfare of the OA fully to ensure that their plight is given due care. The teachers, whose role is critical, will need to be culturally perceptive and should find common ground to make their experience immersive. The lack of communication between teachers and students has compounded absenteeism as, without buy-in from the teachers, the students do not see the need to remain in school as the benefits are not clear to them. This lack of a world-view and the inability to be future focused are barriers that can only be brought down by the teacher. Specific workshops which focus on the psychological, attitudinal and cultural aspects of OA education will go a long way in closing the 'Us and Them' gap which is prevalent. By doing this, it is expected that the dropout percentage in OA children can be reduced gradually. Future research can also be conducted to study the relationship between communication and percentage of dropout.

The infrastructural needs are the final area that requires immediate resolution. Further fact-finding is required to understand the exact nature of the problem. It does not help that the OA are not situated in homogeneous surroundings. Some groups live in the remote interior while others occupy land in rural townships and there are even those who have moved to the town itself. The needs of this diverse group have to be properly identified, so that any solution would not only be effective and efficient but also cost sensitive.

Some stakeholders are unhappy with the ministry's decision to hybridize the national curriculum by including OA-specific items, as they feel that the other races would make similar demands for individual education needs. The national curriculum should be singularly comprehensive and sufficient for all Malaysians regardless of class and ethnicity. It is not clear if a separate curriculum is the best idea, as it might alienate the OA and they might find it difficult to join the mainstream system later in life. A comparative study analysing the local situation with other indigenous groups, for example those in East Malaysia, may yield certain insights which can prove valuable when trying to determine the best course forward for the OA. The link that the OA have with nature needs is to be respected but at the same time the focus of the curriculum should be seen as transitory with the eventual plan to integrate the OA students into the curriculum proper. Perhaps a better solution for this would be to look at where OA children are at this point of time, and bring education to them in a meaningful way.

To conclude, extensive research should be done on education for OA because there are multiple sides to the issues facing them. Formulating policies and implementing programmes that meet the educational needs of the OA children are important to avoid wastage of human resources and funding and most importantly to solve the immediate problem facing them – the high rate of absenteeism and school dropout. As could be seen from the programmes mentioned earlier in the chapter, most of them are one-off programmes which have a short-term effect on OA children's education. For a sustainable education to take place among OA children, their needs and issues revolving in their community have to be analysed thoroughly. This also means including the community in the decision making, rather than assuming what is good and beneficial for them. JHEOA has to play an active and progressive role in designing and implementing programmes for OA and potentially act as the middle party between this community and the government. If JHEOA is able to play their role effectively, the quality and productivity of OA can be improved, especially in the education field. The students have to see the relevance of attending schools for them to stay on and complete their primary and secondary education, and possibly tertiary education too.

Further reading

Endicott, K. and Dentan, R. K. (2008), 'Into the mainstream or into the backwater – Malaysian assimilation of Orang Asli', in C. R. Duncan (ed.), *Civilizing The Margins – Southeast Asian Government Policies for the Development of Minorities*. Singapore: NUS Press, pp. 24–55.

This chapter gives an insight into the different issues surrounding the Orang Asli community such as education, land rights and poverty. The Orang Asli's ongoing fight on land rights is described in detail for better understanding of the issues faced by this community.

Centre for Orang Asli Concerns. Retrieved from http://www.coac.org.my/beta/.

This website has a host of articles and a list of publications on Orang Asli – from land rights to policies and language issues. It also includes current news on Orang Asli.

References

Abdul Razaq, A. and Zalizan, M. J. (2009), *Masyarakat Orang Asli: Perspektif Pendidikan dan Sosiobudaya*. [Orang Asli Community: Education and Sociocultural Perspective]. Bangi: Penerbit UKM.

Abdull, S. H., Nuraini, Y., Mohd, I. G., and Mohd, H. D. (2011), 'Children of the Orang Asli minority in Malaysia: Achieving the Malay language literacy', *Malay Language Journal of Education*, 1, (2), 59–70.

Asian Indigenous and Tribal Peoples Network. (2008), *The Department of Orang Asli Affairs, Malaysia – An Agency for Assimilation*. New Delhi: Asian Indigenous and Tribal Peoples Network.

Hofstede, G. (1984), 'The cultural relativity of the quality of life concept', *Academy of Management Review*, 9, (3), 389–398. Retrieved from http://www.nyegaards.com/yansafiles/Geert%20 Hofstede%20cultural%20attitudes.pdf on 22 February 2013.

Ikram, J. (1997), *Kenyataan Ketua Pengarah Jabatan Hal Ehwal Orang Asli Malaysia pada Perjumpaan dengan Wakil-Wakil Media Massa pada 31hb Oktober 1997*. [Statement of the Director General of the Department of Orang Asli Affairs Malaysia at a Meeting with Mass Media Representatives on 31 October 1997]. Kuala Lumpur: Jabatan Hal Ehwal Orang Asli.

JAKOA Annual Report. (2010), *Laporan Bahagian Pembangunan Minda dan Pendidikan*. [Report by the Mind Development and Education Division]. Kuala Lumpur: Jabatan Hal Ehwal Orang Asli.

Johari, T. and Nazri, M. (2007), 'Bagaimana Kanak-Kanak Orang Asli Gagal di Sekolah. [How do Orang Asli Children Fail in School]', *Jurnal Pengajian Umum Asia Tenggara*, 8, 51–76.

John, E. and Sabaratnam, S. (2002), 'Addressing Orang Asli education needs'. *New Strait Times*, 13 February 2002. Retrieved from http://news.google.com/newspapers?nid=1309&dat=20020213&id =hEs1AAAAIBAJ&sjid=h3gFAAAAIBAJ&pg=1389,1019280 on 20 January 2013.

Kamarulzaman, K. and Osman, J. (2008), 'Education policy and opportunities of Orang Asli: A study on indigenous people in Malaysia', *The Journal of Human Resource and Adult Learning*, 4, (1), 86–97.

Karubi, N. P., Goy, S. C., and Wong, B. W. K. (2011), *The Temiar and the Invisible Wisdom of Taboo: Survival Strategy and Sustainability*. Proceedings of Regional Conference of Local Knowledge: 'Retracing Tradition for a Sustainable Future', Langkawi, Malaysia.

Letchamanan, H. (2010), *Needs and Responses: A Study of Education for Refugee and Migrant Children in Malaysia*. MSc diss., University of Oxford.

———. (2013), 'The education for refugee and asylum seeking children in Malaysia', in L. P. Symaco (ed.), *Education in South East-Asia*. London: Bloomsbury.

MalaysiaKini. (12 December 2012), *Slapping Case: Orang Asli Kids Get only 3 Days at School*. Retrieved from http://www.freemalaysiakini2.com/?p=59740 on 10 February 2013.

Marina, I. M., Rohayu, R. and Arman, A. S. (2009), *Pendidikan Teknik dan Vokasional Dalam Kalangan Masyarakat Orang Asli* [Technical and Vocational Education among Orang Asli Community]. Universiti Tun Hussein Onn Malaysia: Fakulti Pendidikan Teknikal.

Maslow, A. (1954), *Motivation and Personality*. New York: Harper.

Mason, R. and Arifin, S. M. (2005), 'The "Bumiputera Policy": Dynamics and dilemmas', *Journal of Malaysian Studies*, 21, (1&2), 315–329.

Ministry of Education, Malaysia. (2006), *Pelan Induk Pembangunan Pendidikan 2006–2010* [Education Development Master Plan 2006–2010]. Putrajaya: Ministry of Education.

Mohd Asri, M. N. (2012), 'Advancing the Orang Asli through Malaysia's Clusters of Excellence policy', *Journal of International and Comparative Education*, 1, (2), 90–103.

Nicholas, C. (2005), *Integration and Modernization of the Orang Asli: The impact on culture and identity*. Paper presented at the 1st International Conference on the indigenous People, organized by the Centre for Malaysian Pribumi Studies, University of Malaya, Ministry of Culture, Arts and Heritage, Departments of Museums and Antiquities and he Department of Orang Asli Affairs, 4–5 July, Kuala Lumpur, Malaysia.

———. (2006), *The State of Orang Asli Education and its Root Problems. Orang Asli: Rights, Problems, Solutions*. A consultancy report prepared for the Human Rights Commission of Malaysia (SUHAKAM).

Nobuta, T. (2007), 'Islamization policy toward the Orang Asli in Malaysia', *Bulletin of the National Museum of Ethnology*, 31 (4), 479–495.

Orang Asli Foundation. (2012), *Programme 2012*. Retrieved from http://www.yos.org.my/ on 13 January 2013.

Peninsular Malaysia Orang Asli Graduate Association. (2009), *Aktiviti dan Program 2009*. [Activity and Programme 2009]. Retrieved from http://www.psoa.com.my/ on 13 January 2013.

SUHAKAM. (2009), *Report of the Human Rights Education and Promotion Working Group*. Retrieved from http://www.suhakam.org.my/c/document_library/get_file?p_l_id=10408&folderId=23964&name=DLFE-7714.pdf on 15 December 2012.

———. (2013), *Education – Aborigine Origin Rights*. Retrieved from http://www.suhakam.org.my on 13 January 2013.

Wahba, M. A., and Bridwell, L. G. (1976), 'Maslow reconsidered: A review of research on the need hierarchy theory', *Organizational Behavior and Human Performance*, 15, (2), 212–240.

Wong, B. W. K. and Christopher, P. (2012), *The Issues of Teaching and Learning in the Primary School of Orang Asli: A Case Study of Pos Senderut, Kuala Lipis, Pahang*. Paper Presented at BIMP-EAGA Conference.

Indigenous Groups' Education: The Case of North America

7

Lorenzo Cherubini

*Education is like love, we cannot delegate others
to exercise it on our behalf*

Peter Kelly, Grand Chief of the Ojibway in Ontario
(Miller, 1996, p. 400)

Introduction

Similar to many indigenous peoples around the globe, Aboriginal and American Indian and Alaska Native (AI/AN) students in Canada and the United States of America, respectively, are generally disengaged from the learning curriculum in public schools and are confronted by the lingering colonial racism that permeates their formal education (Bowlby and McMullen, 2002; Pirbhai-Illich, 2010). It is worth noting that Aboriginal peoples, consisting of First Nations, Métis and Inuit, represent nearly 4 per cent of the total population in Canada and hence comprise more than 1.3 million people. Aboriginal students 5 to 14 years of age represent 6.2 per cent of the total Canadian population across the latter cohort, while in the United States more than 5 million AI/AN peoples represent 1.6 per cent of the total population, including the 1 per cent of AI/AN school children represented in the major federal databases (National Caucus of Native American Legislators, 2008).

The indigenous peoples who first inhabited North America (identified as Turtle Island by many Aboriginal and AI/AN tribes) included large confederacies, farming nations and small hunting groups. It is estimated that the multilingual population of Turtle Island prior to European contact was in the range of 20 million people. Indigenous peoples across North America had close relationships with the Creator and relied upon elders and community members to teach traditional and contemporary knowledge to children (Hall, 2007). However, the colonial influences in both Canada and the United States targeted education and focused on assimilating Aboriginal and AI/AN peoples to European world-views. The process of assimilation, in both countries, included the compulsory attendance of Aboriginal and AI/AN students in residential and day schools that were subsidized by the federal governments and administered by the churches (Marker, 2000).

The histories of Aboriginal and AI/AN peoples are different. Their respective educational histories include unique testimonies of colonial rule that are rooted in racist actions. Although it is beyond the scope of this chapter to discuss specific nuances, it is useful to offer a broad synopsis of the social anthropology related to the subject.

In both the Canadian and American contexts, Aboriginal and AI/AN children were taken away from their families and educated according to Eurocentric epistemologies and traditions intended to prepare them for the labour market. Colonial authorities distanced Aboriginal and AI/AN children from what they perceived to be superstitious and uncivilized practices learned in traditional indigenous communities and instead educated and socialized them according to Christian belief systems. Common in both Canadian and American educational histories are residential schools that 'were oriented toward eradicating all aspects of the child's ethnic identity and replacing it with a kind of shadow person, neither Indian nor white, who would renounce their past as a dark time of savagery' (Marker, 2000, p. 80). Aboriginal and AI/AN children who spoke in their native tongue or practised traditional beliefs were often corporally punished and imprisoned. The multiple accounts of deviant clergy who sexually abused Aboriginal and AI/AN children are a testament to the atrocities associated with residential schools across North America.

In Canada, the outcomes of such practices amounting to linguistic and cultural genocide have sapped many Aboriginal peoples of their knowledge of cultures of origin and identities as members of Aboriginal communities. The educational policies of the Canadian colonial government, posited as beneficial interventions to assist Aboriginal learners and communities, have resulted in intergenerational consequences for Aboriginal peoples (Ball, 2004; White and Jacobs, 1988).

There are similar outcomes from the AI/AN perspective. These indigenous communities have been devastated by the more than 500 years of contact with European settlers and have witnessed the deterioration of land, identity and traditional and epistemic practices (Duran and Duran, 1995). Residential schools have had adverse generational consequences across AI/AN communities as they severed traditional learning customs (Evans-Campbell, 2008). Much like the Canadian authorities, US governments decreed policy to rescue the 'noble savage' from inadequate living and learning conditions and to domesticate AI/AN peoples into more civilized ways (Warner and Grint, 2012). As in Canada, education in the United States was considered as the legitimate means to sustain Eurocentric values (Calsoyas, 2005). The educational policies in both countries intended to endorse colonial world-views at the peril of eradicating sophisticated Aboriginal and AI/AN ways of teaching and learning that existed well before Europeans set foot on Turtle Island.

In order to situate contemporary educational priorities for Aboriginal and AI/AN peoples in Canada and the United States, it is beneficial first to provide an overview of their respective communities' world-views, including understandings of education from formal and informal perspectives.

World views and education

There are over 600 First Nations across Canada, and 565 tribes in the United States. It is imperative to recognize that Aboriginal and AI/AN peoples are far from homogeneous in their beliefs, languages, cultures, world-views and educational practices. There can be profound variability in each Aboriginal group in Canada as there are varied dimensions of philosophies, languages, cultures and traditions across AI/AN tribes (see Guèvremont and Kohen, 2012). Nevertheless, a broad overview of beliefs and practices is in order.

Generally, Aboriginal world-views are based on contemporary oral, traditional teachings and espouse the values of respect, reciprocity, relationships and responsibility that foster healthy and robust identities across Aboriginal communities (see Ball, 2004). Oral traditions are common among Aboriginal peoples to effectively transmit core world-views. These ideologies frequently share authentic interconnection between all living things (Brill de Ramirez, 1999). Oral traditions and teaching methods can be described as conversive because their focus rests upon the interrelationship and interconnectedness of the elements across the entire universe (Christensen and Poupart, 2012).

Moreover, AI/AN world-views are also founded on certain collective identities of various tribes. Tribal identity is based on indigenous people's land (Warner and Grint, 2012). Elders imparted beliefs and traditional knowledge directly associated with specific places and sacred sites to younger generations of AI/ANs. AI/AN world-views include knowledge about human inspiration, various Deities and Nature itself. Concepts related to the sacred unity that humans share with Nature and the significance of humility in light of one's eternal being are integral to AI/AN world-views. Individuals have special relationships with the universe; hence, AI/AN world-views honour individuals' compatibility with Nature and living perspectives that are spiritually grounded and characteristic of peace and humility (Calsoyas, 2005).

Self-education

The emphasis on self-education to sustain traditional teachings and linguistic practices is a fundamental aspect of Aboriginal and AI/AN world-views. Self-education is understood as the traditional means of education transmitted essentially by family, clan and community (Lomawaima, 1999). Traditional educational paradigms for Aboriginal peoples consisted of being immersed in primarily oral cultures (Weber-Pillwax, 2001). Traditional teachings were intended to impart moral lessons on younger generations of Aboriginal children. Parents, elders and members of the extended family taught Aboriginal children about living a good life. The values and beliefs imparted to Aboriginal children were best epitomized by the grandmothers who taught traditional world-views, including ethics of care and compassion (Kirkness, 1993). Experiences were shared with children in experiential environments since they were considered to be active learners.

Aboriginal children generally participated in the adults' day-to-day activities. The skills taught to children often had social, economic, spiritual and historical significance (Lafrance, 2000). Learning was collaborative and communal. Traditional Aboriginal education often understood learning as integral to living a good life.

Traditional education was, therefore, both informal and experiential. It taught Aboriginal children and youth the necessary skills and values to contribute meaningfully to their communities. The wisdom in the various teachings was informed by the collective knowledge of the particular community (Miller, 1996). Children observed the behaviours and actions of the adults, developed an appreciation for nature and the environment, benefited from the traditional teachings of family and elders, accepted the responsibilities to their communities and understood the significance of being spiritually oriented (Cajete, 1994).

Many of the same characteristics that describe Aboriginal peoples' view of self-education in Canada hold true for AI/ANs in the United States. In the tradition of storytelling, AI/AN children were taught through visual and oral demonstration (Hilberg and Tharp, 2002). AI/AN youth benefited from learning about key teachings in their entirety so they could visualize the important events and formulate conclusions in a holistic manner. Correspondingly, the traditional AI/AN value of reflection contributed to the development of children's holistic perspectives (McCarthy and Benally, 2003). Reflecting upon new learning afforded AI/AN children opportunities to appreciate the traditional values of inclusion, generosity and independence (Brendtro and Brokenieg, 1996). These values are compatible with the same principles of collaboration and co-operation that are significant for Aboriginal peoples in Canada. In traditional contexts, education included hands-on learning activities that focused on perspectives that best served the community instead of individual gain and competition (Strand and Peacock, 2002).

The traditional teachings of AI/AN values were locally determined and espoused by immediate and extended family members, clan and the greater community. Elders and grandparents were considered the carriers of family values and history, and they relied on oral traditions to impart knowledge (Cherubini, 2011). Learning was generally understood by AI/ANs to begin before birth. AI/AN children were 'placed in situations where they were alone for lengthy periods, learning how to subdue their anxieties [and] settle their wandering thoughts ... A mind educated in this fashion carries on a lifelong dialogue with the subtlest elements of Nature' (Calsoyas, 2005, p. 304). In other words, children learned through reflection.

AI/AN education perceived relationship-building skills as very important to children's development. Culturally based stories and non-corporal discipline measures were intended to educate the child about social responsibility as well as both mutual and self-respect (Jacobs and Reyhner, 2002; Two Worlds, 2008). In this fashion, self-education is based on community and determined by cultural practices. It socialized AI/AN children into traditional world-views and knowledge systems. Although disputed by some mainstream educators, self-education in AI/AN communities included organized practices of teaching and learning well in advance of colonial rule (Sumida Huaman and Valdiviezo, 2008).

Education by others

The colonial models of education imposed on Aboriginal and AI/AN peoples in both Canada and the United States provide a striking contrast to the practices of self-education in their traditional communities. The respective policy responses of the colonial governments in both countries focused on the forced assimilation of western languages, cultures and beliefs.

In Canada, the Indian Act (1920) made education compulsory for children and funded industrial schools, operated by Christian churches, to assimilate Aboriginal children into Eurocentric ways (Brady, 1995). There were amendments to the Indian Act until 1951, including the proposal to transfer jurisdiction of First Nations schools from federal to provincial governments. According to Richardson and Blanchet-Cohen (2000), Aboriginal education in Canada has been typified by add-on, partnership and First Nations' control approaches since 1970. In the first approach, Aboriginal content was superficially 'added-on' to mainstream curriculum; the partnership approach, instead, sought to consolidate bi-cultural principles between educational institutions and the various Aboriginal communities (Miller, 1996); lastly, the First Nations' control approach has attempted to devolve secondary and post-secondary education to First Nation authorities (Barsh, 1994), but has been determined to be a failed policy response because traditional assimilation educational practices continue to exist and therefore strengthen western epistemologies and knowledge-systems (Agbo, 2002).

At present, Aboriginal education in Canada is a fiduciary responsibility of the federal government; however, the curriculum of provincially funded schools is a requirement of federally operated reserve schools. Provincial governments across the country have implemented regional-specific policy frameworks related to Aboriginal education. British Columbia, Saskatchewan, Manitoba and Quebec are among these provinces. Ontario, too, has implemented a specific policy framework for First Nation, Métis and Inuit education. The Ontario Ministry of Education's (2007) *First Nation, Métis, and Inuit Education Policy Framework* recognizes that Aboriginal student achievement is often implicated by socio-cultural and socio-historical realities. In turn, the policy document aims to heighten teachers' awareness of Aboriginal students' learning preferences and foster more inclusive and culturally appropriate school and classroom practices. The policy is also in response to the criticism of the Royal Commission of Aboriginal Peoples (RCAP, 1996) report that identified the lack of accountability on the part of the mainstream public educational systems for Aboriginal students.

Yet, the Ontario policy framework endorses, among its objectives, the need to close the achievement gap between Aboriginal and mainstream learners. Included in these measures are externally imposed standardized tests in reading, writing and mathematics. On the one hand, the policy distinguishes Aboriginal students' unique learning styles and epistemic preferences, but paradoxically ignores the fact that external large-scale assessments are often poorly suited to Aboriginal students because the measures are generally informed by Eurocentric teaching, learning and assessment practices (Cherubini, 2009). For Aboriginal peoples, education entails a far larger significance than mere test scores and market-driven initiatives (Friedel, 2011).

AI/ANs have also witnessed the emergence of federal government commitments to work with various tribal organizations to design programmes that cater to the cultural and academic needs of AI/AN students so that they can achieve the same standard as all other students (National Center for Education Statistics, 2005). Like the provincial governments in Canada, the US federal government pledged its support to assist AI/AN students to close the achievement gap (Cavanagh, 2004). The United States Congress's (2001) *No Child Left Behind Act* made this clear. The US federal government promises that education affords all students the 'chance to pursue the American dream ... we want to know which children are catching on and which ones are not' (United States Department of Energy, 2004, n.p.). Equally clear, though, are the ideological conflicts that emerge when AI/AN student achievement is measured by Western-based standardized testing practices (Cherubini, 2010). Patrick (2008) sees the concentration on national standards and student assessment as one of the most pressing dangers for AI/AN students' education in the United States.

Education in the United States is administered by federal jurisdiction with delegation to each state. From a legal perspective, the US government's relationship with AI/ANs is articulated in various sections of the Constitution of the United States, a number of federal statutes, treaties and court rulings. In 1794, the treaty provisions addressed the education of several Iroquois Nations (including the Oneida, Tuscarora and Stockbridge) in an attempt to 'civilize' them from the lifestyles learned 'in the wilderness' (see Warner and Grint, 2012). By 1921 the United States Congress passed the *The Snyder Act* (Public Law 94–482,25USC 13) that authorized the Bureau of Indian Affairs (BIA) both to educate and to acculturate AI/AN students; in turn, BIA schools determined that AI/AN children should be educated in Eurocentric ways and saw no place for traditional linguistic and cultural practices. As the 1960s came to a close, however, AI/AN tribal governments united to protest against their inequitable treatment by the US government in the light of the jurisdiction allotted to the BIA over the governance of land, water and minerals.

Non-committal and sometimes dubious government policy has had adverse historical consequences for AI/AN peoples across the United States (Urban and Wagoner, 2004). The US federal government established approximately 400 treaties with AI/AN peoples between 1778 and 1871 and, of these, more than a hundred included various components related to education (Deyhle and Swisher, 1997).

The Meriam (1928) report concluded that the off-reservation schools conceptualized by the Indian Bureau provided deplorable living conditions and poor instruction. By 1934, the churches' involvement in Indian schools was significantly reduced and it was no longer compulsory for AI/AN children to attend religious ceremonies; they could instead practise traditional Native ways of living. In the 1960s and 1990s, a number of comprehensive reports about the conditions and outcomes of AI/AN education were published in the United States, including, for example, *Indian Education: A National Tragedy – a National Challenge (Report of the Committee on Labor and Public Welfare, 1969)* and *the Indian Nations at Risk Report* (1991). It is difficult to chronicle the destructive influence on AI/AN communities inflicted by the colonial American government in its attempt to solve the 'Indian problem' through education (Galliher, Tsethlikai, and Stolle 2012). Perhaps not until the American *Indian Self-Determination Act* of 1975 did the official policies of mandatory boarding schools and relocation programs come under full scrutiny (Szasz, 2005).

In Canada, and arguably in the United States as well, education has been among the most predominant vehicles of empowerment and control for Aboriginal people over at least the last 25 years (Stonechild, 2006). Moreover, the concept of tribal sovereignty in the United States is a priority to indigenous education because it represents the means for the once independent indigenous peoples to rebuild their nations (Huaman, 2011).

Impending challenges

Kawagley's (1995) assessment of indigenous communities in the northern regions of Canada and the United States is framed in the language of disruption (of traditional world-views) and loss (of epistemic values and beliefs). The challenges faced by indigenous learners across both Canada and the United

States are an integral part of the discussion of education in indigenous North American communities.

Formal educational institutions directed towards Aboriginal students and communities in Canada encompass what some have described as overt racism. In most public schools, Aboriginal students do not have access to Native language learning or to culturally appropriate pedagogical practices (Friedel, 2010; St. Denis, 2004). In many respects Aboriginal students embody what Raibman (2005) describes at the superficial identity imposed on them by mainstream society and educators. Such racism makes it even more difficult for Aboriginal students to have their socio-cultural and socio-linguistic values and knowledges recognized (McConaghy, 2002). As a result, Aboriginal peoples are still faced with the challenge to decolonize their educational practices and epistemic beliefs from the dominant and often racist western views (Dei and Kempf, 2006; James, 2010).

To compound the issue, the educational achievement of Aboriginal students is significantly lower than that of non-Aboriginal learners. According to Statistics Canada (2009), 34 per cent of Aboriginal peoples did not have a secondary school education compared to 15 per cent of the overall population in 2006 (see Guèvremont and Kohen, 2012). Some scholars conclude that the academic under-achievement of Aboriginal students is due in large part to the lingering assimilationist effects of colonization (Pirbhai-Illich, 2010).

Moreover, public schools are criticized for not meaningfully embedding Aboriginal world-views (Malin, 1990), for providing inadequate Aboriginal issues in the provincial curricula across Canada (Godlewska et al., 2010), for the relative absence of culturally respectful curriculum (Malin, 1990), for the lack of culturally appropriate pedagogy (Hudspith, 1996) and for deficit views of Aboriginal learners (Nicklin-Dent and Hatton, 1996). The consequences for Aboriginal students' pride are potentially devastating. It is of little surprise, then, that Aboriginal people are often under-represented in all academic and professional fields of study. This pattern suggests that there is frequently little motivation on their part to master a Eurocentric curriculum that is contextually irrelevant (Wilson, 1994).

In addition, and particularly important to Aboriginal peoples' oral traditions, contemporary colonial practices stifle traditional Aboriginal linguistic diversity. Tove Skutnabb-Kangas (2000) used the term *linguicide* to describe the rapid deterioration of Aboriginal languages and the disappearance of orality that is enacted in contemporary schooling practices. The Aboriginal linguistic tradition is integral to the cultural identity of Aboriginal peoples as it serves as a source of communication but more pressingly as 'a link which connects people with their past and grounds their social, emotional, and spiritual vitality' (Norris, 1998, p. 8). The statistics related to the demise of Aboriginal languages in Canada are staggering. Statistics Canada (2009) reported that 69 per cent of Inuit could speak an Aboriginal language (compared to 72 per cent in 1996), 51 per cent of First Nations people residing on reservation lands knew an Aboriginal language (compared to 56 per cent in 2006), 12 per cent of First Nations people living in urban centres were familiar with an Aboriginal language (compared to 20 per cent in 1996) and only 4 per cent of the Métis population were fluent in an Aboriginal language (compared to 9 per cent in 2006), marking a continuing decline of Aboriginal languages for all groups (Burnaby and Beaujot, 1986).

The challenges facing AI/AN students in the United States are equally profound. The educational disparities of AI/AN students are indicative of Eurocentric education models that promote racist practices and unequal outcomes (Piper et al., 2006). In conditions similar to those of Aboriginal and indigenous peoples in Canada and Australia, AI/AN students are not well served by the dominant educational systems that resonate with colonial histories. Moreover, AI/AN communities and educators are often perceived as barriers to the development of more globalized educational paradigms (Valdiviezo, 2006). The statistics related to academic achievement attest to the inadequacies of contemporary schooling practices. For example, graduation rates for AI/AN students (in the 12 states with the highest number of AI/AN students) are lower than other ethnic groups – 46.6 per cent for AI/AN students compared to 50.5 per cent for Hispanic students and 77.9 per cent for the Asian student demographic (Faircloth and Tippeconnic, 2010). AI/AN students have the highest drop-out rates from formal schooling (15 per cent compared to 7 per cent of Whites). In addition, the achievement levels of AI/AN students in Grades 4 and 8 are lower than those of White students, according to the scores in reading, mathematics and science (United States Department of Education, 2008). Of the 184 Bureau of Indian Schools, a mere 30 per cent are meeting the benchmark standards of the Annual Year Progress measures of student performance across the United States.

Culturally unresponsive school practices, classroom pedagogies and student assessment measures are indeed monumental issues for AI/AN students. Traditional value systems are often relinquished in favour of the ideologies of the Western-dominated educational systems. Such means of cultural annihilation makes issues of preservation especially daunting

(Calsoyas, 2005). Often, the long-term results of racist colonial practices extend beyond low scores on standardized tests and higher rates of school abandonment. AI/AN students have inferior educational opportunities and experiences (Aud et al., 2011), lose confidence in their ability to learn, are more prone to experiment with narcotics and have an increased likelihood of engaging in self-destructive behaviours (Hall, 2007).

A barrier to establishing sustained and culturally appropriate educational systems is the diminishing rates of use of traditional AI/AN languages – a challenge shared by Aboriginal peoples in Canada. The content of AI/AN education also attributes its value to indigenous knowledge; thus, the recovery and revitalization of AI/AN languages is integral to their sense of identity (Huaman, 2011). As Bourdieu (2003) explains, language reproduces the social structure from which it originates, thereby informing how dominant languages can embody the exercise of power in socio-political arenas (like education) and can change a community's relationship to its own socio-cultural and epistemic world-views.

Resilience and determination: Cultural responses

According to Neegan (2005), 'an Aboriginal education is at the heart of the struggle of Aboriginal people to regain control over their lives and their communities' (p. 12). It is clear that the industrial and post-industrial paradigms of Canadian education that are characteristic of positivist and Eurocentric knowledge systems have been detrimental for generations of Aboriginal students and communities. Equally clear, however, is the resistance and determination of Aboriginal peoples to (re)establish their rich cultural identities through culturally relevant and appropriate educational programmes.

The educational leaders across Aboriginal communities will have to be, according to Paquette and Fallon (2011), adamant about the significance of the identities and educational systems they want to establish. In the process, they must persuade governing bodies, educational stakeholders and the general Canadian public of the import on a national scale of culturally appropriate education for Aboriginal learners. This is not unlike the claim expressed by the National Indian Brotherhood of Canada (NIB, 1972) more than 40 years ago that called for the reinforcement of Aboriginal identity. Aboriginal students resist the colonial world-views reflective of mainstream educational practices (Silver and Mallen, 2002). Aboriginal student resilience is particularly admirable since they endure culturally disengaging epistemic practices but simultaneously attempt to integrate into mainstream cultures that have a history of anti-colonial sentiment. Coping with such disengagement is not only very difficult but potentially distressing for Aboriginal youth (Waller et al., 2002).

In this way, self-determination and control of education is the top priority for Aboriginal people in Canada (Kumar, 2009). Various documents, primarily those of the NIB (1972), the Assembly of First Nations (1989), the Senate Standing Committee on Aboriginal Peoples (Parliament of Canada, 1990), MacPherson (1991) and the Royal Commission of Aboriginal Peoples (1996), together with the Senate Standing Committee Annual Reports from 2000 to 2007 (Parliament of Canada, 2013), point to Aboriginal peoples' resilience against oppressive educational policies. Such policies were authored by governing bodies bent on assimilating Aboriginal world-views to Western ways. The Canadian Council on Learning (2007) claims that Aboriginal learning should be reconceptualized in the light of Aboriginal epistemologies and identities.

AI/AN communities' resilience and determination are equally evident; they are determined to structure educational approaches, both formal and informal (public schools and community-based), that are created by AI/AN peoples in culturally appropriate and respectful learning spaces. Within these spaces, AI/AN students can engage in authentic learning environments that prioritize cultural and land-based traditions (Champagne, 2008).

Moreover, AI/AN communities' awareness of their fleeting languages secures the place of traditional languages across these educative spaces. AI/AN people are determined to resist federal policies and accountability interventions that measure student learning on standardized scales of achievement that are not culturally aligned to Native ways of knowing. AI/ANs are dedicated to an education that privileges their ways (Anderson-Levitt, 2003). By positioning traditional heritage and sacred knowledge as central to education, AI/AN communities can exercise their sovereignty – a critical and compelling concept for AI/AN education. As Canby (2004) explains, sovereignty embodies the totality of life for AI/AN peoples in their tradition as independent nations that determine their own educational, political, economic, social and spiritual beliefs. AI/AN people call for participatory educational practices based on traditional epistemic and linguistic values. The role of elders is instrumental to this transformative view of education. Elders are generally perceived by AI/AN people as the cultural links between the past and the present and can transmit culture and language from one generation to the next (Thompson et al., 2008). Learning is not confined to the parameters of a classroom or school and extends into the community (Nieto, 2004).

Concerns and recommendations

There are both commonalities and distinctions in the world-views, histories, educational practices, government responses and respective challenges of Aboriginal and AI/AN peoples. There are also core concerns and key recommendations that can be made from the broad perspectives of both Aboriginal peoples in Canada and AI/AN people in the United States. While not suggesting that the following concerns and recommendations are of equal relevance to each nation across Turtle Island, they underscore six fundamental educational issues that resonate across boundaries.

First, Aboriginal and AI/AN peoples share a concern about including culturally respectful and accurate traditional knowledge into public school curriculum. It is recommended that curriculum design and development consider the hegemonic issues that have implicated power relations in both countries (Neegan, 2005). The curriculum should include accurate historical descriptions of tribes, the struggles between First Nations and settlers and the various stories unique to the people of the particular land (Ngai, 2006).

The second concern rests in the responses and actions of the respective federal, provincial, state and local governing bodies. In effect, it is recommended that the political bodies at each level of governance should recognize, and commit to addressing, the rights of Aboriginal and AI/AN peoples (Neegan, 2005). The Indian Nations at Risk Task Force (1991), as one example, recommends widespread changes to governmental and public institutional organizations to alter deficit views of AI/AN student achievement (see also Gentry and Fugate, 2012). Moreover, programme evaluations specific to AI/AN education, and especially those involving research ethics, need to be designed and delivered in participation with AI/AN students and communities in culturally respectful ways (Caldwell et al., 2005).

A third recommendation deals with Native languages. It is recommended that the rapid decline of Aboriginal and AI/AN languages can be countered by educational practices that connect traditional languages to students' lives. The acquisition of a Native language allows students to understand their own world-views better and fosters a greater sense of cross-cultural understanding between Aboriginal and AI/AN students' mainstream views and their acquired traditional knowledge (Ngai, 2006). Language planning is considered by many

Aboriginal and AI/AN peoples as their community's right to self-determination (Francis and Reyhner, 2002).

A fourth recommendation relates to community involvement in educational matters. It is recommended that Aboriginal and AI/AN communities, parents and elders be directly involved in decision-making processes that involve educational policy and initiatives (McCarty et al., 2006). This requires that publicly funded schools adopt inclusive learning cultures and welcome the necessary dialogue on matters involving traditions and cultures (Patrick, 2008).

There is also a general concern about public school educators' awareness of Aboriginal and AI/AN histories and epistemologies. The recommendation is for teachers to develop and employ culturally relevant educational practices that create learning environments to accommodate students' preferences (St. Denis, 2007). Apart from the actual pedagogy, the recommendation is made that teachers adopt culturally sensitive interpersonal styles as a basis of establishing relationships with their students (Kanu, 2002).

Finally, a consistent concern with honouring the values and character of Aboriginal and AI/AN students in public education also surfaced. Education should draw special attention to students' personal development, strengths and survival. As Ngai (2006) and others discuss, education should help individuals to develop their awareness of community well-being, the integrity of nature and the environmen, and the fact that truth is a focal point of education for Aboriginal and AI/AN people.

Further reading

Ball, J. (2009), 'Supporting young Indigenous children's language development in Canada: A review of research on needs and promising practices', *The Canadian Modern Language Review*, 66 (1), 19–47.

This comprehensive research study underscores the necessity of delivering culturally appropriate education to diverse bodies of students. It also emphasizes the significance of language education and development for Aboriginal learners.

Bruno-Jofré, R., & Henley, D. (2000), 'Public schooling in English Canada: Addressing difference in the context of globalization', *Canadian Ethnic Studies*, 32 (1), 38–53.

This article argues that more attention must be directed towards teachers' pedagogic strategies in order to better address marginalized learners. The authors suggest that educators need to have an understanding of the various approaches to the building of a Canadian polity.

Kanu, Y. (2011), *Integrating Aboriginal Perspectives into the School Curriculum*. Toronto, ON: University of Toronto Press.

Kanu's work and extensive research investigates the challenges and contexts of authentically incorporating indigenous perspectives and epistemologies into public school classrooms. It also offers a concise analysis of why indigenous students struggle with more Eurocentric-based pedagogies and practices.

Lopez, A. & Hall, M. (Fall 2007), 'Letting in the sun: Native youth transform their school with murals', *Reclaiming Children and Youth*, 16 (3), 29–35.

The authors discuss the importance of Aboriginal iconography in places of learning in the United States. They comment upon the place of visual representation in the lives of Native youth, and the necessity for such representation to be extended into public schools. The authors point to the 'No Child Left Behind' policy in the United States as an example of the disregard for these occurrences.

Ngia, P. B., & Koehn. (2010, December), 'Indigenous studies and intercultural education: The impact of a place-based primary-school program', *Intercultural Education*, 21 (6), 597–606.

This study investigates the integration of local indigenous culture into the curriculum of public schools. It is a three-year longitudinal study that points to the improvement of students' knowledge of local indigenous people and to an increase in students' receptivity towards learning about indigenous peoples.

Waller, M. A., Okamotot, S. K., Hankerson, A. A., Hibbeler, T., Hibbeler, P., McIntyre, P., & McAllen-Walker, R. (2002, March), 'The hoop of learning: A holistic, multisystemic model for facilitating educational resilience among Indigenous students', *Journal of Sociology and Social Welfare*, 29 (1), 97–116.

The principles of culturally relevant education and culturally appropriate support for marginalized learners are discussed extensively in this research article. The authors bring to light the various psychological, socio-historical, cultural and economic barriers that often serve as obstacles for indigenous learners.

References

Agbo, S. A. (2002), 'Decentralization of First Nations education in Canada: Perspectives on ideals and realities of Indian control of Indian education', *Interchange*, 33, (3), 281–302.

Anderson-Levitt, K. (2003), 'A world culture of schooling?', in K. Anderson-Levitt (ed.), *Local Meaning, Global Schooling: Anthropology and World Culture Theory*. New York, NY: Palgrave Macmillan, pp. 1–26.

Assembly of First Nations. (1989), *Traditional Education*. Ottawa, ON: Assembly of First Nations.

Aud, S., Hussar, W., Kena, G., Bianco, K., Frohlich, L., Kemp, J., Tahan, K., Mallory, K., Nachazel, T., and Hannes, G. (2011), *The Condition of Education 2011* (NCES 2011-033). Washington, DC: U.S. Department of Education, National Center for Education Statistics.

Ball, J. (2004), 'As if indigenous knowledge and communities mattered: Transformative education in First Nations communities in Canada', *American Indian Quarterly*, 28, (3/4), 454–479.

Barsh, R. L. (1994), 'Canada's Aboriginal people: Social integration or disintegration', *Canadian Journal of Native Studies*, 14, (1), 1–46.

Bourdieu, P. (2003), *Language and Symbolic Power* (7th Printing). Cambridge, MA: Harvard University Press.

Bowlby, J. W. and McMullen, K. (2002), *At a Crossroads: First Results for the 18-20-Year-Old Cohort of the Youth in Transition Survey*. Ottawa, ON: Human Resources and Skills Development Canada.

Brady, P. (1995), 'Two policy approaches to native education: Can the reform be legalized?', *Canadian Journal of Education*, 20, (3), 249–366.

Brendtro, L. K. and Brokenieg, M. (1996), 'Beyond the curriculum of control', *Journal of Correctional Education*, 47, (4), 160–166.

Brill de Ramirez, S. B. (1999), *Contemporary American Indian Literatures & the Oral Tradition*. Tucson: University of Arizona Press.

Burnaby, B. and Beaujot, R. (1986), *The Use of Aboriginal Languages in Canada*. (Prepared for the Social Trends Analysis Directorate and Native Citizens Directorate). Ottawa, ON: Department of the Secretary of State.

Cajete, G. (1994), *Look to the Mountain: Ecology of Indigenous Education*. Durango, CO: Kivaki Press.

Caldwell, J. Y., Davis, J. D., Du Bois, B., Echo-Hawk, H., Erickson, J. S., Goins, R. T., Hill, C., Hillabrant, W., Johnson, S. R., Kendall, E., Keemer, K., Manson, S. M., Marshall, C. A., Running Wolf, P., Santiago, R. L., Schacht, R., and Stone, J. B. (2005), 'Culturally competent research with American Indians and Alaska Natives: Findings and recommendations of the first symposium of the work group on American Indian research and program evaluation methodology', *American Indian and Alaska Native Mental Health Research*, 12, (1), 1–21.

Calsoyas, K. (2005), 'Considerations in the educational process relative to Native Americans', *Cambridge Journal of Education*, 35, (3), 301–310.

Canadian Council on Learning. (2007), *Redefining How Success Is Measured in Metis, First Nations and Inuit Learning*. Ottawa, ON: Author.

Canby, W. (2004), *American Indian Law in a Nutshell*. (Nutshell series, 4th ed.). St Paul, MN: West Group.

Cavanagh, S. (2004), 'No child law poses challenges to Indians', *Education Week*, 23, (34), 32–34.

Champagne, D. (2008), 'Is American Indian studies for real?', *Wicazo Sa Review*, 23, (2), 77–90.

Cherubini, L. (2009), 'Reforming teacher preparation: Fostering critical reflection and awareness in the context of global education', *Excelsior: Leadership in Teaching and Learning*, 3, (2), 43–55.

——. (2010), 'Lessons learned from American educational legislation for Canadian educators: *No child left behind* and the Ontario aboriginal education framework', *Journal of American Indian Education*, 49, (1), 68–85.

——. (2011), 'Honouring the voice of the elders: Interpretations and implications of reflexive ethnography in a digital environment', *The Canadian Journal of Native Studies*, 31, (1), 97–115.

Christensen, R. and Poupart, L. M. (2012), 'Elder teachers gather at Manitou Api, Manitoba: Igniting the fire, gathering wisdom from all nations', *International Journal of Qualitative Studies in Education*, 25, (7), 933–949.

Dei, G. and Kempf, A. (2006), *Anti-Colonialism and Education*. Ann Arbor: The University of Michigan Press.

Deyhle, D. and Swisher, K. G. (1997), 'Research in American Indian, Alaska Native education: From assimilation to self-determination', in M. W. Apple (ed.), *Review of Research in Education*. Washington, DC: American Education Research Association, pp. 113–194.

Duran, E. and Duran, B. (1995), *Native American Postcolonial Psychology*. Albany: State University of New York Press.

Evans-Campbell, T. (2008), 'Historical trauma in American Indian/Native Alaska communities: A multilevel framework for exploring impacts on individuals, families, and communities', *Journal of Interpersonal Violence*, 23, (3), 316–338.

Faircloth, S. C. and Tippeconnic, J. W. III. (2010), *The Dropout/Graduation Rate Crisis Among AI/AN Students: Failure to Respond Places the Future of Native Peoples at Risk*. Los Angeles, CA: The Civil Rights Project/Proyecto Derechos Civiles at UCLA.

Francis, N. and Reyhner, J. (2002), *Language and Literacy Teaching for Indigenous Education: A Bilingual Approach*. Clevedon: Multilingual Matters.

Friedel, T. L. (2011), 'Looking for learning in all the wrong places: Urban Native youths' cultured response to Western-oriented place-based learning', *International Journal of Qualitative Studies in Education*, 24, (5), 531–546.

———. (2010), *Finding a Place for Race at the Policy Table: Broadening the Aboriginal Education Policy Discourse in Canada*. (Aboriginal policy research initiative: Policy research paper series). Ottawa, ON: The Institute on Governance, in partnership with the Office of the Federal Inspector for Métis and Non-Status Indians.

Galliher, R. V., Tsethlikai, M. M., and Stolle, D. (2012), 'Perspectives of Native and Non-Native scholars: Opportunities for collaboration', *Child Development Perspectives*, 6, (1), 66–74.

Gentry, M. and Fugate, C. M. (2012), 'Gifted American students: Underperforming, under-identified and overlooked', *Psychology in the Schools*, 49, (7), 631–646.

Godlewska, A., Moore, J., and Bednasek, C. D. (2010), 'Cultivating ignorance of aboriginal realities', *The Canadian Geographer*, 54, (4), 417–440.

Guèvremont, A. and Kohen, D. E. (2012), *Knowledge of an Aboriginal Language and School Outcomes for Children and Adults*. Ottawa, ON: Statistics Canada.

Hall, M. (2007), 'Mentoring the natural way: Native American approaches to education', *Reclaiming Children and Youth*, 16, (1), 14–16.

Hilberg, R. S. and Tharp, R. G. (2002), 'Theoretical perspective research findings, and classroom implications of the learning styles of AI/AN students', *Eric Digests: Special Edition, Indian Edu/Research.Net* (EDO-RC–03–6).

Huaman, E. (2011), 'Transforming education, transforming society: The co-construction of critical peace education and Indigenous education', *Journal of Peace Education*, 8, (3), 243–258.

Hudspith, S. M. (1996), *Learning to 'Belong': An Ethnography of Urban Aboriginal Schooling*. (Unpublished doctoral dissertation). Darwin: Northern Territory University.

Indian Nations at Risk Task Force. (1991), *Indian Nations at Risk: An Educational Strategy for Action*. (Final report of the Indian nations at Risk Force). Washington, DC: U.S. Department of Education.

Jacobs, D. T. and Reyhner, J. (2002), 'Preparing teachers to support AI/AN student success and cultural heritage', *Eric Digest: Special Edition, Indian Edu/Research.Net* (EDO-RC–01–13).

James, C. E. (2010), *Seeing Ourselves: Exploring Race, Ethnicity and Culture*. Toronto, ON: Thompson Educational Publishing.

Kanu, Y. (2002), 'In their own voices: First Nations students identify some cultural mediators of their learning in the formal school system', *The Alberta Journal of Educational Research*, 48, (2), 98–121.

Kawagley, O. A. (1995), *A Yupiaq Worldview: A Pathway to Ecology and Spirit*. Long Grove, IL: Waveland Press.

Kirkness, V. (1993), 'Giving voices to our ancestors', *Canadian Journal of Native Education*, 2, 145–149.

Kumar, M. P. (2009), 'Aboriginal education in Canada: A postcolonial analysis', *AlterNative: An International Journal of Alternative Scholarship*, 5, (1), 42–57.

Lafrance, B. (2000), 'Culturally negotiated education in first nations community: Empowering ourselves for future generations', in C. Brant, L. Davis and L. Lahache (eds), *Aboriginal Education: Fulfilling the Promise*. Vancouver, BC: UBC Press, pp. 101–114.

Lomawaima, K. T. (1999), 'The unnatural history of American Indian education', in K. Gayton Swisher and J. W. Tippeconnic, III (eds), *Next Steps: Research and Practices to Advance Indian Education*. Charleston, WV: Eric Clearinghouse on Rural Education and Small Schools.

MacPherson, J. C. (1991), *Report on Tradition and Education*. Ottawa, ON: Department of Indian Affairs and Northern Development.

Malin, M. (1990), 'The visibility of invisibility of aboriginal students in an urban classroom', *Australian Journal of Education*, 34, (3), 312–329.

Marker, M. (2000), 'Review essay: Ethnohistory and Indigenous education a moment of uncertainty', *History of Education*, 29, (1), 79–85.

McCarthy, J. and Benally, J. (2003), 'Classroom management in a Navajo middle school', *Theory Into Practice*, 42, (4), 296–305.

McCarty, T. L., Romero-Little, M. E., and Zepeda, O. (2006), 'Native American youth discourses on language shift and retention: Ideological cross-currents and their implications for language planning', *The International Journal of Bilingual Education and Bilingualism*, 9, (5), 659–677.

McConaghy, C. (2002), *Rethinking Indigenous Education: Culturalism, Colonialism and the Politics of Knowing*. Flaxton: Post Pressed.

Meriam, L. (1928), *The Problem of Indian Administration: Report of a Survey Made at the Request of Honorable Hubert Work, Secretary of the Interior*. Baltimore, MD: The Johns Hopkins Press.

Miller, J. R. (1996), *Shingauk's Vision: A History of Native Residential Schools*. Toronto, ON: University of Toronto Press.

National Caucus of Native American State Legislators. (2008), *Striving to Achieve: Helping Native American Students Succeed*. Denver, CO: Author.

National Center for Education Statistics. (2005), *NCES Studies on AI/AN Education*. Alexandria, VA: U.S. Department of Education, Institute of Educational Sciences.

National Indian Brotherhood. (1972), *Indian Control of Indian Education*. Ottawa, ON: Author.

Neegan, E. (2005), 'Excuse me: who are the first peoples of Canada? A historical analysis of Aboriginal education in Canada then and now', *International Journal of Inclusive Education*, 9, (1), 3–15.

Ngai, P. B. (2006), 'Grassroots suggestion for linking Native-language learning, Native American studies, and mainstream education in reservation schools with mixed Indian and White student populations', *Language, Culture and Curriculum*, 19, (2), 220–236.

Nicklin-Dent, J. and Hatton, E. (1996), 'Education and poverty: an Australian primary school response', *Australian Journal of Education*, 40, (1), 42–60.

Nieto, S. (2004), *Affirming Diversity: The Sociopolitical Context of Multicultural Education*. (4th ed.). New York, NY: Pearson.

Norris, M. J. (1998), 'Canada's Aboriginal languages', *Canadian Social Trends*, 51, 8–16.

Ontario Ministry of Education. (2007), *Ontario First Nation, Métis, and Inuit Education Policy Framework*. Toronto, ON: Aboriginal Education Office.

Paquette, J. and Fallon, G. (2011), 'Framing First-Nations education policy: Toward constructing a coherent conceptual "place to stand"', *The International Journal of Interdisciplinary Social Sciences*, 5, (9), 331–374.

Parliament of Canada. (1990), *Introduction to the Standing Committee on Aboriginal Peoples*. Retrieved from http://www.parl.gc.ca/SenCommitteeBusiness/CommitteeAbout.

———. (2013), *Standing Committee Annual Reports*. Retrieved from http://www.parl.gc.ca/Search/Results.aspx?Language=Edsearch_term=annual%20reports.

Patrick, R. (2008), 'Perspectives on change: A continued struggle for academic success and cultural relevancy at an American Indian school in the midst of No Child Left Behind', *Journal of American Indian Education*, 47, (1), 65–81.

Piper, B., Dryden-Peterson, S., and Kim, Y. (eds). (2006), *International Education for the Millennium: Toward Access, Equity and Quality*. Cambridge, MA: Harvard Educational Review.

Pirbhai-Illich, F. (2010), 'Aboriginal students engaging and struggling with critical multiliteracies', *Journal of Adolescent and Adult Literacy*, 54, (4), 257–266.

Raibman, P. (2005), *Authentic Indians: Episodes of Encounter from the Late Nineteenth Century Northwest Coast*. Durham, NC: Duke University Press.

Report of the Committee on Labor and Public Welfare. (1969), *Indian Education: A National Tragedy*. Washington, DC: United States Government Priority Office.

Richardson, C. and Blanchet-Cohen, N. (2000), *Survey of Post-Secondary Education Programs in Canada for Aboriginal Peoples*. Victoria, BC: Institute for Child Rights and Development and First Nations Partnerships Program.

Royal Commission on Aboriginal Peoples (RCAP). (1996), *Report of the Royal Commission on Aboriginal Peoples—Vol. 3: Gathering Strength*. Ottawa, ON: Canada Communication Group.

Silver, J. and Mallen, K. (with Greene, J. and Simard, F.). (2002), *Aboriginal Education in Winnipeg Inner City High Schools*. Winnipeg: Canada Centre for Policy Alternatives—Manitoba.

Skutnabb-Kangas, T. (2000), *Linguistic Genocide in Education—or Worldwide Diversity and Human Rights?* Mahwah, NJ: Lawrence Erlbaum.

Statistics Canada. (2009), *Aboriginal Peoples in Canada in 2006: 2006 Census*. Ottawa, ON: Minister of Public Works and Government Services.

St. Denis, V. (2007), 'Aboriginal education and anti-racist education: Building alliances across cultural and racial identity', *Canadian Journal of Education*, 30, (4), 1068–1092.

———. (2004), '7 real Indians: Cultural revitalization and fundamentalism in Aboriginal education', in C. Schick, J. Jaffe and A. M. Watkinson (eds), *Contesting Fundamentalisms*. Halifax, NS: Fernwood, pp. 35–47.

Stonechild, B. (2006), *The New Buffalo: The Struggle for Aboriginal Post-Secondary Education in Canada*. Winnipeg: University of Manitoba Press.

Strand, J. A. and Peacock, T. D. (2002), 'Nurturing resilience and school success in AI/AN students', *ERIC Digests: Clearinghouse on Rural Education and Small Schools* (EDO-RC-02–11).

Sumida Huaman, E. and Valdiviezo, L. (2008, December 8), *Rethinking Indigenous Learning Spaces: At the Crossroads of Formal and Nonformal Education in the Americas*. Paper presented at the World Indigenous Peoples Conference on Education, Melbourne, Australia.

Szasz, M. (2005), '"I knew how to be moderate. And I knew how to obey": The commonality of American Indian boarding school experiences, 1750s–1920s', *American Indian Culture and Research Journal*, 29, 75–94.

Thompson, N. L., Hare, D., Sempler, T. T. and Grace, C. (2008), 'The development of a curriculum toolkit with AI/AN Communities', *Early Childhood Education Journal*, 35, (5), 397–404.

Two Worlds, W. (2008), 'The first gift from the Creator was love … the second was a child', *Smoke Signal News*, XII, (7), 869.

United States Congress. (2001), *No Child Left Behind Act—Public Law 107-110*. Washington, DC: Author.

United States Department of Education. (2008), *Status and Trends in the Education of American Indians and Alaska Natives*. Alexandria, VA: National Center for Education Statistics, Institute of Education Sciences.

United States Department of Energy. (2004), *Executive Order—American Indian and Alaska Native Education*. Washington, DC: Author.

Urban, W. and Wagoner, J. (2004), *American Education: A History*. (3rd ed.). New York: McGraw-Hill.

Valdiviezo, L. (2006), *The Construction of Interculturality: An Ethnography of Teachers' Beliefs and Practices in Indigenous Quechua Schools*. (Doctoral dissertation). New York, NY: Columbia University.

Waller, M. A., Okamoto, S. K., Hankerson, A. A., Hibbeler, T., Hibbeler, P., McIntyre, P. and McAllen-Walker, R. (2002), 'The hoop of learning: A holistic, multisystematic model for facilitating educational resilience among indigenous students', *Journal of Sociology and Social Welfare*, 29, (1), 97–116.

Warner, L. S. and Grint, K. (2012), 'The case of the noble savage: The myth that governance can replace leadership', *International Journal of Qualitative Studies in Education*, 25, (7), 969–982.

Weber-Pillwax, C. (2001), 'Orality in northern Cree indigenous worlds', *Canadian Journal of Native Education*, 25, (2), 149–165.

White, L. and Jacobs, E. (1988), *Liberating Our Children, Liberating Our Nation. Report of the Aboriginal Committee*. Victoria, BC: Family and Children's Services Legislation Review Community Panel, Aboriginal Committee.

Wilson, P. (1994), 'The professor/student relationship: Key factors in minority student performance and achievement', *Canadian Journal of Native Studies*, 14, (2), 305–317.

Intercultural Bilingual Education, Self-Determination and Indigenous Peoples of the Amazon Basin

Sheila Aikman

Introduction

Intercultural bilingual education is invested with expectations for the inclusion, self-determination and development of indigenous learners and their communities promoted through a diverse range of educational aims, policies and practices. This chapter considers the growth of intercultural bilingual education (IBE) in the Peruvian Amazon and asks about the nature of the expectations of IBE for those actors debating and shaping the concept, those drafting the policies and not least indigenous leaders, parents and learners engaging with IBE as a practice. It explores the histories and contexts in which IBE has flourished in Peru and more widely in Latin America, examining how it has been experienced by indigenous peoples of the Peruvian Amazon. Since the late 1980s, IBE has been part of national educational policy frameworks in Andean and Amazonian countries oriented to providing a culturally and linguistically relevant education for indigenous groups (Hornberger and López, 1998).

'Intercultural education' is a term that is used to discuss and describe a wide range of educational policies, programmes and approaches across the globe. This chapter considers intercultural bilingual education (IBE) as a politically, historically, socially and culturally embedded form of intercultural education associated with indigenous peoples, rights claims and debates on coloniality. For this chapter and its focus on Peru, along with its neighbouring Latin American countries, IBE is associated with primary schooling for indigenous children (López, 2009; Zavala, 2007). While in recent years there has been a rapid development of intercultural universities and intercultural higher education programmes in Latin America (Llanes Ortiz, 2009) intercultural bilingual education has emerged most strongly from debates over models of formal schooling. Notions of interculturalism, intra-culturalism, plurilingualism and pluriculturalism are historically embedded in different country contexts and recent political and social struggles for new forms of democracy and plural societies, notably Bolivia and Ecuador (Escobar, 2010; López, 2005). In Peru, however, debates about interculturalism are confined mostly to the field of education and expressed through IBE, whether viewed as an organizing principle of the curriculum, a competency or, as in the *National Education Project for 2021, 'The Education We Want for Peru'* (Ministry of Education, 2007), an ill-defined aspiration. In Peru, then, a commitment to intercultural education for all remains elusive (López, 2009) and IBE is first and foremost an educational modality for indigenous children.

The chapter aims to provide depth and breadth of understanding of the concept of IBE in the Peruvian Amazon by investigating it through three 'lenses' which offer different insights into its promises and the expectations for it as well as its successes. It looks first at ways in which IBE is seen as a strategy to aid economic development and as a means of aiding the inclusion of indigenous peoples in the global stride towards education for all (EFA). It then examines IBE as emergent from a pro-indigenous movement of, primarily, intellectuals of the twentieth century, denouncing indigenous peoples' marginalization and their ongoing situation of internal colonization. This anti-colonial perspective has been more recently enriched by discussion of the 'coloniality' of power (Quijano, 2000). A third perspective comes from the indigenous movement in the Peruvian Amazon and its relationship with the global social movement for indigenous rights. In Peru, IBE has been and continues to be negotiated and shaped by non-indigenous and indigenous actors and through complex relationships, alliances and networks, which evolve and change over time. Two examples of indigenous-run IBE programmes in the Peruvian Amazon are discussed which offer grounded reflections on the school practice of IBE, illustrating the changing nature of its meanings, the expectations of it and its practices.

Poverty and indigenous peoples: IBE for economic and social development

Debates about the relationship of the indigenous peoples to national society and non-indigenous populations across Latin America have a long history and over the last century formal education has been viewed as a means of addressing the 'Indian problem' through strategies variously aimed at their assimilation, integration and inclusion (Stavenhagen, 2002; Varese, 1980). With the economic growth of the 1950s and 1960s came increased investment in formal education – schooling – to promote the expansion and development of national capitalist economies and to invest in Spanish language schooling as a means of overcoming economic gulfs between urban and rural regions and between *mestizo, campesino* and Amazonian Indian populations.

Education as a means to increased human capital is a pervasive rationale for expanding educational access. It is seen as a means of overcoming indigenous poverty: poverty linked to the exclusion and marginalization of indigenous peoples from the market and productive employment. In the 1980s, economists cited research indicating that in rural areas of Peru 70 per cent of Quechua speakers had no schooling, compared with 40 per cent of Peruvians who spoke non-indigenous languages (Hernandez, cited by Hall and Patrinos, 2006). Links between indigenous status and low levels of education persist today and indigenous students across not only Latin America but the globe have lower enrolment rates, higher dropout rates and poorer educational outcomes than non-indigenous people in the same countries (Champagne, 2009). Indigenous peoples in Latin America also have poor socio-economic conditions and high poverty rates in relation to the population as a whole, understood as linked to their exclusion through labour market discrimination and limited access to public education and health services

(Psacharopolous and Patrinos, 1994). Seen as a means by which economically and socially disadvantaged and marginalized people can 'lift themselves out of poverty', educational investment is urged upon states as 'one of the best long term financial investments that States can make' (United Nations and Expert Mechanism on the Rights of Indigenous Peoples, 2009, pp. 4–5, 25).

In the context of the current global educational discourse on EFA, intercultural education is seen as an important strategy for tackling multidimensional marginalization in education and IBE is seen as a model of good practice for inclusive schooling for young indigenous learners (Aikman, 2012; UNESCO, 2010). In relation to the Peruvian Amazon, the World Bank (2001) views the persistence of disparity in levels of educational achievement between indigenous and non-indigenous populations as problematic and supports the expansion of 'bilingual and multicultural education' to promote poverty alleviation and social cohesion, 'despite high costs due to the large number and small population size of Amazonian ethno-linguistic communities' (pp. 62–63).

However, although over the past 50 years extensive efforts and resources have been devoted to overcoming the poverty and marginalization which many indigenous communities experience, the economic, social and human development levels of these communities generally remain very low (Stavenhagen, 2008).

Education for social and cultural integration

Peru was at the forefront of advocacy of educational reform, as early as the 1940s, by *indigenistas* (non-indigenous pro-indigenous actors) concerned with the historic social and cultural marginalization of the indigenous population. Primarily researchers and philosophers, *indigenistas* in Peru were part of an intellectual elite which established an agenda for indigenous peoples and education, based on respect for the dignity, sensibility and moral interests of indigenous people, including recognition of their native languages as an aspect of their personality, thus instigating debate about the hitherto acculturative and assimilationist nature of education (Citarella, 1990). Through the work of the Inter-American Indigenist Institute over subsequent decades, educational policies called for the 'gradual, effective and harmonic integration of the ethnic minorities into national societies' (Masferrer, 1983, p. 524). Reflecting political and social critiques of the deficiencies of formal education, such as the work of the socialist philosopher Mariategui and the influence of pedagogies for liberation (Freire, 1972; Tauro, 1970), they urged that there should be indigenous participation in educational planning and management and that education should be bilingual and intercultural.

In UNESCO's Latin American *Proyecto Principal* for education in the 1980s, we find aims for raising levels of educational access and quality for the population as a whole expressed in terms of goals for an eight-year minimum education for all by 1999, the eradication of adult illiteracy and the improvement of educational efficiency and quality by 2000. Alongside this are concerns to ensure that education – schooling – not only reflects the nature of indigenous people's economic and social lives but promotes respect for indigenous peoples' rights as citizens and their right to defend their 'indigenous cultural heritage' (Quintanilla and Lozano, 1983, p. xi). Their call was for the 'decolonization' of indigenous education. In Peru, the Education Reform Law of 1972 under the Velasco military government recognized Peru as a multilingual country and the 'intercultural' concept was established in educational policy in 1989 (Ministry of Education, 1989).

Writing in the same publication as Quintanilla and Lozano, Varese and Rodriguez (1983) ask about the apparent contradictions of policies and discourses which would try to maintain cultural plurality at the same time as trying to achieve economic integration of indigenous peoples into national society (p. 9). This is a question which challenges IBE, as we explore in subsequent sections through the diverse and divergent aims, policies and practices of IBE in the Peruvian Amazon. As Stavenhagen (2002) notes, debates about relationships between class and ethnicity, about internal colonialism and about the social construction of categories continue today through the guise of post-modern discourse. We find it given a new potency and expression through the work of Peruvian anthropologist Anibal Quijano and his use of the term 'coloniality of power' to refer to ways in which power continues to operate to subordinate indigenous peoples to an assumed superiority and universality of European cultural models – including schooling (Mignolo, 2011; Quijano, 2000; Walsh, 2009).

Peru's neighbours in Ecuador and Bolivia have more recently taken strides in new directions, with radical moves which challenge and suggest structural transformations to advance new social and political projects. In Ecuador the 2008 Constitution offers a vision of development as *buen vivir* ('living well'), offering a philosophy of life that suggests a rupture with the dominant neo-liberal model, and of identity as pluricultural and the nation as plurinational (Escobar, 2010; Walsh, 2009). In Bolivia the 2009 Constitution provides for culturally appropriate language and education policy based on principles of 'decolonization', plurinationality, social decentralization and territorial autonomies (Escobar, 2010; Gustafson, 2009; Howard, 2009).

In contrast, in the views of political analyses of the 'fractured politics' of Peru, the country's acute political instability, socio-economic and political crises and about-turns in government have led to a shallow democracy with weak linkages between state and society and to a situation where political contention frequently results in the use of violence (Cotler, 2011; Crabtree, 2011). Where gains were made in terms of influencing the concept and importance of intercultural education, the impact of these on the vision for and nature of Peruvian citizenship and pluriculturalism still remains to be felt despite expectations raised in earlier times. The optimism of the 1980s produced only an inconsistent and fragile institutionalization of IBE within the Ministry of Education and a continual vulnerability to shifts in political support. While leading educationalists worked at the national policy level to scrutinize and discuss the meaning of 'intercultural' for IBE, this came to be reflected in subsequent Ministry of Education policy documents. The concept shifted from a paternalistic and static notion of 'culture' and IBE as a contribution to 'recovering indigenous cultures and so avoid[ing] their deterioration and disappearance (Ministry of Education, 1989) to a relational and a political notion of a 'dialogue between cultures' (Ministry of Education, 1991, Defensoria del Pueblo 2011). Today the literature on meanings of interculturalism is extensive, and in Latin America it is largely focused on challenging the perpetuation of oppression of indigenous groups through the persistence of discriminatory stereotypes and racially defined inequalities. In Peru, the debates have mostly taken place within the educational sphere and developments in IBE (Dietz, 2009; Heise et al., 1994; Oliart, 2011; Rodriguez Vargas, 1996).

Indigenous rights, IBE and self-determination

So far this chapter has examined debates and influences shaping the emergence of IBE in Peruvian national educational discourse and policy as a form of education *for* the indigenous population. But what of indigenous peoples themselves and their role as protagonists in the development of IBE that respond to their analyses and demands? Across the Peruvian Amazon indigenous peoples have been on the receiving end of a very patchy offer, diverse in terms of providers and in terms of aims, quality and outcomes. Catholic missionary organizations have provided their own brands of 'civilizing' and Christianizing schooling agendas and public schooling has expanded its reach slowly and inconsistently (Cueto et al., 2009). Here we examine the significance of the 'arrival' of formal education in the form of primary schooling for indigenous peoples in three ways.

First, schooling in the official language of Spanish offered the promise of developing a proficiency in this language, which was a key to engagement with wider Peruvian and Latin American societies, as well as a lingua franca between different indigenous peoples both from the Amazon and the Andes. The demand for access to education was shaped, then, by indigenous peoples' desire and increasing requirement over the late twentieth century to engage with the surrounding national society and its diverse representatives and members. Their experiences with migrants and new incomers, with commercial traders as well as with the burgeoning bureaucracies in regional centres of administration, demanded the ability to express themselves, not only through diverse forms and registers of Spanish but through different Spanish literacy forms. As one outcome of this changing wider social and cultural environment, schooling became valued for its promise of access through the Spanish language to diverse modernities (Aikman, 2001). Linked to the demand for schooling in Spanish, was a promise of a new status and identity, that of being Peruvian and of being 'educated', as distinct from being 'uneducated' and in a state of savagery.

Another significant advantage of education for indigenous peoples is that it fosters the ability to manage knowledge, skills and practices that are crucial for defence of rights granted by the state and maintained and defended through the state's own institutions and mechanisms. The debates about citizenship, democracy and indigenous rights taking place in the 1970s and 1980s in the universities of Lima were happening alongside the drafting of a new law which guaranteed inalienable rights for indigenous peoples to their territories (Decree Law 22175, *Ley de Comunidades Nativas y de Desarollo Agrario de la Selva*, 1978). However, protecting the rights embedded in this Law has been difficult in the face of uncontrolled migration and unregulated resource extraction (oil, timber, gold), alongside equivocal support for indigenous rights from successive governments through the 1990s and outright hostility under the second Alan Garcia government (Chirif and Garcia Hierro, 2008;

Gray, 1997). Success in the public school system was, then, viewed a starting point on the road towards the acquisition of capabilities and professional qualifications (e.g. in the fields of law, agriculture, health and forest management), needed for the articulation of legal claims and formal denunciation of injustices and rights abuses.

A third way in which formal education has been significant is in the development of a critique of its colonial nature, of indigenous peoples' marginalized situation and the role of missionary and public schooling in the perpetuation of Amazonian peoples' position at the bottom of the ladder in a racially stratified society (Laurie and Bonnett, 2002). Indigenous representative organizations and federations were formed through the 1980s to fight against the injustices of national models of development and unregulated migration and depredation in indigenous territories. They raised an outcry against top-down and undemocratic institutions and a prejudiced and biased judiciary and police system. In this struggle, they also placed the transformation of schooling at the top of their organizational agendas with a view to ensuring that schooling recognized and valued their cultural, social and linguistic heritages.

The educational context for the rise of demands for IBE also has roots in the indigenous experience of the linguist-missionaries of the Summer Institute of Linguistics (SIL), who developed orthographies, grammars and dictionaries of indigenous languages, translating the Bible and opening bilingual schools under the auspices of the Ministry of Education (Larson and Davis, 1981). A young, formally educated, indigenous elite emerged alongside a cadre of indigenous, SIL-trained, bilingual teachers who formed the backbone of the indigenous movement, active in the establishment and growth of their local organizations and federations and allied with the emergent Amazon indigenous organization, AIDESEP (*Asociación Interétnica de Desarrollo de la Selva Peruana*).

Peruvian Amazon indigenous organizations have been in the vanguard of Amazonian wide indigenous politics, forging alliances and actively participating in transnational and regional networks for the articulation and advancement of indigenous rights. These include both rights embedded in ILO Convention 169, and ones of increased access to public secondary and further education, as well as to IBE. AIDESEP and Amazonian federations actively participated in over two decades of meetings, negotiations and discussions at the United Nations (UN) which resulted in the *Declaration on the Rights of Indigenous Peoples* (A/RES/61/295) adopted in 2007 (UN, 2008).

This Declaration sets out a legal framework for linguistic and cultural rights of indigenous peoples and constitutes an important legal landmark in the shaping of institutional action and national laws on education which recognize indigenous peoples' self-determination (Allen and Xanthaki, 2011; Gray, 1997; Stamatopoulou, 2011).

Importantly, the Declaration outlines three kinds of education rights. It states that indigenous individuals, particularly children, have the right to all levels and forms of education provided by the state, without discrimination. Indigenous peoples have the right to establish and control their own educational systems and institutions, providing education in their own languages, in a manner appropriate to their cultural methods of teaching and learning. States shall, in conjunction with indigenous peoples, take effective measures in order for indigenous individuals, particularly children, including those living outside their communities, to have access when possible to an education in their own culture and provided in their own language (UN, 2008, Article 14). It confirms that 'education' is more than schooling, recognizing the contribution that indigenous ('informal') educational processes and pedagogies make in terms of intergenerational transfer of knowledge and their intimate association with indigenous cosmologies, territories and languages. Realization of these educational rights is predicated on indigenous peoples' right to self-determination: that is, freely to determine their political status and freely to pursue their economic, social and cultural development (Article 4).

Indigenous peoples' expectations of IBE in the Peruvian Amazon are informed by many processes and experiences. These include their direct contact with schooling in many guises in their communities and their organizations' activism in the field of education and indigenous rights, local, national, regional and international. The next sections take this exploration from discourses, concepts and policy development to IBE as an educational practice in indigenous communities.

The practices of IBE in the Peruvian Amazon

Much of the discussion in this chapter so far has been about tracing the twists and turns of the development of IBE and identifying different meanings and aims for IBE. While this discussion has drawn on the extensive literature on IBE and the indigenous movements' demands in Peru and the Peruvian

Amazon, there is less academic discussion of the concepts of IBE as expressed in classroom practice (Trapnell et al., 2008). What exists is often focused on technical issues of teacher supply, teacher training and the delivery of IBE (López, 2009) rather than the political, philosophical and social challenges which the practice of IBE presents. Here we investigate two distinct experiences of IBE in the Peruvian Amazon, both teacher training and primary school programmes. One is ongoing today with a 20-year history; the other was short-lived and swiftly rejected by indigenous parents, in a fast-changing social, cultural and political landscape. While the first offers insights into the processes of analysis and reflects on the development of IBE as a pedagogical model, the second offers insights into the wider socio-cultural and economic context of the indigenous school.

The 'Bilingual Teacher Training Programme of the Peruvian Amazon' (*Programa de Formación de Maestros Bilingües de la Amazonía Peruana,* FORMABIAP) was established in 1988 by AIDESEP in collaboration with educationalists, linguists and anthropologists and the Loreto Teacher Training College. It was recognized as an experimental programme by the Ministry of Education and viewed as a step towards a new educational practice for indigenous peoples of the Amazon at a time when IBE was viewed by indigenous and non-indigenous peoples as offering great promise for change. Notable for its longevity and persistence in the face of financial and educational change alongside fluctuating political support from the Ministry of Education, the programme has been training teachers, both in-service and pre-service. It is also notable for the analysis and evaluations promoted by those directly involved in its practice and the ways in which this analysis has not only enriched discussion and debates on IBE in the Peruvian Amazon but fed back into FORMABIAP practice.

The publications of Trapnell and her colleagues (Trapnell, 2003, 2007; Trapnell et al., 2008) provide the source of analysis for this section. She discusses the radical nature of this FORMABIAP programme at a time when IBE meant little more than some adaptations to the national curriculum. Rather, it aimed to reorient the institution of the school to address indigenous peoples' needs and demands in the context of the loss of indigenous knowledge and social and cultural values as well as the need to prepare indigenous children for their participation in national society (Trapnell, 2003, pp. 168–169). In a break with bilingual education, this IBE programme saw 'the biggest educational problem in indigenous communities, not as that of language, but the role that the school has been assigned as a mechanism for ideological domination' (Trapnell et al., 2008, p. 28). Its aims included narrowing the gap between the school and the community and recognizing the value of active community participation through, for example, drawing on elders and leaders to teach and help affirm the respect of the younger generation for their cultural heritage. Its innovative curriculum for primary education was organized around community social and productive activities such as fishing, basket making, healing and curing recognizing that these spaces and activities were the locus for children's appropriation of the knowledge, values and skills of their people. It considered indigenous knowledge and worldviews and their forms of social, economic and political organization as the starting point of an educational process, to be enriched by the contribution of Western science (Trapnell et al., 2008, p. 42).

The aims, structure and content of the early years of this programme reflect the political and intellectual situation of the time. IBE was valued by the government, the indigenous organizations and communities for training indigenous teachers in the scientific disciplines without leaving aside their own knowledge. It was assumed that science would help the indigenous peoples empower themselves, in terms of understanding their realities and acquiring elements to help them overcome relations of inequality (Trapnell et al., 2008). This was at a time when indigenous peoples were demanding recognition and respect, a time for indigenous peoples to show the nation and the world that they too could be professionals and take their place in the political life of the nation with their own linguistic and cultural heritage.

As a result of evaluations and reflections on the Programme through the late 1990s, FORMABIAP broke away from its approach which articulated indigenous knowledge with scientific knowledge. This was criticized as being 'bipolar' and under-emphasizing the hierarchical relations between these different types of knowledge and how they played out in teachers' and students' everyday lives (Trapnell et al., 2008, p. 40). In 2004 IBE underwent a revision in the light of changes in conceptualizations of intercultural education and interculturalism as well as feedback and discussions with teachers. Increasingly their jobs were being carried out, not in schools and communities that were homogeneous and mono-ethnic, but in multi-ethnic schools where relations were complex, diverse and often contentious. The new programme set out to work with the diversity of schools as well as the diversity of teachers themselves, their own identities and sense of what being indigenous meant for them, addressing pedagogical and social problems from the reality of the school and learners' experiences. As Trapnell et al. note (2008, p. 175), when teachers had registered for their training, indigenous collective rights were becoming consolidated, but by the time they graduated and began teaching, the socio-cultural and linguistic diversity of Peru had become an established dimension of intercultural education. New discussions of interculturality and relational, multiple and shifting identities were emerging from a post-structural social science that was concerned with hybridity, positionality and intersectionality and with questions of state as pluricultural and plurilingual (see, for example, Gupta and Ferguson, 1997; Werbner and Modood, 2000).

As the programme participants (Trapnell et al., 2008, p. 113) discuss, FORMABIAP took up the challenge of stepping outside of a western matrix of knowledge and pedagogy to shape a critical intercultural education approach, using the concepts which learners employ in their own languages to talk about how they live, what they value and about the universe. Such a challenge leads inevitably and importantly to the task of considering the relationships between indigenous oral language and forms of knowledge and the hegemony of literate schooling traditions. It also implies the need for renewed efforts to expose the majority society through national education to diverse forms of knowledge and narratives and reinvigorating the notion of 'interculturalism for all'.

The FORMABIAP experience has provided insights into the complexities of *doing* IBE in the Peruvian Amazon and of the importance of a strong analysis of the fluid and reflexive relationship between IBE as a concept and programme design and IBE as practice. The reflection above helps with exploring and explaining some of the contradictory responses to the practice of IBE in schools in the Peruvian Amazon. The experience of the introduction of an IBE programme into primary schools in Arakmbut communities in the SE Peruvian Amazon offers insights into the hugely challenging contexts in which IBE is carried out. It also emphasizes the need for educational models and practices which reflect this complexity and diversity of indigenous peoples' lives, their histories of exclusion and discrimination and weak democratic structures.

The indigenous federation of the southern Peruvian Amazon (*Federación de Nativos del Río de Madre de Dios*, FENAMAD) decided to develop its own IBE programme independent of FORMABIAP, beginning with a programme for five Arakmbut communities. These communities had experienced Spanish-language civilizing and assimilationist schooling since the 1950s, provided by Dominican missionaries and then through lay missionaries of the Dominican School Network (*Red Escolar de la Selva Sur Oriente Peruana*, RESSOP) (Aikman, 1999). In the period between the decision by FENAMAD to promote

IBE in the mid-1980s and the emergence of the first Arakmbut bilingual teachers in the early 2000s, there had been huge transformations in the lives and territories of the Arakmbut communities. Their territory, which had been a source of their economic subsistence – hunting, gardening and fishing – as well as the foundation of their cosmology, history and language, had become physically transformed through unregulated migration and artisan gold mining.

At its Third Congress in 1985, FENAMAD (1985) had identified two urgent educational needs. The first was for access to, and funding for, secondary and further education, in order to support the growth of indigenous professionals who could work with the Federation in its land demarcation, legal challenges, health needs and schooling. The second was intercultural bilingual primary schooling, in response to schooling that was seen to be authoritarian, teaching facts from an undiversified national curriculum which discriminated against rural and indigenous students (Aikman, 1999, Gray 1996). In the late 1990s, FENAMAD was successful in getting funding for IBE training for the Arakmbut people. But by the time the first teachers took up their positions in the village schools, ousting the lay missionaries, the Arakmbut had become dependent on gold panning for their subsistence as the forest resources had been exhausted and habitats laid to waste by the many gold mining operations. Alongside these changes there had been a gradual intermarrying of Arakmbut with migrants from many parts of Peru, and Spanish was becoming the dominant language of communication (Aikman, 2009).

The IBE training programme was inserted into the mainstream teacher training programme in the regional teacher training college and support from anthropologists, linguists, educationalists and indigenous professionals was limited. FENAMAD's own human resources were stretched and slowly the programme merged into the mainstream teacher education programme. New 'IBE' teachers were poorly trained and equipped to initiate intercultural education in their community schools and communities were ill-prepared to support it. The IBE teachers lasted only a couple of years because community members made clear their opposition to IBE and sought missionary support for the return of the lay-missionary teachers. For the Arakmbut in the 2000s, IBE represented a marginalizing form of education. Indeed it compounded their sense of exclusion at a time when their lives had become intricately entangled and integrated with the lives of the gold mining migrants living with and around them, and their struggle had become one of protecting their gold panning installations within their community territory in order to secure their future livelihoods.

The IBE which the teachers followed was little more than the insertion of a few indigenous language components into the national curriculum. Its aims were formulated around teaching in and through the Arakmbut language, offering a stark contrast to the FORMABIAP emphasis on 'being more intercultural than bilingual' (Trapnell et al., 2008, p. 28). The Arakmbut communities have never considered the school as a suitable space for the transmission of their language or knowledge. They have always been quite clear that the school is a non-Arakmbut, non-indigenous institution and have valued it for its promise of acceptance as 'Peruvians' and as a means of shedding their identity as indigenous, which has become, for some, the basis of deep-seated discrimination that they experience on a daily basis (Aikman, 2012).

These examples offer some insights into the complex contexts in which indigenous organizations are working to shape IBE practices. They serve to raise important queries for those policy makers who would propose IBE as a solution to educational 'problems' of access and inclusion.

Concluding discussion

The forgoing sections of this chapter have examined expectations of and for IBE in the Peruvian Amazon from the perspectives of three main players in the education field: government and donor agencies; academics and researchers; and the indigenous movement. Coming from different ideological and theoretical positions and starting points, they interrelate over time and space to influence the possibilities and nature of IBE programmes on the ground.

The two programmes we have examined – FORMABIAP and the Arakmbut experience – have both emerged from indigenous activism and claims for rights to self-determination and recognition of the indigenous movement. While the UN Convention on the Rights of Indigenous Peoples identifies three dimensions to rights to education – the right to have access to state education, to control their own educational systems and to educate their children in a manner appropriate to their cultural methods of teaching and learn – in Peru these different rights and different forms of education have been collapsed into one form, that of institutionalized and schooled IBE. The FORMABIAP programme has looked to schooling to assert indigenous educational rights to access without discrimination and indigenous peoples' right to control their own educational system, through the development of IBE teacher training programmes and IBE school curricula. This approach aims to operationalize the right to an education which respects indigenous cultures and languages. The FORMABIAP model has been shaped by indigenous organizations of the Peruvian Amazon and their demands. Its aims are to decolonize education for the indigenous peoples living in the culturally and linguistically plural societies of the twenty-first century. The programme faces this huge task through processes of self-reflection, action research and probing evaluations of its work, both conceptual and empirical. In this way it aims to renew its critical intercultural education practice continually so as to respond to the fast changing social, cultural, political and economic environment of the Peruvian Amazon.

The FENAMAD sponsored programme, working independently of the FORMABIAP programme, has developed out of different circumstances and dynamics. The IBE programme which emerged reflected for the Arakmbut a conception of IBE reminiscent of debates of the 1980s and early 1990s when there was a strong need for indigenous peoples to be able to gain acknowledgement and recognition as valid actors, in and through the institutions of the national society. Its bilingual education programme aimed to teach Arakmbut language literacy, but was severely hampered by very meagre learning and teaching materials in the indigenous language. The limitations in its design and its training programme were obvious from its inception in community schools, where its teachers were unable to offer little more than folkloric additions to a dominant national curriculum and pedagogy. While there is not space here to enter into discussion of how this situation emerged, it can be said that the dominance of institutionalized educational structures, together with the weakness of democratic institutions in this region of the Amazon, has meant that conditions have not been favourable for indigenous self-determination of education.

And what of the expectations of the Arakmbut people themselves in the gold mining region? They rejected the IBE school in the 2000s, as they have resisted any bridging of the gap that has always existed between the community and the school (Aikman, 1999). Their expectations for schooling and their rights lie firmly in realizing access and participation in the educational institutions of the state at all levels. They have internalized the pervasive and persistent message that schooling is for learning about how to be Peruvian and become a fully recognized member of Peruvian society, which precludes the possibility of retaining pride in being Arakmbut. Governments – nationally and through global agendas such as Education for All – subscribe to the notion that inclusion in formal education is a means to overcoming poverty and promoting national economic and social development. However, since the Arakmbut, in the late 1980s, gained access to primary schooling, in their villages, run by missionary teachers with good formal qualifications, their standard of living, their levels of nutrition and their well-being have plummeted (Roberts, cited by Ward, 2004). It is not their lack of 'education' but structural causes that underlie the ways in which schooling marginalizes the Arakmbut as indigenous peoples, as Stavenhagen (2008) reminds us, directly linked to the failure to recognize, protect and guarantee observance of their individual and collective human rights.

For the Arakmbut, an education that offers a means of understanding their intercultural lives today amidst social and economic marginalization, violence and conflict is beyond their expectations of what schooling can do, or indeed what it is for. Their enactment of their self-determination today is to reject this IBE model as further stigmatizing them on their own lands which have been transformed into a mining zone where conflict is rife, discrimination endemic and poverty in its many dimensions is widespread. While the dominant discourse is one of IBE as a means to improve access and retention of indigenous students, the Arakmbut, however, have never been marginal to schooling, due to the indefatigable efforts of the Dominican mission since the 1950s. On the contrary, their educational inclusion has compounded their social exclusion as indigenous Arakmbut. They have claimed the right to state education, but have failed to see how this education, this schooling, can be used to add value to their cultural or linguistic practices. Moreover, they have always exercised the right to determine their own forms of education appropriate to their own cultural methods of teaching and learning – as something quite distinct from and beyond the grasp of schooling. This has never been in dispute for them. What is in doubt today, however, is how these non-schooled forms of learning can be sustained in this mining environment.

Further reading

Aikman, S. (1999), *Intercultural Education and Literacy: An Ethnographic Study of Indigenous Knowledge and Learning in the Peruvian Amazon*. Amsterdam: John Benjamins.

Gustafson, B. (2009), *New languages of the State: Indigenous Resurgence and the Politics of Knowledge in Bolivia*. Durham, NC: Duke University Press.

Hornberger, N. (1988), *Bilingual education and language maintenance: a Southern Peruvian Quechua case*. Dordrecht: Foris Publications.

These three ethnographies offer in-depth insights into context and processes around educational change and national 'development' in South America. Hornberger's ethnography considers questions of bilingual education in the Peruvian Andes while my ethnography from the 1990s expands on the context discussed in this chapter. Gustafson's work on Bolivia in the 2000s focuses on the Gurarani of Bolivia at a time of indigenous mobilization and reform. See also Hornberger's more recent and extensive publications on multilingual languages in education.

Compare, 42 (2) *Special Issue on Education and Marginalisation*, S. Aikman and C. Dyer (eds) This Special Issue arose out of debates around the 2010 UN Global Monitoring Report on 'Beyond the Mainstream'. Articles investigate the concept of educational 'marginalization' and problematizes questions of educational inclusion.

Crabtree, J. (ed.). (2011), *Fractured Politics Past and Present*. London: Institute for the Study of the Americas, University of London.

For a book on the Peruvian political situation more generally, chapters in this accessible edited volume examine the nature and working of the Peruvian political system, considering a range of key issues including questions of identity, social exclusion and power.

References

Aikman, S. (1999), *Intercultural Education and Literacy: An Ethnographic Study of Indigenous Knowledge and Learning in the Peruvian Amazon*. Amsterdam: John Benjamins.

——. (2001), 'Literacies, languages and developments in Peruvian Amazonia', in B. Street (ed.), *Literacy and Development: Ethnographic Perspectives*. Routledge: London, pp. 103–120.

——. (2009), 'The contradictory languages of fishing and gold panning', *Maritime Studies/MAST*, 8, (2), 53–72.

——. (2012), 'Interrogating discourses of intercultural education: From indigenous Amazon community to global policy forum', *Compare*, 42, (2), 235–259.

Allen, S. and Xanthaki, A. (2011), 'Introduction', in S. Allen and A. Xanthaki (eds), *Reflections on the UN Declaration on the Rights of Indigenous Peoples*. Oxford: Hart Publishing, pp. 1–10.

Champagne, D. (2009), 'Contemporary education', in United Nations (ed.), *State of the World's Indigenous Peoples*. New York: UNST/ESA/328, pp. 130–154.

Chirif, A. and Garcia Hierro, P. (2008), 'Peruvian Amazon: Indigenous organisations: Challenges and achievements', *Indigenous Affairs*, 8, (3–4), 35–47.

Citarella, L. (1990), 'Peru', in L. Citarella, M. Amadio, M. Zuniga, and F. Chiodi (eds), *La Educacion Indigena en America Latina*. Vol. 2. Santiago: PEBI&Abya Yala/UNESCO/OREALC, pp. 7–226.

Cotler, J. (2011), 'Paradoxes of development', in J. Crabtree (ed.), *Fractured Politics Past and Present*. London: Institute for the Study of the Americas, University of London, pp. 53–66.

Crabtree, J. (2011), 'Preface', in J. Crabtree (ed.), *Fractured Politics Past and Present*. London: Institute for the Study of the Americas, University of London, pp. xvii–xxii.

Cueto, S., Guerrero, G., Leon, J., Seguin, E., and Munoz, I. (2009), *Explaining and Overcoming Marginalisation in Education: A Focus on Ethnic/language Minorities in Peru*. Background paper for the EFA Global Monitoring Report 2010. Paris: UNESCO.

Defensoria del Pueblo. (2011), *Aportes para una Politica Nacional de Educacion Intercultural Bilingüe a Favor de los Pueblos Indígenas del Peru*. Lima: Republica del Peru.

Dietz, G. (2009), *Multiculturalism, Interculturality and Diversity in Education: An Anthropological Approach*. Munster: Waxmann.

Escobar, A. (2010), 'Latin America at the crossroads: Alternative modernisations, post-liberalism, or post-development?', *Cultural Studies*, 24, (1), 1–65.

Federation of Natives of Madre de Dios (FENAMAD). (1985), *III Congreso de la Federacion Nativa del Rio Madre de Dios y sus Afluentes, Resolutions of the III Congress*. Unpublished manuscript, December.

Freire, P. (1972), *Pedagogy of the Oppressed*. Harmondsworth: Penguin Press.

Gray, A. (1996), *Mythology, Spirituality and History: The Arakmbut of Amazonian Peru*. Oxford: Berghahn Books.

———. (1997), *Indigenous Rights and Development*. Oxford: Berghahn Books.

Gupta, A. and Ferguson, J. (1997), *Culture, Power, Place: Explorations in Critical Anthropology*. Durham, NC: Duke University Press.

Gustafson, B. (2009), *New Languages of the State: Indigenous Resurgence and the Politics of Knowledge in Bolivia*. Durham, NC: Duke University Press.

Hall, G. and Patrinos, H. A. (2006), *Indigenous Peoples, Poverty, and Human Development in Latin America*. Basingstoke: Palgrave Macmillan.

Heise, M., Tubino F., and Ardito, W. (1994), *Interculturalidad – un Desafio*. 2nd ed. Lima: CAAAP.

Hornberger, N. and López, L. E. (1998), 'Policy, possibility and paradox: Indigenous multilingualism and education in Peru and Bolivia', in J. Cenoz and F. Genesee (eds), *Beyond Bilingualism: Multilingualism and Multilingual Education*. Clevedon: Multilingual Matters, pp. 206–242.

Howard, R. (2009), 'Education reform, indigenous politics, and decolonisation in the Bolivia of Evo Morales', *International Journal of Educational Development*, 29, (6), 583–593.

Larson, M. and Davis, P. (1981), *Bilingual Education: An Experience in Peruvian Amazonia*. Washington, DC: SIL/ Centre for Applied Linguistics.

Laurie, N. and Bonnett, A. (2002), 'Adjusting to equity: The contradictions of neo-liberalism and the search for racial equality in Peru', *Antipode*, 34, (7), 28–53.

Llanes Ortiz, G. (2009), *Indigenous Universities and the Construction of Interculturality: The Case of the Peasant and Indigenous University Network in Yucatan, Mexico*. D. Phil. thesis, University of Sussex.

López, L. E. (2005), *De Resquicios a Boquerones. La Educación Intercultural Bilingüe en Bolivia*. Cochabamba/La Paz: PROEIB-ANDES/Plural Editores.

———. (2009), *Reaching the Unreached: Indigenous Intercultural Bilingual Education in Latin America*. Background paper for the EFA Global Monitoring Report 2010. Paris: UNESCO.

Masferrer, E. (1983), 'El movimiento indigenista y la educacion indigena (1990–1980)', in N. Rodriguez, E. Masferrer, and K. Vargas Vega (eds), *Educacion, Etnias y Descolonizacion en America Latina*. Vol. 2. Mexico: UNESCO/III, pp. 521–528.

Mignolo, W. (2011), *The Darker Side of Western Modernity: Global Futures, Decolonial Options*. London: Duke.

Ministry of Education. (1989), *Politica de de Educacion Bilingue Intercultural*. Lima: Ministry of Education.

——. (1991), *Politica Nacional de Educacion Bilingue e Educacion Intercultural 1991–1995 (PEBI)*. Lima: Ministry of Education.

——. (2007), *National Education Project for 2021 'The Education We Want for Peru'*. Lima: Ministry of Education.

Oliart, P. (2011), *Políticas Educativas y la Cultura del Sistema Escolar en el Perú*. Lima: Instituto de Estudios Peruanos.

Psacharopolous, G. and Patrinos, G. (1994), *Indigenous People and Poverty in Latin America: An Ethnographic Analysis*. Washington, DC: The World Bank.

Quijano, A. (2000), 'Coloniality of power, Eurocentrism, and Latin America', *Nepantla: Views from the South*, 1, (3), 533–580.

Quintanilla, O. and Lozano, S. R. (1983), 'Presentacion', in N. Rodriguez, E. Masferrer, and K. Vargas Vega (eds), *Educacion, Etnias y Descolonizacion en America Latina*. Vol. 2. Mexico: UNESCO/III, pp. xi–xxv.

Rodriguez Vargas, M. (1996), *Educacion Intercultural: Aproximaciones Hacia una Propuesta Educative para la Realidad Peruana. Documento de Trabajo*. Lima: CAAAP.

Stamatopoulou, E. (2011), 'Taking cultural rights seriously: The vision of the UN declaration on the rights of indigenous peoples', in S. Allen and A. Xanthaki (eds), *Reflections on the UN Declaration on the Rights of Indigenous Peoples*. Oxford: Hart Publishing, pp. 387–412.

Stavenhagen, R. (2002), 'Indigenous peoples and the state in Latin America: An ongoing debate', in R. Sieder (ed.), *Multiculturalism in Latin America; Indigenous Rights, Diversity and Democracy*. Basingstoke: Institute for Latin American Studies, Palgrave Macmillan, pp. 24–44.

——. (2008), 'Building intercultural citizenship through education: A human rights approach', *European Journal of Education*, 43, (2), 161–179.

Tauro, A. (1970), 'Prologo', in A. Tauro (ed.), *Temas de Educacion: Jose Carlos Mariategui*. Biblioteca Amauta 14. Lima: Ediciones populares de las Obras Completas de Carlos Mariategui.

Trapnell, L. (2003), 'Some key issues in intercultural bilingual education teacher training programmes – as seen from a teacher training programme in the Peruvian Amazon', *Comparative Education*, 39, (2), 165–184.

——. (2007), 'La educacion intercultural bilingue en el Peru', in V. Zavala (ed.), *Avances y Desafíos de la Educación Intercultural Bilingüe en Bolivia, Ecuador y Perú*. Lima: CARE/IBIS, pp. 193–274.

Trapnell, L., Calderon, A., and Flores, R. (2008), *Interculturalidad, Conocimiento y Poder*. Lima: Instituto del Bien Comun.

UNESCO. (2010), *EFA Global Monitoring Report: Reaching the Marginalised*. Oxford: Oxford University Press.

United Nations (UN). (2008), *United Nations Declaration on the Rights of Indigenous Peoples*. New York: UN.

United Nations, Expert Mechanism on the Rights of Indigenous Peoples. (2009), *Study on Lessons Learned and Challenges to Achieve the Implementation of the Rights of Indigenous Peoples to Education:*

Report of the Expert Mechanism on the Rights of Indigenous Peoples to the Human Rights Council. New York: UN Doc. A/HRC/EMRIP/2009/2.

Varese, S. (1980), *Restoring Multiplicity: Indigeneities and the Civilizing Project in Latin America.* Paper for the 9th World Congress of Sociology, Uppsala, Sweden. Reprinted in A. Chirif (ed.) (2006), *Witness to Sovereignty: Essays on the Indian Movement in Latin America.* Copenhagen: International Work Group for Indigenous Affairs (IWGIA), pp. 140–153.

Varese, S. and Rodriguez, N. (1983), 'Etnias indígenas y educación en America Latina: Diagnostico y perspectiva', in N. Rodriguez, E. Masferrer, and K. Vargas Vega (eds), *Educacion, Etnias y Descolonizacion en America Latina.* Vol. 2. Mexico: UNESCO/III, pp. xi–xxv.

Walsh, C. (2009), 'Interculturalidad, plurinacionalidad y razon decolonial: Refundares politico-epistemicos e marcha', in S. Albagli and L. M. Maciel (eds), *Conocimiento, capital y desarrollo: Dialécticas contemporáneas.* Buenos Aires: Editora la Crujia.

Ward, P. (2004), 'From the marginality of the 1960s to the new poverty of today', *Latin American Research Review*, 39, (1), 183–195.

Werbner, P. and Modood, T. (2000), *Debating Cultural Hybridity: Multi-cultural Identities and the Politics of Anti-racism.* London: Zed books.

World Bank. (2001), *Peruvian Education at a Crossroads: Challenges and Opportunities for the 21st Century.* Washington, DC: World Bank Country Case Study.

Zavala, V. (ed.). (2007), *Avances y Desafíos de la Educación Intercultural Bilingüe en Bolivia, Ecuador y Perú.* Lima: CARE/IBIS.

Index

Note: Page numbers followed by *t* and *f* refer to pages containing tables and figures respectively